D0512567

PENGUIN BOOKS
LOVE IS THE DRUG

John Aizlewood was born of mining stock in South Yorkshire and now lives off the North Circular Road. He is married to Lorna and has a stroppy cat called Cabbage. He believes, among other things, that Sheffield Wednesday will win the Premiership 'soon-ish' and that Dexys Midnight Runners were genuinely great. He works for *Q* Magazine and doesn't have any hobbies.

Love

is the Drug

Edited by JOHN AIZLEWOOD

PENGUIN BOOKS

PENGUIN BOOKS

Published by the Penguin Group
Penguin Books Ltd, 27 Wrights Lane, London W8 5TZ, England
Penguin Books USA Inc., 375 Hudson Street, New York, New York 10014, USA
Penguin Books Australia Ltd, Ringwood, Victoria, Australia
Penguin Books Canada Ltd, 10 Alcorn Avenue, Toronto, Ontario, Canada M4V 3B2
Penguin Books (NZ) Ltd, 182–190 Wairau Road, Auckland 10, New Zealand

Penguin Books Ltd, Registered Offices: Harmondsworth, Middlesex, England

First published 1994
10 9 8 7 6 5 4 3 2 1

The acknowledgements on page vii constitute an extension of this copyright page

Typeset by Datix International Limited, Bungay, Suffolk
Printed in England by Clays Ltd, St Ives plc
Filmset in 11.25/14 pt Monophoto Janson

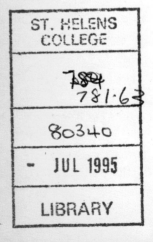

Contents

Acknowledgements

The publishers would like to thank the following for permission to reproduce copyright extracts from song lyrics:

Dexys Midnight Runners: to EMI Music Publishing Ltd, London WC2H 0EA, for 'Keep It' (Geoffrey Blyth/Kevin Archer) © 1980, and 'Plan B' (Kevin Rowland/James Patterson) © 1981.

Bob Dylan: to Special Rider Music for 'Mr Tambourine Man'.

Billy Fury: to EMI Music Publishing Ltd, London WC2H 0EA, and BMG UFA Musikverlage, for 'Jealousy' (music by Jacob Gade, words by Winifred May) © 1926, Editions Karl Brull, Denmark; to Skidmore Music Ltd for 'In Summer' (Valerie & Elaine Murtagh/Ray Adams) © 1963, Skidmore Music Ltd, 8/9 Frith Street, London W1V 5TZ, all rights reserved.

Gram Parsons: to TRO Essex Music Group and Len Freedman Music for 'Hickory Wind' (Gram Parsons/Bob Buchanan) © 1970, Tickson Music Co., USA. Assigned to TRO Essex Music Ltd, London SW10 0SZ.

Teardrop Explodes: to International Music Publications Ltd for 'Passionate Friend' (Julian Cope).

The The: to Complete Music Ltd for 'Slow Train to Dawn' (Matt Johnson).

The Triffids: to International Music Publications Ltd for 'Lonely Stretch'; to International Music Network for 'Bright Lights, Big City', 'Field of Glass', 'Beautiful Waste' and 'Monkey on My Back'.

Introduction

Imagine that consultant surgeons had fans. That everywhere they went, they were hassled, that they constantly had strangers coming up to them in the street and asking about this or that operation, that they couldn't go to a restaurant and have a normal meal because their very presence made the whole situation abnormal. Why not? It's not such a far-fetched notion. The work is tough, only a select few can do it, and saving people's lives is as important in the wider scheme as 'things' can be. Better yet, consultant surgeons are (probably – best not put these things to empirical research) an urbane, sexy, intelligent bunch. If your life is sufficiently sad, you can take time to construct a similar set of arguments around miners or teachers or almost anyone bar the terminally unsexy plumbers. Yet, give or take a few actors and sportsfolk, hardly anyone actually has fans.

Musicians aren't always desperately attractive (step forward, difficult skins, big bones and all, Elton John, Bonnie Raitt, anyone in The Farm, Shara Nelson, Meat Loaf, Chrissie Hynde and Take That), but they all have fans. It's not strictly how things should be if we were working on the objective scale of looks, personality and the X Factor that women's magazines witter on about. There must be something else.

Obviously, musicians touch people's lives in a way that consultant surgeons simply can't. A good pop song, say something by Ace of Base, has a catchy tune which bears repeated listening, and that's about it. People don't go mad about Ace of Base, they just like them (forgetting, if we can, the theory-undermining German bloke who stabbed one of the women). Yet there's something else: there are songs that touch people's lives, and this is the first part of the point.

Once you've touched someone's life with a song, you've got them. Dylan seemed to touch a whole generation, Kurt Cobain, the stupid, stupid man, touched a different generation but in a remarkably similar way. So did The Clash, The Rolling Stones, the *Bat Out of Hell* albums, Elvis Costello and the rest. For some people that's enough. Others want more, others are touched by more than one song by the same artist. Then they start to push further, to burrow deeper, to become obsessed. That's what *Love is the Drug* encapsulates, the rather stomach-wrenching moments where band and fan are (in the fan's mind only) one. It feels great.

It's a matter of luck in the end. The groups and singers anyone likes, as in *really really likes*, aren't down to 'good taste', whatever that's supposed to be. It's all a matter of chance, a fluke moment. An elder sibling's record collection, the parental record collection (never to be snorted at derisively: imagine the unmitigated joy of owning every Dean Martin album) are both possible starting points for your own obsession. More likely is the self-discovery of hearing something, almost accidentally, on the radio or television, or at a friend's house. The way to obsession is, as Ferdinand Magellan might have put it, a voyage of discovery. You like someone (I like The Stranglers, Neil Diamond and Shabba Ranks, but I don't care if I never hear them again), and that's all. Sometimes, some people go further. Sometimes, someone takes over your life: someone you've probably never met, probably never will, someone who may very well be dead.

It's a funny feeling, it really is. You function normally, you hold down a job or your studies. You look normal (although in my case a stupid Dexys T-shirt, emblazoned with a frankly wretched poem, raised a few eyebrows when I walked it through Rotherham town centre) and to most outsiders you're perfectly ordinary. You're not, you're sort of mad and your head is spinning with all sorts of nonsense, other people's nonsense at that. You are (and we shall return to this subject time and time again) highly unlikely to be having any kind of sexual relationship.

Almost floating above yourself, like those people who seem to make a living from talking about near-death experiences on BBC 2 documentaries, you see yourself hectoring innocent people getting on with their everyday business about something as indefinable as musical taste. You don't really like yourself but you just can't quit. Perhaps you really don't want to. This is what the outsiders, the ones who haven't felt like us – and surely there can hardly be any, unless they're in denial – are missing: it feels fantastic and your life is easier. You don't have to think. Enver Hoxha understood this notion brilliantly – he'd have been a top pop svengali . . .

Imagine your whole life being governed by a principle that you know, despite what everyone else knows, to be absolutely, unutterably, unalterably right. It's almost born-again-Christian, and this 'I am right, you are wrong' attitude is exactly the same mantra by which Margaret Thatcher seemed to live her life. Don't knock it. I know I've only just said it, but it bears speedy repetition: it feels fantastic. It's like ruling the world.

You grow out of it, almost always. I can't feel so intensely now, but I know exactly what it felt like. Other things come into your life, adult things. You discover sex and, assuming hetero-sexuality, it's highly unlikely your partner will share your obsession with the same intensity (if at all) and if they do, then one of you must be fantasizing. Bands tend to attract followers of one sex, depending on how they deploy the traditional pop ingredients: what they look like, what they sound like and what they say. This further limits your chances of finding a partner with your obsession. Any new partner sentient enough to dress themselves in a morning or clean their own teeth isn't going to put up with a perfect, invisible rival. You make your choice for real life, real sex and really washing the pots, and if there's any regrets, at least you've 'known' your obsession for longer than your partner for life. Could anything be more comforting?

Let me, off the top of my head, tell you some of the things I've done. I know it sounds like name-dropping but wait a while, there's a valid reason. I've 'sung' with Iron Maiden in a football stadium in Brazil; Sharon Finn, wife of Crowded House's Neil, once invited me into her lovely Melbourne home and cooked me and the whole Finn tribe dinner; I have sat on Sinitta's waterbed with Sinitta herself; I was given a tour of LA by Poison; I went to a diner in New York with Jim Steinman on the night he ordered 'everything'; I have sat freezing in a hotel room in Siberia with Nitzer Ebb, drinking Cup-A-Soup; I have played childish games with Kurt Cobain's baby; I 'sang' on a Hothouse Flowers record with the cream of South Africa's musicians; I saw a member of UB40, accompanied by a Tina Turner lookalike, blow up a condom until it burst in a Jakarta night-club. Sounds great? It was, all of it, but none of it felt quite the same as the things I and others have written about in this book. They were things that happened because I happen to have written for some magazines and that's the rather bizarre life music journalists are supposed to lead, not because I'm a great bloke, although, hey, I have my moments. The Dexys business happened because I cared a lot, I cared about Dexys more than anything in my life at that point. The same applies to almost every story in this book.

From the band's point of view this is all very different. When they start out, they're desperate for fans, gagging for them. Anyone who shows the slightest smidgen of interest is immediately clasped to the band's bosom. They play what songs you like on stage, they give you lifts home, they buy you drinks and put you on guest lists, even if there's only two people in the audience. The drummer will explain how he plays that solo note for note, thud for thud.

Then, suddenly, things change. The band gets a little success, say at the stage where they're playing universities and just breaching the Top 40, and fans suddenly become an irritant unless the band are sleeping with them. Fans give and the band takes, except that the band are not that interested in taking what the fans want to give. Worse, the fans are acutely confused as to what they want from bands. Ostensibly, I just wanted a few autographed Dexys singles, but it was more than that, as it's more than that with everyone else in this book.

These are complex emotions we're dealing with; these bands are singing the fans' lives. The lyricist understands them better than anyone else. A meeting isn't always necessary. Fans watch over bands, defend their interests in debate, justifying the let-down new album, pretend they've always liked Paul Anka because in a moment of drunken, druggy mischief the band has decided to cover 'You're Having My Baby'. No wonder there's no irony in a fan's make up – although distance brings it. Oh, and the fans don't want to be in the band.

All this confusion, this lack of focus, makes the bands shy away further. They know they probably won't get John Hinkley at the next show but, because fans look normal, bands don't know if the next person to accost them is a bore, a quick-autograph-and-off merchant, an 'I just wanted to say . . .' type or someone who really wants to talk about himself: 'You don't know how much that song meant to me. My parents were getting divorced and. . .' Usually, it's 'When are you going to play Hereford?' to Pink Floyd, who neither know nor care quite frankly. If they talk at all, most bands just want to talk about football ('I don't go as much as I should now but . . .'), sex ('I know I shouldn't but . . .'), the music industry ('You know *him*? What a wanker!') or, God help us, computer games. Mostly, they just want fans to buy the records, see the shows and go home.

If I'd been a Dexy, I would have ignored my whingeing letter about their cancelled tour, and I bet they wish they had. If, however, I had been a Triffid, playing to nobody, I'd have welcomed David Cavanagh as the font of all that was believable. In David's story, when the newly popular Triffids return from Australia, they effectively snub him. I'd have done that too. I wouldn't want to be reminded of playing to nobody, not now there were numerous David Cavanaghs saying the same things. If I'd been a Bay City Roller, I'd have been terrified of all my fans, every one of them, although not as much as I'd have been afraid of my manager. If I were Bob Dylan, well I'd have put 'Series of Dreams' on *Oh Mercy* and released it as a single. But I'm not and that's another part of the point: fans can't be their heroes and don't want to be.

Then it finishes, the feeling goes. Not everyone grows out of it, and that's sad. Go to a Barry Manilow or Bob Dylan concert and you'll see facial expressions to make you weep, but in the main people move on. Maybe it's sex (again) or maybe it's work and age. It's hard to be obsessive, like a kid, when you've a couple of your own screaming for attention. What once brought a certain weird kudos from peers – feeling desperately for a band is the first adult emotion some of us were capable of – quickly becomes a point of ridicule: get on with your life, the invisible voices say. But you never forget, never ever, and I'd still like 'Knowledge of Beauty' by Dexys Midnight Runners played at my funeral. And that's perhaps the final part of the point.

I'm sorry there aren't more women writing for this book. I can think of a couple of possible reasons. Firstly, being more mature than men, maybe women reach and discard their obsessions earlier. Secondly, music journalism is a macho thing and, shamefully, women aren't made welcome enough to see it through. Decide for yourself. I genuinely don't know.

I'm less sorry that there's hardly anything that's on-going with life-altering fervour. It's not because today's scene is rubbish, that's arrant nonsense, of course: all eras are roughly equal in proportions of good, bad and indifferent. It's more a case that there has to be a distance between having the feelings and being able to write about them with humour and irony without chuntering on about greatest bands in the world and 'you ought to listen to. . .' Nobody *ought* to listen to anything, except those three Dexys albums. There's a disproportionate number of music journalists here, but that's simply because the happy coincidence of having these lunatic feelings and the ability to write about them occurs almost exclusively in music journalists. Sad, isn't it?

Giving of yourself is never easy; writing about it for several thousand words is even harder and that's why the contributions here are so special. Thanks, everyone, for caring so much.

Others especially helped too. I'll be brief: Kate St John provided some lovely food; Sean Hughes provided some nice wine; Lucy O'Brien got me tipsy; Sheryl Garratt missed a weekend of raving; Mike Edwards sent some marvellous Arabic music and I went to the pub with Tom Hibbert, who filled me with confidence, David Cavanagh, Danny Kelly and Stuart Maconie. Lee Haynes was in the right place at the right time (again).

Simon Majumdar was the first person to say what a good idea *Love is the Drug* might just be, and without him it simply wouldn't exist. Thanks too to everyone else at Penguin. Their encouragement and complete lack of interference has made *Love is the Drug* even better.

In my dark and distant past, I'd like to thank Robbi Millar, Steve Sutherland, Debbi Voller, Phil McNeill and Paul Du Noyer, who all said yes to my writing when they could have said no. Presently, Danny, Andrew, Tim, Bill, Kim and Clare at *Q* are a joy to work with.

Finally, there is Lorna, who deserves eternal thanks for everything.

John Aizlewood
London, June 1994

Get Happy!

STUART MACONIE

Once a computer operator at the Elizabeth Arden cosmetics factory, Elvis Costello established a career on a rather contrived geek look – National Health glasses, a hangdog demeanour which suggested he was about to be beaten up, ill-fitting suits and, almost, spittle dripping off his chin. He didn't need all that nonsense for he was one of the great songwriters of his generation. He suffered when he dispensed with his backing band and musical soul-mates The Attractions. He couldn't do country properly, and at one stage – the stage significantly where he had another silly image, this time involving a beard encrusted with food particles – it appeared that the muse had permanently deserted him. A reunion with The Attractions suggests this isn't the case.

I remember punk rock like it was only yesterday, to borrow a phrase from Vic Reeves. To borrow another from the Poet Laureate, it swooped into my adolescent life like a hawk into a dovecote and I was never really the same again.

Somewhere worryingly over the horizon loomed O levels and, less worryingly, girls, shaving, wages and the unlimited freedom and temptations of adult life. We were roughly between the three-day week and the Winter of Discontent and times were not good. Music, the mainstay of my life since buying The Scaffold's 'Lily the Pink' as a precocious and presumably demented toddler, was letting me down badly. Northern Soul had fizzled out in a slew of novelty records, progressive rock had come to mean the dismal Genesis, and elsewhere The Eagles held fell dominion over the land. Disco hadn't been invented so I spent my time listening to old Beatles records and eccentrics such as Split Enz, Deaf School, Aphrodite's Child and Syd Barrett. Salvation, however, was just around the corner.

John Peel's was a fairly tired selection of records that evening as I recall, culminating in his rather apologetically playing Poco's 'Rose of Cimmaron' twice when, with the air of a kindly and adventurous uncle, he put on 'Neat Neat Neat' by The Damned. The effect was electrifying. As I remember it, I had cut my hair and sold all my Yes records before the end of that first simple bass guitar phrase. A keen student of the music press, I had suspected punk to be a scam perpetrated by shallow London trendies. Now, as Dave Vanian sang out in his attractive monotone, I realized it was all our futures.

Being a punk rocker was hard work in the Wigan of the time. A lot of my friends thought that this brave new sound was a joke lacking the musical substance of, say, Rory Gallagher or Ritchie Blackmore's Rainbow. Overnight, such types were dismissed as 'boring old farts' and dispensed with. Then there was the matter of the clothes. We would get changed in the toilets of the Bees Knees pub, entering as rather conventional seventies teenagers in Birmingham bags and Simon shirts, and emerging as, so we thought, art terrorists of the new Bohemia festooned with pins and cheap jewellery hanging from torn T-shirts. Such apparel rendered our already slim chances of getting served approximately nil.

It's easy to forget in our post-everything, free-for-all Britain, where young people routinely eat fire in the streets dressed as Arapaho Indians, just how shocking punk rock was. The entire top deck of a passing bus once gave me 'the finger' as I set out to see Slaughter & The Dogs at Wigan Casino. A jeering mob of children shouted, 'Look at fucking Johnny Rotten,' as I tried to make my innocent way through a public park. There was one pub that would shelter us, the Bier Keller on King Street, and each week – Tuesday nights to be specific – a score of us punks would revel in our secret vice, encouraged by a supportive overweight DJ called Tommy. It would be visited by gangs of Teds, bikers, soul boys and the merely curious, all keen to study (with a view to later kicking in) some punk rockers. It was unbearably exciting.

But if being a punk rocker was hard, being a punk rock intellectual was murder. Strummer and Rotten had suppressed their intelligence for the good of their art. There was Wire and Howard Devoto, but they were kind of aloof and short on toe-tapping tunes. The Damned were clearly berks. Enter, sneering and blinking owlishly, Declan McManus.

I first saw Elvis Costello on *Granada Reports*, our teatime magazine show. Presenting this programme was the youthful Tony Wilson's day job (by night he owned Factory Records, future home of New Order, Happy Mondays and a singing hairdresser called Andrew Berry) and he could be guaranteed to upset your dad by slipping in a short set by This Heat between the weather and an item on rates increases in War-rington. Costello played a couple of songs backed by himself on electric guitar. He wore a pastel blue suit and horn rims and made ugly faces throughout. I think he played 'Welcome to the Working Week' and 'Alison' and maybe 'Red Shoes'. I wasn't sure whether I liked it but I felt some kind of kinship.

Costello was obviously punk rock. His terse and pungent little songs had nothing in common with Eater but even less with Dean Friedman or Camel. He looked awkward and unbe-lievably pissed off. He leered. Besides, *Sounds* had said that he was punk rock. Later that week the self-same paper featured a picture of his legs. I was baffled until I realized that it was a part of a composite poster that you could only assemble by buying all that week's Big Three rock weeklies, *Sounds, Melody Maker* and the *NME*. I did ... simply because I always did.

Costello quickly became an honorary member of my list of acceptable musicians. My friend Nigel, however, with whom I had formed a punk combo called The Idiots, was yet more keen and quickly acquired a copy of Costello's debut album, *My Aim is True*. We would listen to it in his bedroom while marvelling at the picture of Elvis on the back of the sleeve, looking perhaps crapper than anyone has ever done as a publicity gambit on their own record. He wore a tie and jeans with big farmboy-style turn-ups and an Oxfam jacket. He looked like someone who would get his dinner money stolen on a regular basis.

I didn't really like *My Aim is True* for what I now know to be a very pertinent reason. It isn't very good. 'Sneaky Feelings' and 'Pay it Back' are awful old pub singalongs, and a general mood of bar-room downhomeness prevailed. This was not what I wanted at all, pedal steels and tinkling pianos. But there was something about it. '(The Angels Wanna Wear My) Red Shoes' was ace. 'Less than Zero' was catchy and had an unfathomable lyric about Oswald Mosley. More importantly, there was a song called 'I'm Not Angry', which struck some very peculiar chords in me as Elvis railed with lust and acidic contempt against the monstrous regiment of women. And there was 'Alison', a song lovely enough to melt the hardest of punk rock hearts even with its kernel of bitterness. Astute readers will have already guessed what was afoot. Girls were on the verge of arriving into my life big time, and if ever there was a songwriter to map out with certainty the hazardous emotional terrain of the teenage Bohemian and *bon vivant* it was the Elvis Costello of the late seventies.

The Idiots had become Les Flirts, but sophistication was still not high on our agenda, even though we were, perhaps for want of competition, Wigan's premier intellectual punk outfit. We had a song called 'New Society' whose lyric was largely compiled from sociology text books. We had songs called 'Who Needs Karl Marx?' and 'Prague' about armchair socialists, something I seem to have been unduly preoccupied with. These would be supplemented for live performances with a range of improbable covers: the Cole Porter standard 'Anything Goes' in punk idiom, Lou Reed's 'Satellite of Love', 'Mannequin' by

Wire, and the easiest and punkiest Costello tune we could find, 'Mystery Dance'. A barbed rocker about sexual dysfunction, it could have been written for us, and ours was actually a very faithful version sung by me in my best stifled sneer. We played several times at a club called Trucks, where the wiring was so poor that the electrician would not return to the building. We were paid £9 between the three of us, and the manager, a character for whom the word nefarious might have been coined, once claimed that he 'could make you boys bigger than The Dooleys'. Once, we got cocky and essayed a version of 'Alison' that went completely out of control. Someone threw a glass and Jem, our drummer, leapt off his drumstool into the under-nourished throng and proceeded to punch the offending youth insensible as a dancefloor full of Lancashire's hippest cheered and pogoed.

Things were happening. I started my A Levels and fancied myself as something of a dissolute intellectual, a budding poet and novelist who nevertheless combined all this with a keen interest in drinking, girls, politics and sport. A renaissance toyboy, if you like. With consummately brilliant timing, Elvis released *This Year's Model* that spring. In terms of its cultural significance in our teenage lives, it ranked between Picasso's *Guernica*, Beethoven's Ninth and the painting of the Sistine Chapel ceiling.

It was a hot afternoon and we had convened at Nigel's house for a band practice. Nigel and I were on Easter holiday, but Jem had recently been sacked from his job at Rathbone's Bakery for nicking a tray of loaves. Nigel had been into town that morning and bought *This Year's Model*. It was a moment to savour. We all agreed that the cover was excellent, Elvis striking a character-istic pose in a dark suit behind a photographer's tripod. Inside were some odd visuals that we felt sure were of major signifi-cance: a line of bright plastic torsos in string vests stood before a row of washing machines; elsewhere Elvis & The Attractions stood looking aghast at something in a hotel room and played

with a tiny hand-held TV clutched in a rubber mitt. We put
the record on Nigel's mum's music centre and watched as the
bright green Radar label rotated.

It was obviously the best album that had ever been made in
the history of recorded sound. Gone was the hoary old tradition-
alism of *My Aim is True*, gone were the country stylings of US
country rockers Clover (later, appropriately, to become The
News, Huey Lewis's backing band), who had been so anony-
mously competent on that first album.

This was the stuff, fierce and modern and unpretentious, the
full-blooded rock attack of the music augmented by almost
baroque keyboard embellishments by a man called Steve Nieve,
clearly one of the most talented musicians since Liszt. The
Attractions were a proper band and, best of all, they all looked
the part. Faintly geeky but with something abrasively cool
about them. Two of them were called Thomas but weren't
brothers. One of them was about eight foot tall and a drummer
of great skill, while the other was blond, wore glasses and
played bass lines of fearsome complexity, particularly when
measured against the low standards of The Lurkers. Nigel, a
thoughtful musician, was delighted. It was his liberation. He
would no longer have to pretend to be partially deaf and three-
fingered for the sake of our punk credentials. In fact, punk
ended that day as far as I was concerned. It had been a glorious
and bloody revolution. And we had won. Deep Purple would
dangle upside-down from lamp-posts, Robert Plant's hair would
be forcibly cut. But now it was time to move on. *This Year's
Model* pointed to a new and bright future. Of Farfisa organs,
knitted ties, demob jackets and songs about guilt, deception and
having girls you fancied go off with man-apes in IDONTGOTO
UNIVERSITY sweatshirts. And they did, the bastards. And they
were studying geology. Always.

Even 1994's remastered, restructured, orthopaedically contoured
and ergonomically streamlined CD version of *This Year's Model*

sounds bloody fabulous. Unlike all albums before, it seemed from my limited vantage-point, there was no billing or cooing or macho posturing or any of the stand-bys of the typical rock song about human relationships. Remember that there were only two kinds of love song in the seventies: 'Big Legged Woman With My Dinner Ready When I Get Home on Mars', as sung by some preening ninnie in tight flares and golden ringlets, or 'I'm Gonna Do it to You All Night Long, Honey', as sung by a vast black man in a tuxedo. Oh . . . and 'Annie's Song'.

Costello was no John Denver. He took, it seemed, a dim view of human relationships. Well, perhaps not dim but certainly an off-kilter one. He was lustful, ireful, spiteful. 'No Action', 'Hand in Hand' and 'Living in Paradise' were abrasive and petulant little takes on the romantic myth. '(I Don't Wanna Go to) Chelsea' (the *Top of the Pops* performance of which was a highlight of 1978) was a vicious assault on trendies. Even in such exalted company, a couple of tracks stood out.

'Lipstick Vogue', even by his own twisted standards, was, shall we say, vituperative. He referred to love as a tumour and spent the whole song in a state of apoplexy over the tortuous route of his emotional affairs. There was a mad piece of drumming during which you could imagine the vein in Elv's temple bulging. My other big fave was 'Night Rally', a very scary song about Nazis, of whom there were a surfeit in late-seventies Britain. The National Front were folk devils, third placed in many constituencies, leering out at us even from the normally staid confines of the Party Political Broadcast (does anyone else remember this?). The country was in a sour and claustrophobic mood. Joe Strummer announced that the Tories 'are just the NF in good suits'. Happy days. And 'Night Rally' was both a call to arms and a brooding harbinger. Costello's Nazis were not just the bull-necked skins of the NF, but emotional bullies, office backslappers, rugby bores and fat-cat capitalists. It was and is a startlingly great track containing some haunting images. On the American version of *This Year's*

Model – which, obviously, I had to have, even if it meant a drastically reduced beer intake one week – 'Night Rally' was taken off for fear that the kids in Boise, Idaho, wouldn't want to hear it on the radio and replaced with 'Radio Radio', a snarling put-down of the entertainment business. It was an irony not lost even on a Northern teenager.

As I was saying, the National Front upset me and a lot of my peers. They were run by two goons called Tyndall and Webster, who looked exactly like the kind of people who would eventually get arrested for stealing women's underwear from British Home Stores. Webster bought a house in Billinge, near Wigan. Lord knows why, unless he was a rugby league fan or a connoisseur of fun-pubs, night-clubs and taxi-rank violence. Anyway, each night, local folks would go round chucking rocks and putting the occasional window through until eventually he decided not to move in. It made me inordinately proud of my town.

A network of music fans, enraged by some stupid (later retracted) racist comments by Eric Clapton and a hilariously dim piece of political analysis by David Bowie (Britain needs a fascist dictator, yes, yes, haven't you got any mime workshops you could be running, David?) founded an organization called Rock Against Racism which, in cohort with the Anti-Nazi League, mobilized great chunks of Britain's youth against the NF. A huge outdoor anti-racist gig was organized in Brixton on the same day that the NF were holding some kind of think-in for low foreheads. I thought it my duty to be there, as a committed libertarian socialist, particularly since Costello & The Attractions were topping the bill.

The coach left Wigan Gas Showrooms at some unearthly hour, and as we assembled it became obvious that it was to be a trying day. One of our party was a cartoon punk who made Sid Vicious look like Noël Coward. During the five-hour journey to London, he belched, swore, farted and attempted to evacuate all his internal organs via his nose. He hummed tunelessly, gurned upsettingly at the several pretty young women on the bus and held forth on a variety of subjects, most notably his contention that Elvis Costello was 'not a proper punk'. I smouldered and occasionally engaged him in witty badinage of the 'Get fucked' variety.

Upon arrival at Hyde Park, we sat dutifully through some rather dull speeches by left-wing luminaries. During Tony Benn's speech, Smeggy – or whatever his bloody name was – bellowed like an elk. Bathed in righteous glory, we marched to Brixton. Smeggy had found a stick (he was the sort of person who would always find a stick), which he rattled against railings and banged on dustbin lids every inch of the way. Bearded, compassionate, liberal types looked on with pained expressions and entertained highly unright-on, authoritarian fantasies.

Once in the park, we got some good news. For the benefit of those of us making the return trip to the frozen North, Costello and Aswad had swopped places on the bill. This meant that Costello would appear soon and with any luck we would be at Watford Gap before Aswad came on. The sun shone and Jimmy Pursey made a heartfelt but incomprehensible address.

When Costello strolled on to the stage and announced 'Welcome to The Black & White Minstrel Show' I was staggered. Not by the rather fey quip but by the way he was dressed. Red drape jacket, brothel creepers, bootlace tie. Here was my first in-the-flesh experience of the great man and he was dressed as a Ted, the kind of stupid boozy reactionary nitwit who thought that the fat Elvis was king and who used to come mobhanded to the Bier Keller intent on disrupting our fun by throwing tables at us. What had gotten into him?

This rather petty objection soon passed however. He began with 'Night Rally', the perfect choice under the circumstances, even if some late-developing pogoers and crap reggae dancers were somewhat wrong-footed. Even on that cloudless day, it still sounded darkly sinister, particularly since legions of NF skins were rumoured to be converging on us even as we sat and tanned. Obviously, they didn't.

The only problems we had were from the legendary SPG (folk devil, militaristic, imperialist scum of the day, as name-checked on Tom Robinson Band albums), who tried to misdirect us into pockets of lurking skinheads by Brick Lane, and, of course, Smeggy, who had brought no money but managed to obtain enough Skol (i.e. an egg-cup full) to render him doubly obnoxious and pushy. I remember nothing more of Costello's set except a few asides ('Met some of those nice chaps from the National Front earlier, on the way to the Nazis Against Everybody rally') and a song called '(What's So Funny 'bout) Peace, Love and Understanding' that I thought was rotten. When I found out he hadn't written it I was delighted, even if it did call his taste into severe question. He did what I soon learned to be the standard six or seven minute 'Watching the Detectives'. Naturally, I did not do the crap reggae dance.

Once more, Jimmy Pursey made an emotional, not entirely logical speech about Sham 69 and the worldwide struggle for freedom, so we left. There was a major conflagration at Brixton tube station involving the SPG, a few Sieg Heilers and hundreds of Anti-Nazi League supporters. With a bit of embellishment, it was the kind of first-hand involvement in direct political action that would make us the toasts of the sociology class for weeks. Soon, it was time to board the coach back to Wigan. Now are we all here, asked the coach driver, as coach drivers will. 'Yes,' we answered wearily before it dawned on us that Smeggy was absent. One of us, Jeff, made as if to speak. He was met with a huge collective glower. 'Yes, we're all here,' we repeated, some of us whistling brokenly.

It meant leaving the pretty girls behind too (one of whom couldn't get home for days, hunted me down on her return to Wigan and subsequently became a great pal), but it was worth it. We had fought the good fight, we had seen the greatest living Englishman, we had triumphed over the forces of darkness and ignorance. It had been a wonderful day.

By now, I was modelling myself on Costello to an alarming

degree. The ripped and aerosoled punk gear – never, it must be said, a winner with what Michael Bolton would call 'the ladies' – had long gone, to be replaced by a style nicked wholesale from EC. He had refined his image considerably since *My Aim is True* and now resembled a vengeful bookie's runner turned mod, rather than Jethro Clampett's dwarf idiot half-brother turned out for the school dance. We (myself and my mate John who shared my lunatic obsession) would scour Oxfam shops in search of the right kind of Trutex button-down shirt of the early sixties, demob jackets and vented fifties suits, knitted ties in unpalatable hues of cerise and salmon pink and odd accoutrements that we thought added to the effect, such as cuff-links, tie-pins and those elasticated nickel armlets. By great good fortune, I was hopelessly short-sighted and still not vain or rich enough for contact lenses. Finally came the obligatory Oxblood Doctor Marten shoes. Shoes, mark you, never boots, which were set to become the ubiquitous youth footwear of the nineties but back then were still the preserve of football hooligans and hod-carriers.

Stylistically, this sort of thing marked you out. For this was the era when flared Wranglers and large collars with small quantities of shirt attached were the off-duty choice of the day. Prince Charles, Noel Edmonds, Lindsay Wagner, Racey, Norman St John Stevas, Jan Leeming ... they all had rugby shirts and cowboy boots. The sporty, passed-his-test-at-17, dad-a-successful-builder, stupid-moustache types hated us, especially because their girlfriends didn't. Costello was never and will never be a sex symbol, but back in 1978, it was surprising how many girls preferred blokes who'd modelled themselves on him over blokes who'd modelled themselves on the Bee Gee with the big hair.

I'd embarked on a novel and unorthodox approach to my studies – disastrous, needless to say – which involved staying out every night till 2 a.m. at Bluto's club in downtown Wigan. This had become our Algonquin Round Table, a place where creatures of the night would come and disport to the cool tunes of the day, drink, canoodle, vomit and sit on the stairs crying. There were a lot of trenchcoats and a lot of *Station to Station*. One record was inescapable in the last few days of the 1970s and that was 'Oliver's Army'. That breezy, almost corny piano melody was everywhere, not just in Bluto's but in Asda and chip shops and even in the tacky pubs where the beer-monsters hung out. Its success meant that Costello was no longer our personal property. Suddenly he belonged to brickies and clip-pies, rugby lads and the pony-owning girls of Standish and Wrightington. One night I watched in disbelief and horror as Cannon & Ball (whatever happened to Cannon & Ball, by the way?) did a sketch that mentioned Elvis. 'You mean the poor man's Buddy Holly, Tommy?' asked the puppy-doggish Bobby Ball in answer to some disparaging remark from the thin one. It was the same slightly hollow feeling I'd had that same year when I'd seen my first awful Janet or maybe Faith Brown impression of the lovely Kate Bush, whose spell I was also under, except for slightly different reasons. If you're honest, you've probably known that feeling too, the snobby teenager's jealousy at seeing his pet pleasures lured into Sharon and Tracy and Darren's public domain. You never grow out of it.

For all that it became a beer-boy anthem, 'Oliver's Army' was a queer, complex little song. It was probably sung lustily by the same squaddies whose culture it coldly dissected. It hung around at Number 2 for ages and remains Costello's biggest hit. The album it came from, *Armed Forces*, was a strange affair, which only served to make it all the more fascinating. It was covered in terrible drawings of soldiers and had a picture of some elephants on the front like you see on the walls in dilapidated boarding houses. The Attractions stood around in front of a posh semi and Elvis was buttoned into a tight black suit, draped over a diving board. The caption read 'Emotional Fascism', which had been the album's working title. Nobody knew what it all meant. The record sounded like Abba, though.

Or at least Abba during the throes of a particularly messy nervous breakdown. In amongst the military metaphors were a song allegedly about Angela Rippon ('Green Shirt'), a song about the Sunday papers ('Sunday's Best'), and a song called 'Party Girl' that I, with my incisive nascent journalistic skill, assumed to be about his new flame, the all-purpose rock girlfriend Bebe Buell. He was pictured turning up in disguise with her at various gigs. She said, 'Sex with him was more than physical, it was spiritual,' which was extremely flattering but it blew the avenging nerd angle. I imagined the arse-clenchingly private Costello reading it with steam coming out of his ears.

Before going away to college, I managed to get myself embroiled in a very messy, very secret, very improper love affair. It was all very Costello and tremendously exciting, if bad for the nerves. Right on cue, he released 'Radio Radio' as a belated single. On the B-side is 'Tiny Steps', one of the blackest and best things he's ever done. The tune is a pretty sixties thing, but the lyric is a car-crash of half-formed feelings and horrible little images of wounds and gashes and funeral urns. I played it all night every night right up until I went off to college and promptly forgot all about everything except cheap beer and the poems of Thom Gunn.

It was a good time to be young and pretentious. I went to a college on the outskirts of Liverpool which proved handy when The Teardrop Explodes and Echo & The Bunnymen flowered into life that first term, as Eric's club was only twenty minutes away. My prime loyalty was still to Costello, and although I was showing worrying tendencies to sporting a bandanna and flying jacket, I still looked in the main like an extra from *Saturday Night and Sunday Morning*. This enraged the Human Groovers, our pet name for the moustachioed and tracksuited oiks studying Human Movement. I couldn't believe that a grown man would do a degree in PE and I couldn't believe that a grown man could drink pints of still orange and like Wings.

Coming from Wigan, I was naturally a soul boy at heart. This came in very handy when Elvis released an album called *Get Happy!*, a *hommage* to Stax and Motown and, stretching a point, Bluebeat and Merseybeat: *hommage* right down to the cover and its smart-alecy ready-embossed coffee rings and worn cardboard. Actually having heard of Sam and Dave, Lamont Dozier and Betty Wright came in handy when seeking to impress. Looking back, it's obvious that Costello was at the height of his powers. *Get Happy!* was a masterpiece and he still had a couple more in him before it all started to go wrong.

Three or four of us shared a weird, beach-front bachelor pad in Southport, a kind of genteel, sea-less Blackpool where Scousers go to die. The house reverberated daily to King Horse and Hi Fidelity, plus other approved listening such as Dalek I, Wire and The Human League. It was a strange old existence that looks more Bohemian and idyllic in retrospect than it ever was in reality. Fiddling the electricity meter, trying to get the landlord to mend the hole in the roof and living off fags and curry and Martini.

Life took a weird twist when my friend Vourneen got a job at the United Biscuits factory in Huyton and claimed to be working alongside Elvis Costello's mum. Vourneen had been known to embroider the truth before, but this sounded odd and prosaic enough to be true. Costello toured again and, fortuitously, included Southport Floral Hall (or was it the Theatre) on the itinerary. I don't remember much about the gig except that he played 'Moods for Moderns' and a new song called 'Watch Your Step' and danced in that knock-kneed, pigeon-toed way that was his trademark. I'm rather more clear on the events afterwards. I'm sitting in the bar, having a fag, when a gangling, sweaty, familiar looking man sidles by me. It's Pete Thomas, The Attractions' drummer. On impulse, I decide to follow him. He wanders through a couple of doors and just at the point where ninety-nine times out of a hundred the burly security man would gently put his hand into my face, we turn a corner and there's Costello. Guitar case, glass of wine, long overcoat. He fixes me that raised-eyebrow quizzical look – not unreasonably, I'm practically in his dressing room – and I say for want of anything more apposite or intelligent, 'Can I have your autograph?' He sort of chuckled. 'On what?' I have nothing in my hand but a packet of Benson & Hedges. 'On this,' I announce, holding it out. 'Well, all right. I'll sign it, but you have to promise to give up smoking.'

I broke the promise within five minutes but I still have the packet. My mates wouldn't believe me when I got back. I remember the chest-busting feeling holding that little gold oblong out and watching their eyes widen. Just then Vourneen – who we had no idea was coming – walked past us with a middle-aged woman, waved and casually announced, 'This is Mrs McManus. We're just going to the after-show party in town. If I'd known I could have got you a pass. Oh well.' I was sick to the pit of my stomach. I could have been clinking glasses with The Attractions and grilling Elvis, who was practically my best mate now, on the inner meaning of 'Goon Squad'. It was for the best. I would have been a horrible gauche little twerp I now realize but at the time I was inconsolable.

My flatmates and I stood in the icy street and looked at the huge and luxurious tour bus. We looked back at the hall, a sometime cinema, and at the large red letters on the illuminated white background above the main doors reading, 'Elvis Costello And The Attractions Tonight'. Though I already had his auto-graph, I was feeling cheated and souvenir-hungry.

It took about half an hour, standing on each other's shoulders, falling down a lot, giggling, smirking, shrieking in pain and hiding behind wheelie bins. But we did it. From then on, we ate our tea nightly under the ludicrously large Elvis Costello And The Attractions Tonight legend on the wall. It stayed there until we moved, which coincided almost exactly with the landlord finding out about the electricity meter.

*

College went by in a blur. I moved in with three radical feminists. I started to eat properly and spend my evenings reading *Women's Voice* or *Spare Rib* and discussing Gramsci, The Au Pairs, Martin Fry, the myth of the vaginal orgasm and how to make kedgeree. They were the wildest, hardest-drinking bunch I ever met, and I learned more in that year than in my previous twenty. Costello brought 'New Amsterdam' out, on an EP backed by a couple of the strangest and most striking songs he's ever done. Hunt them down, they're marvellous. 'Ghost Train' may be his finest moment, and we would sing it lustily as we walked back from the Shakespeare pub, where each night an implausibly named organist/drummer combo named Roy Rocket and Mr Personality would entertain us.

Costello made a country record that we all pretended to like, and during a documentary about the making of it we saw him almost in tears of joy at the string arrangement producer Billy Sherrill had put on it. A wonderful moment. *Almost Blue* kept us reasonably occupied until he made a proper record, *Trust*, which had real gems on it like 'Clubland' and 'Shot With His Own Gun', another piece of pitiless emotional wrangling, just right for those 3 a.m. lowspots.

I didn't know it, but the love affair was almost over. Costello had one indubitably great album left in him, *Imperial Bedroom*, released in the same week as ABC's *The Lexicon of Love*. Some week, eh? My best mate John bought both albums on the same day that he got a Dear John letter from his fiancée, and we sat in his front room, me trying to be supportive and philosophical and both of us listening with increasing interest to these two magnificent LPs. By the end of them, John was whistling and cracking jokes, and since then I've never underestimated the therapeutic and restorative capacity of a good tune.

Imperial Bedroom is Elvis Costello's best LP – ignore any statements to the contrary. It spans genres, plays games, tells jokes and uses state-of-the-art technology and complex arrangements in a humane and clever way. It's the sort of record you don't get very often (Prefab Sprout's *Jordan: The Comeback* is one, and Blur's recent *Parklife* is another): a kind of instant record collection, a record that would sustain you through long desert-island afternoons.

Of course, it was all different before the war. A gang of scrap-metal dealers planted a flag on some godforsaken rock in the South Atlantic and before we knew it, Prince Andrew and his chums were steaming out of Portsmouth. A funny time to be a young man. You had to give the fascists what for, naturally, but no one fancied losing a leg for that callous bloody harridan. You fancied it would be all over by Christmas but still you fretted. Maybe it was nothing more than paranoia, but none of the lads I knew could get a passport that summer. They'd lose the forms, there were staff shortages. Come the Argie surrender, they began plopping on to the mat.

Considering that Britain was effectively at war for the first time since 1945, British songwriters didn't really rise to the challenge. The best song about the Falklands, indeed one of the best social documentary songs of our time, is Elvis Costello's 'Shipbuilding'. A lesser songwriter would have gone in for some blether about the senseless waste of human life. Costello rooted it somewhere we could all understand, in the life of a little man who felt scared and disheartened by the thought of another war but knew that it would mean more work at the shipyards and a new winter coat for the wife.

These were the kind of men who would frequent working men's clubs. During the summer of 1983, I too, became that kind of man when I finally got my own back on Vourneen and became, briefly, the mate of Elvis Costello's dad. It was, as we say up North, a queer how do you do.

I'd known for some time that Costello's father, Ross McManus, had been the singer with Joe Loss's band in the fifties. It was something I happened to mention one day round at my parents' house. 'Oh, yes,' said my mother without looking up from her knitting, 'Ross McManus. He does the clubs now. He's always round here. In fact, let me check the book.' I ought to point out that The Book, in our house, was not *The Holy Bible* but *Spotlight*, a listings mag that told you exactly when Peter Firmani (Well Respected Tenor) was next playing Garstang Soldiers & Sailors Club. 'Yeah, he's on at Worsley Mesnes Labour Club next week.'

Next week found me and John drinking mild at five pence a pint and filling in a bingo card each. At about eight, we were asked to give best of order, and a pixieish man in a white jacket and glasses came on. It was Ross McManus, Elvis Costello's dad, and we loved him instantly. He played trumpet in 'Georgia on My Mind', sang a few standards and did a weird little dance in a strobe light during The Strawbs' 'Part of the Union'. Then he went off for the break. During which, something must have happened. My mother must have pulled in some arcane favour in the Wigan entertainment industry Mafia, for when Ross returned he announced – and I can remember these words almost verbatim – 'It's come to my knowledge that there are some fans of my son's in the audience. For those of you who don't know, my son Declan metamorphosized into the rock and roll phenomenon that is Elvis Costello. And for them and for the rest of you, I'd like to do a few of his songs now.'

He passed around some sheet music to the organist and drummer, who looked at each other, shrugged and then launched into 'Oliver's Army'. It was ace. Then he did 'Good Year for the Roses' and then, unbelievably, he did 'Alison'. 'Alison'! After that, it came as almost no surprise when, later in the evening, a man sidled up to us and muttered, 'Ross says join him for a drink backstage.'

And so, for a summer, we became Elvis Costello's dad's mates. We humped gear, we stood him barley wines, we listened enraptured to tales of Steve Nieve's musical prowess ('He's chock-full of tunes, that lad') and how Elvis had bought a grand piano as a tax loss. He gave me a hand-made T-shirt that an

American fan had made with a silk print of Elvis on the front and the slogan 'Almost Blue Almost Out Now' that Elvis had left behind in a dressing room in New York. And he would try to throw in a few Costello numbers each time for us. The last time I saw him was at a Falklands Benefit at St Cuthbert's Catholic Club, Pemberton. We moved his amp for him and he said sheepishly, 'No Elvis tonight, lads. This bloody organist and drummer aren't up to it.' So, we contented ourselves with Ross's own tunes and an extraordinary set from a miner in a frilly shirt with his arm in plaster. It was a happy summer of cheap beer and nice people and full houses and jackpots and all the twos, twenty-two. And if you're reading this, Ross, I hope you're well.

Let's go back to 'Shipbuilding' a moment. A modern classic, everyone agrees, which is ironic since its parent album, *Punch the Clock*, was his first real false move, at least in our house. There was some fashionable flirting with funk and soul which delighted the wanna-be black men on the staff of the *NME*, who made it their album of the year. It was more straightforward than *Imperial Bedroom* and had about an eighth as many good tunes. During 'The World and His Wife', you finally got some idea of how irritating Costello's relentless punning had always been to those who didn't like him. It was boring, it had no style and little grace. Plus there was a group around whose songs had. They were from Manchester and they were called The Smiths, and when I heard 'Hand in Glove', it was the same feeling I'd got when I heard 'Neat Neat Neat' and *This Year's Model* all those years before.

Like a lot of couples who marry too young, we drifted apart. I couldn't bear the company he'd taken to hanging around with, The Pogues and beery country singers and the rest. The records went from bad to worse, at first just patchy (*Goodbye Cruel World* and *King of America*) and then self-obsessed and charmless (*Spike* and *Mighty Like a Rose*). In a series of shock

moves, I became a music journalist and Costello became a prize
nana, hell-bent, it seemed, on making himself wilfully unattrac-
tive, piling on weight, dressing like James Robertson Justice and
growing a crap beard. Costello hates people going on about the
beard, but what the hell were we supposed to do? Here was my
sharp-dressed New Wave mentor looking like the fat old self-
important windbags he was supposed to have annihilated. Everyone at the *NME* where I now worked thought he was still a
major player. I thought he was a prannock. Hell hath no fury,
etc., etc., etc.

In late 1993, I was enjoying the delights of the freelance
lifestyle and spending the afternoon at the Edvard Munch
exhibition at the National Gallery. Like everyone else I went
out of my way to see *The Scream*, that potent symbol of the 20th
century. I scrutinized a while from different angles just in case
anyone was watching me before realizing that someone was. It
was Elvis Costello. He looked great. He'd lost weight, cut his
hair and he wore a rather smart leather jacket. He gave me a
look which said, quite clearly, 'Stop gawping, you arse,' and
went back to listening to the commentary on his Walkman.

He'd just made *The Juliet Letters*, which, despite some carping
from critics, was terrific and, although I didn't know it, he must
have been working on *Brutal Youth*, the excellent reunion album
with The Attractions, for which praise has been unanimous and
which heralds a welcome return to a more direct and communi-
cative style.

I suppose I ought to have pulled the headphones from his ear
and said, 'You won't remember me but you signed my cig
packet in 1980,' or 'I know your dad,' or something. But I didn't.
I just let him go on to the other paintings. We'd had our
differences along the way, fallen out of love and sought comfort
in the arms of others. But it was still nice to see him looking so
well. It was nice to think that in the end we both got happy.

Thankfully Not Living in Yorkshire it Doesn't Apply

JOHN AIZLEWOOD

When Kevin Rowland ceased flirtations with glam rock in Lucy and the Lovers and punk as leader of The Killjoys, he discovered a blend of Stax horns, vocals that Chairmen of the Board's General Johnson ought to have sued over and some distinctly pithy lyrics. Dexys Midnight Runners had a British Number 1 with 'Geno' in 1980, but Rowland's essentially obstreperous attitude led Dexys to refuse to speak to the press, play alcohol-free venues in seated theatres and eventually split up for the first time.

They would rise on one more occasion, as 'Come On Eileen' reached Number 1 in both Britain and America, before Rowland changed image for the fourth time in three albums and adopted a slacks and pullover look for *Don't Stand Me Down*. Unfortunately, nobody wanted to know and Dexys petered out. Rowland's solo career ended in tears after a poorly received album, and by 1993 he was drawing the dole in North West London. A television appearance on Jonathan Ross's *Saturday Zoo* by a revitalized Dexys performing new songs confirmed that the re-formation rumours could, for once, be true.

Sheffield's Virgin Records store was hardly mega. It was a dank place, situated at the bottom of the city's main shopping thoroughfare, The Moor, and played deafeningly loud music and only extended a warm handshake of welcome to Cabaret Voltaire disciples. To peruse the records you had to contort your upper body, while shuffling through badly felt-tipped marker cards, highlighting sections by This Heat, They Must be Russians or The Flying Alphonso Brothers. On the walls, there were hand-written postcards from Artery, Vice Versa or The

Scarborough Antelopes looking for guitarists, who 'must be into Wire'.

Virgin's January 1981 sale wasn't the great Polish car-boot style extravaganza I'd anticipated. There were albums by Shooting Star, Slaughter & The Dogs, Rose Royce, Lou Reed, Darling, Slade, Straight 8 and Fingerprintz. Somewhere at the back, between Vivabeat and Manfred Mann's Earth Band, lurked a guilty copy of *Searching for the Young Soul Rebels*, the first Dexys Midnight Runners album. It was a purchase born of frustration; I was hoping for a cheap Skids album, but if you've got Christmas money in your pocket, it has to be spent. And that's how it really began.

I was rather taken by the second wave of British punk bands, like The Clash, Buzzcocks, Adverts, Damned – anyone in fact on a medium to big tour who passed through Sheffield – and I wore a frighteningly tatty leather jacket festooned with tour badges just to prove it. To me, Dexys were half-joke, half-intriguing: no more, no less.

I'd bought the first single, 'Dance Stance', for 50p from Rotherham Woolworth's. The follow up, 'Geno', went to Number 1, so I lost interest and concentrated on willing The Clash into the Top 20. 'There There My Dear', with its lyrics in letter form, was so purely superb that it eclipsed the latest Ruts offering, although I didn't summon up the anti-fashion statement to buy it. I only heard 'Keep It Part One (Inferiority Part Two)' once, on Dave Lee Travis's morning show on Radio 1. He hated it and said so. I merely admired him for having an opinion and somehow missed Kevin Rowland's astonishing vocal performance. I didn't bother with the tour.

Dexys took adverts in the music press to explain why they weren't doing interviews. I thought this was silly, so I'd no idea what a driven man Kevin was or that they wouldn't shuffle their way into soft soul like Simply Red or Spandau Ballet would later do. Dexys were woolly-hatted bozos with a few catchy singles. In my bedroom, The Members had more potential.

There is no group picture of Dexys anywhere on *Searching for the Young Soul Rebels*. The front cover shows a Belfast boy, looking frightened. He'd been evacuated after the British army moved in during the late sixties. If the picture hadn't been cropped so closely, you'd have seen soldiers wielding guns at the boy. He looked a little like the young Kevin Rowland, but it wasn't. I found this out by mistake, while browsing through a British Empire partwork – not something I usually did. I attributed the remarkable coincidence to the Lord and could have wept with joy. At the bottom right-hand corner of the album's back cover was someone, probably a Dexy, walking away, woolly hat intact, sports bag in hand. Around the song titles, except 'Geno' and the sole cover version, '7 Days Too Long', were helpful words like: 'Reality – I don't think so, not yet.' I was hooked.

I was to spend hours analysing the title – the bloody title for God's sake – of 'Thankfully Not Living in Yorkshire it Doesn't Apply'. Did it mean aspiring to reality? Had reality been achieved and then spurned? Was reality trying to peep through the door and was our Kevin having none of it? Or did he simply not like Yorkshire, and it had nothing to do with reality at all? I still don't know and, yes, I wouldn't mind knowing. You never quite lose this stuff, you know.

On one side of the inner sleeve, there was a rather pompous essay, romanticizing the founding of Dexys in cod Dashiell Hammett style. On the other side of that cardboard, scratch-inducing sleeve were the lyrics. On my way home, I read them atop the 69 bus to Rotherham, still unhirsute enough to pay the 2p child's fare, although I was nearly seventeen. I could have written those words myself, if I'd been able to string a sentence together. When it said, 'Some of the words are not necessarily used in the songs but we think they add to the picture,' my life was changed. And I hadn't even played the thing.

Sorry to harp on, but oh, those lyrics. I believed the lot. It was a rotten time. I was trying to get into university, my parents were splitting up and I could no more lose my virginity than fly to the moon, or, indeed, fly anywhere. Here was a lyricist who appeared to feel as quietly desperate and alienated as I was. 'You're feeling a loss but you're not fit to make it,' sang Kevin on the first version of 'Keep It'. 'You're offered so much but you're frightened to take it.' That it didn't make strict grammatical sense never troubled me. Here was my soul mate, and, better yet, the tunes were lovely too.

I fed my obsession. I bought the three singles I hadn't bothered with and discovered that the new 'Keep It', the one that so distressed the Hairy Monster, was the most intense vocal performance I'd ever heard. Try to listen to it now – if it doesn't contort your stomach, you probably don't have a pulse rate. I stopped listening to other groups, I'd lie on my bed with the lights turned out, singing the whole album as quietly as my tone-deaf bellows would allow. Downstairs my parents would be shouting at each other and I'd be under my duvet mumbling, 'You might need sympathy but that's not what I'd tell you.' It's best they never knew.

The choruses of 'Burn it Down' (née 'Dance Stance') and 'There There My Dear' were lists of names. 'Burn it Down' was an anti-Irish-joke song – I applied it to myself of course, as I did almost everything – and its refrain was one of Irish writers: Oscar Wilde, Brendan Behan, Sean O'Casey, George Bernard Shaw. I started to discover these people, most of whom I'd never heard of. I read Behan's *Borstal Boy*, Beckett's *Waiting for Godot*, and anything I could find by Edna O'Brien, partly because I fancied her, partly because she always seemed to be encouraging young writers and partly because *The Country Girls* trilogy was spectacularly readable. I discovered who Laurence Sterne and Sean O'Casey were and, after many years, gave up on Frank O'Connor, Jimmy Hiney and Catherine Rhine. I was mesmerized by the writers I did track down, but with a Dexys

endorsement there was no other option. How fortunate Kevin
Rowland never had much in the way of irony.

'There There My Dear' I saw as an indictment of the
pseudish Cabaret Voltaire groupies who frequented Virgin.
Thus I developed a burning hatred for William Burroughs
(hopefully Kevin didn't mean Edgar Rice Burroughs on that
song's shitlist), Berlin (Isaiah, not the city), Kerouac, poor old
Kirkegaard and J. G. Ballard. I still carry these prejudices I
deliberately acquired from the shelves of Rotherham's excellent
public library.

A new single, the first since my conversion, was released in
March. 'Plan B' referred to Bill Withers' 'Lean On Me'. In a
moment oozing style and taste I bought it; I'd only known
Mud's version previously. 'Plan B' confirmed how right I was:
'Hold out your hand, we'll make a stand,' suggested Kevin. I
was holding and standing like nobody before or since. It was
patently the best song there had ever been and it reached
Number 58.

I was turning into a Dexys bore. A frankly fiddled election saw
me on my sixth-form college's student shop committee. I had no
interest in serving my fellow students Opal Fruits and coffee. I
had considerable interest in commandeering the shop stereo and
letting everyone hear the majesty of Dexys. Soon, everyone
knew 'Plan B'. They didn't seem to like it though. 'Supper's
Ready' by Genesis soon returned to the top of the college airplay
chart, closely followed by 'New Face in Hell' by The Fall.

None of this mattered the day Dexys announced a tour, the
Projected Passion Revue. They only played seated venues and
banned alcohol, which was a shame for me as theatres were one
of the few places a youthful under-eighteen-year-old like myself
could be served beer. Dexys were to be supported by dance
troupe Torque and comedy duo The Outer Limits, featuring
Comic Strip leader Peter Richardson and Nigel 'Neil' Planer.
My nearest show was Doncaster, where a promoter with a sense
of humour had booked them into the Odeon. How I rejoiced.

I enlisted a brace of friends whose curiosity certainly hadn't been raised by me, but who did know that *Searching for the Young Soul Rebels* was genuinely great. I begged one of their mothers to use her credit card and, a mere two days after the dates were announced, we had the tickets. Indeed, so marvellously situated were those tickets that there can't have been general hats in the air in South Yorkshire at Dexys' appearance. I, though, was beside myself with excitement.

Meanwhile, in London, unbeknown to me, Dexys Midnight Runners were having difficulties. Most of the band had left Kevin and trombonist Big Jimmy Patterson before 'Plan B' to form The Bureau, whose album was never released in Britain, to my great delight (I bought it though. Just to be safe.) Now Kevin wanted to escape from EMI, the record company, on whom he blamed the failure of 'Keep It' and 'Plan B'. EMI were reluctant to finance the tour. Relations were what Gerry Adams and Ian Paisley might have referred to as 'strained'. All I knew was that, unless you lived in Chelmsford, London or Birmingham, your opportunity to see Dexys was no longer available, for they had cancelled most of the tour.

I was incandescent with rage, bloody livid in fact. Dexys were honest, I believed in them, they owed us a tour and my friends wouldn't have the opportunity to see and believe. Blah, blah, blah. All because they couldn't finance a few poxy dates. Pah!

On the back of the 'Plan B' sleeve, there was an address that sadder Dexys fans could write to, somewhere in Sutton Coldfield, where, it was implied (and even I wasn't naïve enough to believe this twaddle) a band member was waiting to receive harsh criticism and laudatory praise.

I didn't usually do this sort of thing, but I was genuinely humiliated. The Clash had always been the best live band in the world, closely followed by the last people we'd been to see. Like a Jehovah's Witness, I was waiting in supreme confidence for a visitation of the band I knew to be the Christ to Strummer's John the Baptist. I couldn't even hang on to the tickets in the hope of a re-scheduling.

I telephoned the Odeon. A woman with saint-like patience explained the situation: 'They just did it to get their names in the papers, love.' I played my neglected punk records once more, wrote to Sutton Coldfield to explain, as forcibly as I could, my feelings of betrayal. High horse professionally saddled, I referred to myself in the third person as 'student' and taunted Seb Shelton, who'd drummed for Mod revival leaders Secret Affair, for probably having a parka. A few days later a letter arrived with a London postmark. Do I still have this hand-written missive? Oh yes. Sad isn't it?

Dear Student,
   Thank you for your criticisms. Please consider this:
1. Aug 1980. Kevin Rowland asks drummer to join his group.
2. Sep. Drummer agrees. Sincerity and integrity mean more to him than fat wages and hollow sloganeering.
3. Drummer leaves his group.
4. Two weeks before drummer is due to join Kevin's group, it disintegrates whilst touring in Europe.
5. Drummer feels sick; lost; redundant.
6. Kevin, Jimmy and drummer begin to rebuild group.
7. Meanwhile Kevin insists that single recorded before split is released.
8. Record company reluctantly agree but see this as an ideal time to teach Kevin a lesson; break his spirit and put group under their control.
9. Kevin asks record company for money to rebuild group and stresses importance of current record.
10. Record company not sympathetic; offers peanuts and makes minimal efforts to promote newly released record.
11. Repeat 9 & 10 for 2–3 months.
12. Kevin, Jimmy & drummer are determined not to be dictated to by record company and continue to audition and rehearse

five new players in warehouse with no heating, throughout winter.

13. Dec 10, 1980. Group has full line-up again. Begin intensive rehearsals.

14. Jan 1981. Group records single but withholds tapes from record company. Company regains tapes.

15. March. Record company releases record against group's wishes. Again fails to promote it properly – new group seems stroppier than old one if anything.

16. Group believes it would be better to stop playing music altogether rather than release any more records via their record company. Kevin decides enough is enough. It's time to leave record company – at any cost.

17. Group hopes to sign with another company in time to finance tour.

18. Negotiations slow. Group cancels most of tour they've been working towards for three months. Group not very happy.

John; this little story covers my eight months involvement with this group. In this time, the group has received no financial help from the record company. Were it not for Kevin's determination and the strength and belief of the members and our manager (who isn't a millionaire incidentally), the group would have disappeared before Christmas under a cloud of despair and frustration.

This is no sob story though. I've enjoyed most of the past eight months (despite the lack of cooperation from the rock press) – being part of this group, which is not part of the rock'n'roll circus, is worthwhile.

I really don't want to go through your letter point by point, but there's a couple of things I've got to comment on.

Firstly, since when was 'the lady who sells tickets at the Doncaster Odeon' an authority on us?? What could we possibly gain by setting up a tour that we didn't intend to play? Publicity??!! If we wanted that we'd do interviews in the rock press and be guaranteed the front page of every one of them!

Secondly, regarding the three shows which have been salvaged:

for London, if it sells out, we'll get £1,800. For Chelmsford and Birmingham we get sod all because our fee of £1,000 in each case will go to the two promoters who we've cancelled dates on elsewhere. Weigh that against the cost of PA, lights, accommodation, transport, paying the dance troupe, stage props etc – £6,000 give or take a couple of quid. Believe me, not bollocks but a big loss.

There's a lot more I could say but I think you'll understand now that you are not the only disappointed one.

All that remains now is to say that we are sorry you made an effort to get tickets and that the shows had to be cancelled. If you feel that you can make another effort to get to either Chelmsford, London or Birmingham, we'd be pleased to see you and I think it'll be worth it.

If you can, then please phone:
1. Jenny at Intense Emotions before Wednesday midday.
2. The Letchworth House Hotel up until about Thursday midday.

We'll put you on the guest list and find a floor, at least, for you to sleep on.

> Sincerely,
> Seb Shelton.

PS. I've never had a parka and two of the singles were re-recordings!!!
PPS. I tried to get you on the phone but you're ex-directory, so I hope the postperson pulls his/her finger out.

I shook with fear and excitement. They'd noticed! Truly, they cared. And I could go to London for the day.

I phoned Jenny that minute. She wasn't in. The post came at 7 a.m. at our place. Two fretful hours later, me and Jenny were chatting like old pals. I jabbered at her for some time. She suggested I might like to take a friend along. I was having none of it, I wanted Dexys' undivided attention. Jenny told me my ticket would be at the door of the Dominion Theatre.

I couldn't afford the train, so a National Express coach was the only option. I wasn't going to chance hitching. Clutching my 'Plan B' sleeve, I found what we called a beer-off, which was willing to serve me, and bought a four-pack of Stones bitter for reasons which forever must remain a mystery. They didn't have toilets on coaches then and, after the stop at Leicester Forest East, I was in an agony only those who've had hernia operations without anaesthetic could possibly understand. How sensible Kevin Rowland's ban on alcohol now seemed.

London was where I wanted to live. I'd been there a few times, mainly to see Sheffield Wednesday slug it out with Brentford or Orient. My idea of exploring London involved getting to the Dominion as soon as I'd got off the coach and visiting the toilets. Then I'd go to the Virgin Megastore, for about six hours.

By 6.30, I was the only person in the Dominion queue. Every fifteen minutes I'd tell the door man I had a ticket and backstage pass on the door. Since he was the door man, I thought he would have them. I assumed he'd be impressed. Other than mutely pointing at the ticket office, he ignored me.

When the doors opened, I was first inside. The ticket was at the box office. With it was a pass. Now, a backstage pass marked 'Access All Areas' has magical powers. It entitles the bearer to go anywhere he wants at any time. I went on to the stage, which was hidden from view by the curtain Dexys would start their set from behind. There was nobody around so I sat on Seb Shelton's drumstool, twanged Steve Wynn's bass, and tapped Kevin Rowland's microphone, without seeing anything repressed or sexual in such action. There were lifts to the dressing rooms, but what with the (possibly apocryphal) tales of pre-gig chanting and press-ups, I didn't take them. Sensibly, I waited in my seat, blissfully happy and with my pass so prominent it might as well have been stuck to my forehead.

A dance troupe was, is and always will be a dance troupe. I felt impossibly worthy sitting through Torque. The Outer Limits were terribly funny: they impersonated Space Invaders and the Neil character said 'orgasm', which was hilarious. Anyway, if Dexys found them funny, then I had little option other than to fall around, asking for a nurse to stitch my sides together.

Dexys, as I knew they would be, were the best thing I'd seen. They dressed in hooded, monkish tops, wore Lonsdale boxing boots and looked intense. The press had suggested Kevin's grimness meant that nobody was allowed to dance. Midway through 'Until I Believe in My Soul', a dancing deputation sauntered down the aisles. 'Why can't we dance, Kevin?' their leader demanded. This was mutiny! I wouldn't have budged if they played Liquid Gold's 'Dance Yourself Dizzy'. 'Go ahead,' smiled Kevin, rather like Saddam Hussein smiling at his kiddy hostages, 'be my guest.' Phew! A moment of rock'n'roll tension defused. Nobody else seemed to think this was one of the best few seconds of their lives.

I assumed that after shows, bands scampered into a waiting limousine and drove off at high speed, because I'd once seen Whitesnake do this after a Sheffield City Hall gig. Therefore, I sprinted backstage after the final encore, pass flashing like a Belisha beacon. There were still assorted sweat-encrusted Dexys waiting for the lifts – Kevin had long gone, of course. I smiled weakly, safe in the knowledge that they hadn't a clue who I was or why I was staring so. I anxiously waited until the lift was free, without the precious knowledge that anyone with a pass like mine is never challenged.

The dressing room was crowded and my pass was suddenly devalued. Shockingly, beer was being drunk; less shockingly, Kevin Rowland was arguing with what I presumed to be fans; nobody was signing autographs and nobody paid me any interest. I searched out Seb Shelton – he'd tell me what to do.

He was friendly and behaved in a manner which suggested he didn't see me as anything but perfectly normal. I apologized for all the trouble I'd caused. He introduced me to the others, eventually. They'd all seen 'that letter', which pleased me

immensely. I'd never assumed I'd been the only one the cancella-
tion would have provoked into writing. Even at my most
gauche – and I would never be quite so gauche ever again – I
scurried round getting my freshly creased 'Plan B' and the
programme signed. Kevin Rowland was combative and I wilted.
I was honoured to be there and told him so directly. I think he
was disappointed I didn't spar more. Surely he, of all people,
would have cared enough to write if he'd been in my position.
Seb Shelton tapped me on the shoulder. I was going home with
him. Joy beyond words.

Somewhat unglamorously, we left the Dominion through the
back, edging around the roadies packing stuff away, to board
what I now know to be a 134 bus. Seb Shelton was still wearing
his stage gear, although I didn't find this remotely incongruous.
We went upstairs and sat at the front. I can't remember if there
was anyone else on the top deck, for I was plying the poor man
with question after question, which, despite having drummed to
within an inch of his kit's life, he answered unfailingly. His
girlfriend was with us. I forgot her name instantly and never
bothered to re-learn it. She was lovely, too, and if she was
distressed about sharing her home with me, she never let it
show. She'd chip in with something wise every so often, but I
was oblivious. God, I was happy, if surprised he wasn't surrounded by autograph-seekers.

We alighted on Fortis Green Road, at the top of Muswell
Hill. I was hungry now after all that jaw ache. Seb suggested a
Chinese takeaway which he would pay for. Being northern, I'd
never eaten Chinese food before and, neck-reddening, I committed the *faux pas* of ordering chips on their own. I knew it was a
mistake as soon as I opened my mouth, but I didn't know any
different. We didn't have foreign food in our house. We weren't
paid-up racists, it just never occurred.

The rock star's pad was a first floor flat above a futon centre.
Chips in hand, I set about asking more questions. I noted sagely
how great Dexys guitarists had looked when they jointly

straddled monitors, and Seb said they'd worked on it for ages. I generously admitted that maybe Secret Affair weren't that bad and kept quiet about liking football. He wondered why I hadn't hitch-hiked, showed me a Stax budget-priced double album (I bought it the next week and it was wonderful) and revealed he was teetotal. They put me in a room of my own but before I went to bed I made sure he did the signing. 'In case there's no time tomorrow,' I offered, feebly. I wouldn't have slept so well otherwise, I really wouldn't.

The morning was similarly sweet. Seb was up early on good-bloke duties. I was offered breakfast and, as a ridiculous commitment to the newly Spartan me, I accepted only an orange. He said, 'Are you sure?' in a manner which suggested he now knew I was bonkers. Dexys were playing Birmingham that night. Unbelievably, Seb asked if I wanted to go. Even more unbelievably I declined, genuinely not wanting to push my luck and be a burden. What a fool.

As I walked to the bus stop, I saw the other Dexys pass by in a cheap Transit van, on their way to pick up my friend Seb. They were all in stage gear but I didn't think this was especially unusual. I didn't wave, but I knew then I'd made a rotten decision not to go with them.

I wrote a second time to Sutton Coldfield on my return, after beginning to purchase all the records they'd recommended in the programme. This was a thank you letter – I got Seb's girlfriend's name wrong once more (I think I called her Doris) and joined the Intense Emotions Circle. It provided a directory with everyone's name and address and proved to be a Dexys fans' Dateline. Funnily enough, I only wrote to women, and I met the fairly lovely Julie from North Wales for an afternoon's hard but innocent snogging under the shadow of Chester city walls. I felt guiltier than ever when I listened to other groups, and my Dexys bore factor reached new heights now they were all close personal friends. I hadn't finished with them yet though.

They supported The Teardrop Explodes in Nottingham for a TV broadcast. I said hello to Big Jimmy Patterson, Seb and ex-guitarist Al Archer as they hung about the bar while The Teardrop Explodes played. The Projected Passion Revue never toured again and closed with a few dates in London, at the Old Vic. Again I met Seb and several other Dexys who were watching the support acts from the gods. I'd been confident enough of meeting them, so I brought another single to be signed. They seemed friendly enough. In their position, I'd have hidden from me.

Two days before my friend Hugh's A level history exam, Dexys played a Radio 1 show in a Newcastle tent. Hugh was game for anything that distracted him from revision and agreed to come, partially to test my tale of pop star kinship. I'd virtually sunk to stopping innocent strangers on the street to tell them I knew Dexys.

At this show (released as a Radio 1 In Concert album in 1993), Dexys unveiled the raggle-taggle gypsy look and played 'Come On Eileen' for the second time, the first one having been the previous night at a working men's club. Already I was sufficiently above my station to wonder why I hadn't been invited. Kid Jensen introduced the band and I booed loudly enough to put him off, because I hated 'my' band getting tainted by the business.

Somehow I managed to meet Seb Shelton, yet again. This time he was signing autographs (this reassured me in itself), passing signed pieces of paper through the backstage fence. I let slip to him that the only trains left were mail ones, taking hours. Catching them would involve a long wait, I mused. He did the decent thing and offered to put us up at their hotel. Hugh was impressed; I was beginning to get a touch blasé.

The Holiday Inn bar was packed, so I sat and talked to Seb — and his girlfriend, who was far friendlier than I deserved, as she must have known I'd called her Doris by now — and he intimated that the brass section wasn't happy at being usurped by a fiddle section. I loved hearing this kind of thing, I felt close to the centre. Hugh behaved himself (although he was Apprentice Satan, his dad was a priest, so he knew how to pretend to have benefited from being well brought up; besides, he was humbled too) and said all the right things, i.e. he followed my lead and agreed with everything Seb said. In the bar itself was a journalist from the *NME* and one from *Record Mirror*. This was impressive stuff. I'd made it now, for we talked with the journalists as if we were equals.

Seb had earlier suggested we might end up sleeping in the same room as him and his girlfriend. Common sense had prevailed and we were dumped with the Intense Emotions Circle organizer (Jenny had been mysteriously sacked). I hated him – he seemed jaded by all this hanging around with Dexys and I was profoundly jealous he'd seen the working men's club show. I tried to get him to give me his job but he wasn't *that* jaded. Hugh was embarrassed for me and shut me up. As if in punishment, the organizer went to sleep with the radio still on. We left early the next morning without saying goodbye, in a desperate mission to try and salvage Hugh's A level, although as he'd been revising for the wrong one, any kind of effort on this subject was pointless. I didn't know it then, but I wouldn't get any closer to Dexys.

There were two more meetings. A few weeks after the Newcastle show, 'Come On Eileen' was Number 1, *Too-Rye-Ay* was about to be released (Seb Shelton becoming Seb Shilton in the process, I wasn't just imagining that nobody cared as much as I did), and HMV had a shop to be opened in Sheffield with some of Dexys (Seb, Kevin and Kevin's fiddler girlfriend, Helen O'Hara) doing the honours, along with antichrists Dollar. The queues were huge – pop stars didn't appear at such close quarters in Sheffield, and everyone now loved Dexys, much to my chagrin. My pop star chums recognized me and I got yet more things signed. I didn't know it then, but their real friends didn't bother with all this autographing lark. Once a fan always a fan, you see, and that gap is not for bridging. I flexed my friendship muscle by saying I wanted to talk. I had nothing to say, of course, but I needed the contact. There'd be some time afterwards they reckoned, and so I waited around the back.

Three hours later, they emerged and were bundled into a taxi. 'If you need to talk, you'd better get in that cab,' said a security man I'd spent most of those three hours convincing I was a friend of Dexys. I knew it was the wrong thing to do and that it was all over when they looked astonished to find me still there and said a quick hello. I'd gone with two friends who'd deserted me for the pub after ten minutes waiting. I put on the bravest face I could muster when I rejoined them, but I think my friends knew.

Within a few months I was at university in Southampton. Dexys were having their best run of hits. I saw them at Poole Arts Centre. Seb's predictions had unsurprisingly been proved right and personnel had changed. John Edwards, who's in Status Quo to this day, was on bass, and although I went through the motions of trying to like the new arrangement, I couldn't. I too wasn't there at the beginning, I reasoned, but I'd made up for a late start with sheer passion. They did a signing afterwards. I got my programme scrawled on and told Kevin he'd sold out. He wasn't impressed at all, but I felt much better for saying it and started listening to other bands at last. I even interviewed some of those other bands for the university newspaper occasionally, and only rarely brought Dexys into it. I had a bloody degree by the time the next Dexys album appeared.

Years later I interviewed Kevin around the time of *The Wanderer*, his ill-fated but still OK solo album. He's a shocking interviewee, throwing every question back with 'Why are you asking that?' or 'What do *you* think?' but without any sense of levity and with less small talk than the least-friendly rapper. He stopped the interview at one point: 'Don't I know you?' I confessed as cheerily as I could how he'd changed my life and that I was fairly sorry for always having a go at him, but I cared so much. He carried on as if nothing had been said.

Seb Shelton never played drums after Dexys. There seemed no point. He would never be in a band as good, so why bother? I read one week that he was doing a little PR work for Rough Trade, so I rang him for some records to review. He sent a splendid Floy Joy (or was it Float Up C.P.?) single, 'Joy's Address', but he didn't acknowledge me. Later though he had no choice. He went into management – The Woodentops, Julian Cope and Adrian Sherwood. I interviewed Adrian Sherwood for *Number 1* magazine after the producer had put out a Tackhead record about football. He obviously couldn't afford a PR so Seb did it. The one-time drummer now lived in Crouch End, about 100 yards from me. He dropped some records round but I wasn't in and that was that.

I have Kevin Rowland's autograph eleven times.

Simple Twist of Fate

JOHN BAULDIE

Everybody has heard of Bob Dylan. They might not know whether he's alive or not, they might think his sinuses need a good scrub, they might not own any of his albums, but they know who he is. His father owned an electrical store in Hibbing, Minnesota, and, according to legend, in 1951 the ten-year-old Robert Allan Zimmerman ran away to Chicago, changed his name and wisely learned to play guitar. In the sixties he was the voice of a generation like nobody before or since; in the seventies he discovered God and divorce; in the eighties he became a Traveling Wilbury and released some under-rated albums. Now he's on the all-too-appropriately titled Never Ending Tour, but a song like 'Series of Dreams' (1991) shows he's not completely washed up even when he's releasing albums of blues covers.

It began with a poke in the back. I think that it was during history, though looking back to those cap-and-blazer schooldays from a distance of thirty years, I wouldn't swear to it. Nonetheless, that simple finger jab in the small of my back was to prove The Poke That Changed My Life.

The poker was called Pete Bryan. He was a Mod-ish friend of mine who commanded a good deal of my respect and, to be honest, some adolescent envy. Pete was cool in every way: his ginger hair was always neatly cropped, with an off-set parting that looked as though it could have been cut in by a butcher's knife, his clothes were impeccable – his shirt collars always had buttons or studs and his trousers were narrow and Sta-Prest, he was a great dancer and, most impressively of all, Pete seemed to have more records than you'd believe any one person could possibly own.

My own record collection, at the time, was as risible as my haircut, my fashion sense and my dancing ability. When, a couple of years before, my parents bought our first record player, a portable model, beautifully finished in crimson and cream leatherette, I was allowed to choose one LP of my own. I picked *Kent Walton's Honey Hit Parade*, a selection of singles by various artists often played on a Radio Luxembourg programme that was sponsored by – oh, how could I have chosen it? – a soppy girls' magazine called *Honey*. The LP was on the Pye Golden Guinea label and thus cost a mere 21 shillings. I had wanted it primarily because it included Benny Hill's hilarious 'Garden of Love', a song positively stuffed, you may remember, with a series of vegetable puns. The only defence I can offer today for this awful *faux pas* is that at least it proves I had some awareness of the felicities of word-play and I was only eleven at the time, but I still feel annoyed at my own childish idiocy and wish I could claim to have actually chosen a Buddy Holly LP. But I can't.

By 1963, my tastes had matured with astonishing rapidity. I liked The Beatles. OK, I wasn't on my own, but I do remember being enthusiastic about 'Love Me Do' when I heard it on the radio, and I'll never tire of telling people that I actually had to order their first LP, *Please Please Me*, from my local record shop.

'I'd like to order the Beatles LP,' I remember piping. 'I didn't know they'd made one,' replied the shop owner, Mr Bennett, whose son Norman had been in my class at primary school. Being one of the first-ever copies, it had an old black-and-gold Parlophone label and is now apparently worth about £150, several golden guineas more than *Kent Walton's Honey Hit Parade*. I still have it, and cherish it for the way it reminds me of childish times. My name on the back of the sleeve – rubber-stamped with a John Bull printing kit – confirms that it will forever be mine, and hopefully will not be tutted over by an unsympathetic Sotheby's auctioneer in years to come.

But, though intense, my love affair with the four mop-tops was to be short-lived. I was introduced to a much wilder, much more grown-up sort of music shortly after I'd unwrapped my Christmas-present copy of *With The Beatles*. For some reason, Pete Bryan began to lend me some of his own records, most of which seemed to be on the red-and-yellow Pye International label. They were, I was told, 'rhythm and blues' records, and featured such mysterious artists as Sonny Boy Williamson, Chuck Berry, John Lee Hooker, Jimmy Witherspoon, Little Walter and, my favourite, Howlin' Wolf. I'd never heard anything like this stuff before. It was never played on the radio – not even on Radio Luxembourg, to whose crackly, swooshy programmes my ear was glued most nights – and none of my other friends knew anything about it. Nor did they like it. But I did. I'd borrow a handful of records at a time and play them repeatedly (much to the irritation of my dad, who liked only Frank Sinatra and Doris Day – the latter probably not so much for her singing), before returning them to Pete a few days later. I looked forward to each new batch with increasing hunger and trusted Pete's judgement absolutely. He was my man, my benevolent musical pusher, and at fourteen I was a hopelessly addicted R&B junkie. That's when the poke came.

I leaned backwards, with practised casualness.

'Have you heard Bob Dylan?'

I muttered a reply that I had neither heard, nor heard of, Bob Dylan.

'He's new, and good, and a bit bluesy, but he sings his own songs too – weird songs, some about warmongers, like Winston Churchill, and stuff.' While hardly the most succinct summary of what I was soon to discover for myself, it was enough to intrigue me. A day later, I hurried home with two LPs, *The Freewheelin' Bob Dylan* and, imported from America, the just-released *Times They Are A-Changin'*. It must have been March or April 1964.

That's exactly how it started. I can honestly say it was love at first hearing. Lots of people would blather later that Dylan had a funny voice and couldn't sing properly, but I'd been listening for months with enormous delight to Howlin' Wolf. Compared to him, Dylan had a voice like Mario Lanza. And those songs! Pete had been talking, of course, about 'Masters of War', but on that same record there was also 'A Hard Rain's A-Gonna Fall', a tumbling torrent of words – of poetry! And that was it really, because I was, simultaneously, being seduced by literature, and actually enjoying English lessons, devouring poets and plays with the kind of ravenous hunger for new knowledge and excitement that is only truly experienced in adolescence. So it was that my two true loves, music and poetry, came together in one croaky-voiced singer. My immediate, irreproachable idol. My distant, unapproachable hero.

Having been a fan of this 'secret' singer for well over a year, I was none the less delighted when, in 1965, Bob Dylan became a big star in Britain – bigger, for a few wonderful weeks in the summer, than even The Beatles. Folk music was happening. Arguments raged in the pop papers between washed-up old popsters and newly hip folkies about the merits of their respective musics, but when it came to Bob Dylan, most people agreed that he was a genius, a poet, a hero. I had always known this, and felt impossibly proud and enormously grown-up. I learnt that Dylan was to play a concert in Manchester and made plans to go and see him, live.

I didn't go to the concert. I don't really know why. It's something that seems to have been forever blocked from my conscious mind. The same is true of his second coming to the Free Trade Hall in 1966. By that time, of course, the furore over Dylan 'going electric' had been raging for a good year. He'd put out *Bringing it All Back Home* and *Highway 61 Revisited*, and I loved them both. Bob was no folk-singing traitor, no rock'n'roll quisling for me. My faith was total, absolute, unswerving. But once again I didn't go to see him play his concert in

Manchester. If I had, I would be able to tell you about the guy who shouted 'Judas!' – where he was sitting, perhaps, maybe even what he looked like. But I can't, because I wasn't there.

I suspect that my mother didn't think it was a good idea that I went to Manchester at night when I had to be at school the next day. After all, I was only sixteen, and sixteen-year-olds didn't go too far afield at night back in 1966. At least, sixteen-year-olds like me didn't. I must have suppressed the memory of that suppression ever since, for I don't rightly recall it. I don't remember sulking or shouting, protesting or pouting. I just didn't go. Let's leave it at that, shall we? Otherwise it gets too painful, thinking about what I missed.

I was at the Isle of Wight, however, in 1969. I was at university by then, boring my friends with my Bob Dylan obsession but nevertheless basking in a reflected coolness, because Dylan, man, was still where it was at, *Nashville Skyline*, or even the soon-to-be-released *Self Portrait* (which I loved, of course) notwithstanding. What do I remember of the Isle of Wight? Well, lots, but not much that would interest you. I do remember, however, that by the time Dylan came on (around 11 o'clock at night) I was just about asleep on my feet, knocked out by a combination of the physical exhaustion of getting there in the first place and inhaling far too much smoke for my own good. Ragged, jingle-jangle, laughing, sleep, sleep, sleep, wanna sleep – such is my report from the Isle of Wight, August 1969. I can tell you that Bob wore a white suit and didn't sound like himself at all, but you probably know that already.

The idea that one day I might meet, and talk to, Bob Dylan, never crossed my mind. By the turn of the seventies, I had all his records (no big deal, actually – there were only ten of them), and had begun collecting bootleg records of unreleased material – white-label mysteries which seemed, magically, to come out of nowhere, and tapes of other rare, unissued stuff – and age-old concerts, and press cuttings, photographs, books, badges, posters. I'd never done any of this in my few months of

Beatles fixation, but now, at twenty-one, a graduate in English Literature and apprentice existentialist, I was a screaming groupie, more fanatically interested in another human being than might be deemed healthy. I lived and breathed Bob Dylan. I could answer any question anyone asked me about him. I knew all his lyrics off by heart. Give me a line, any line, and I could give you the next one. Give me a word, any word, and I'd give you a context. Play me three seconds of any track – two seconds – one second – and I'd tell you what it was. No hesitation. Easy.

The bubble burst a little in 1974. Dylan played his first shows, in the USA, for eight years. I had a complete tape collection at the time, but couldn't be bothered gathering up cassettes of forty shows that sounded pretty much the same. In any case, for the first time I wasn't totally thrilled by what I was hearing. It wasn't that my faith was wavering, it was just that my passion was no longer all-consuming. Completely coincidentally, I'd met this girl . . .

Of course, I was there at Earl's Court in 1978, five shows out of six (don't ask), having queued up all night for tickets in Manchester. I didn't go to Blackbushe – the idea of seeing Bob in a field with 200,000 other people didn't appeal then and still doesn't and I've never regretted not being there. Although I was shocked when he became a born-again Christian in 1979, I stuck by him. I liked *Slow Train Coming* a lot, and anyway, I never let religion interfere with my liking of the poetry of George Herbert, John Donne or T. S. Eliot.

It was at this time that it became increasingly difficult to keep in touch with Bob Dylan's doings. In the post-punk years, the music papers, who'd always been on Bob's side, turned against him. First they ridiculed, then – worse – they ignored him. For those of us who needed to be kept informed of what he was up to, these were dark days indeed. Then – praise be – a quirky English newsletter, *The Wicked Messenger*, came into being. It was circulated privately, but it was full of the sort of

Bob Dylan gossip and information that people like me needed, and I lapped it up gratefully.

That's really how *The Telegraph* began. *The Telegraph* is a Bob Dylan fan magazine I've been editing and distributing since November 1981. During that time it's developed from being a badly photocopied, clumsily stapled newsletter – and, for a while, vehicle for the wider distribution of *The Wicked Messenger*, which is, incidentally, also still current – to its present form, a smart, laminated, full-colour, perfect-bound, almost professional-looking miniature magazine of which I'm enormously proud. It has news, reviews, interviews, historical perspectives, set lists, photos, letters, essays – anything and everything to delight those who've retained or developed an enthusiasm for Dylan's (continuing) work down the years.

Directly because of *The Telegraph*, I've met people and been places and done things that I could never have dreamed of doing. I've rattled through Manhattan in the back of a van with Allen Ginsberg gleefully spouting William Blake lyrics at me; I've stared, not a little apprehensively, down both barrels of a loaded shotgun waved towards me by A. J. Weberman, fabled raider of Bob Dylan's dustbins and the world's first self-proclaimed Dylanologist; I've knelt by the moaning, prostrate body of Maria Muldaur, sexy singer of 'Midnight at the Oasis' – I'd tell you the full story, but this really isn't the right time; I've sat outside the walls of the old town of Jerusalem in an ancient amphitheatre called the Sultan's Pool, under a beautiful moon, and seen Bob Dylan's PA explode, bringing a marvellous concert to a premature conclusion. I've also seen him play on a mountain top in Greece, the air heavy with heat and perfume; in a park in Paris with the sun setting bloody and pink against a lovely chateau; in a football stadium with a positively frenzied crowd in Barcelona with fireworks bursting overhead; in a tiny market square in Switzerland in the middle of a deluge. I've seen him drunk and stumbling; I've seen him awesome and amazing; I've seen him delighted and dancing; I've even seen him leap from the stage at the end of a show into the arms of bewildered admirers; I've dipped into cupboards and seen films and heard tapes that even the hardest of hardcore Dylan fans couldn't begin to dream of; I've even been nominated for a Grammy Award for my liner notes to a boxed set collection of unreleased Bob Dylan tracks (dicky-bowed and dinner-jacketed, I was brave-faced but disgusted when I didn't win) ... and yes, I have got to meet, and speak to, Bob Dylan. Should I tell you how it happened? Do you really want to know? OK. I'll tell you of the episode I have subsequently come to call my own Simple Twist of Fate, after the *Blood on the Tracks* song. It happened like this ...

It was in Hartford, Connecticut on 11 July 1986. I'd been spending some of my summer holiday following the Bob Dylan/Tom Petty & The Heartbreakers tour through Northeast USA, and this particular night at the Civic Centre was much like any other, save that Bob seemed a little more animated than usual, slightly drunk perhaps, insisting on performing 'Lay Lady Lay' even though it was clear that he hadn't even thought of the song for a couple of years. He didn't know the words, but hammed it up with hilarious enthusiasm, conducting his bewildered backing singers through the chorus while The Heartbreakers fell about behind him.

The Civic Auditorium was in the middle of a shopping mall, and we'd had to park our car some way away, down a side road at the back of the mall. I was travelling with Christian Behrens, a friend from Germany. Immediately after the concert, we made our way out through the mall and back to where our trusty Subaru was parked. There was a traffic jam in the surrounding streets, with various happy concert-goers queuing to get away into the night, and there, twenty or thirty yards ahead of us, in the middle of the queue, was a small white Volkswagen van. The vehicle was familiar because we'd seen it just about every night during the previous week, shuttling Bob

Dylan from his hotel to various concert halls and arenas in New England. Obviously tonight, his usually rapid post-concert escape to his big tour bus had been thwarted by the auditorium's inconvenient location, and so there he sat, behind the van's darkened windows, stuck in the traffic just like most of his fans, probably tapping his fingers in frustration. Or maybe not. There was no way of telling, of course. All you could do was imagine.

Don't get me wrong. We weren't hanging around this street deliberately, in the hope of catching a fleeting glimpse of Bob Dylan. We weren't interested in that sort of behaviour, and generally would frown at those who took special pleasure in playing such popular fans' games as Chase the Tour Bus or Hang Around the Hotel. It was by complete chance that we happened to be about to walk past the little van inside which our curly-haired hero was sitting. Immediately behind the van was a very nice convertible, in which four girls were bopping about to a stereo playing *Bringing it All Back Home* at full blast. We smiled as we walked past them.

'Hey!' I shouted. 'Bob Dylan's in the van in front of you!' 'Ha ha ha!' they laughed, which probably meant, 'Who the hell's he kidding?' or 'What's the crazy English guy on about?' or some such thought. 'No, no, really. He is!' I laughed back at them. 'Ha ha ha!' they went again. 'Ha ha ha!' So Christian and I strolled on, unaware that an event of cataclysmic proportions was about to take place in this murky street on this warm July evening.

At the very moment that we reached the van, the sliding side door opened, and out hopped Bob Dylan, right next to us, still in his leather stage clothes and clutching a small plastic cup of what smelled like very strong whisky . . .

Now, Bob must have known that if he got out of his van, chances are someone or other would rush up to him and babble at him, or ask for autographs, or follow him down the road – I mean, we weren't too far away from the hall in which he'd just played a show, so anyone who happened to be walking down this particular street would have had to be something of a fan.

So he must have been prepared for that. What he couldn't have been prepared for was hopping out of his bus and bumping straight into a guy from Germany who'd been on the road for over a month, following the tour from California, through Texas, up to Minnesota, and now down through New England heading towards New York City, and a guy from England who for the past fifteen years had edited a fan magazine about him with an enthusiasm that occasionally had veered towards the fanatical but had never been obsessional, despite how it may sometimes have looked from the outside.

But that's exactly what happened. So there we were, the three of us, Christian on the left, me on the right, and Bob loping along between us, occasionally sipping from his cup of whisky, and still wearing his prescription Ray-Bans, despite the fact that it was a fairly dark street and a fairly dark night. We'd no idea at the time where he was going or what he was doing or how long this extraordinary escapade was to last. Knowing, however, that Bob was quite likely to disappear again, and probably sooner rather than later, I decided to plunge right in . . .

OK, so what's the first thing you say when you meet Bob Dylan? 'Hi, Bob, I'm a great admirer of your work.' No points. 'Oh, it's Bob, isn't it?' Minus one. 'Bob, one thing I've always wanted to know. . .' Minus two. 'Pretty dark night to be wearing shades, isn't it? Ha ha!' Minus three. It's a real problem, isn't it? So what was my doozy — the opening gambit that I'd never even imagined being able to play, the statement or question that would immediately grab Dylan's attention, capture his imagination, let him know that this guy ambling along with him wasn't just some lame-brain bozo but a real fan, yet not a drooling groupie, a knowledgeable, intelligent, understanding kind of fan, someone who meant him no harm, who didn't want a piece of him, who was himself worth talking to . . . Oh dear.

In fact, there was no time to think. Like a racing driver, or a lover, I improvised. 'Hey! "Lay Lady Lay", Bob! Last time I heard you sing that was in Barcelona!'

Well, what do you think? This immediately brought the night's concert into play — Bob was still sweaty, and high, from the performance and the 'Lay Lady Lay' encore had been outrageously funny — but also, importantly, it demonstrated my impressive career awareness (it was true, he hadn't actually performed the song since the show in Barcelona in 1984) as well as my enthusiasm (I'd been there in Spain and here I was now, in Connecticut) and my Englishness (Bob would be able to recognize that from the way I talked). Pretty good, eh? Well, it worked. Bob laughed and spoke to me.

'You were at that show?' he asked, with genuine interest and surprise.

'Yes,' I replied. 'It was one of my favourite shows ever. Do you remember it?'

'Yeah, I do remember,' Bob mused. 'It was with Santana. Me and Carlos both liked that show.'

'It was very late and there were fireworks. . .'

'Yeah,' Bob remembered, albeit vaguely. 'Why was that? Why was it so late?'

'Because it was so hot, I guess. You had to wait for it to cool down. . .'

OK, I admit it. The thing about it being hot was my first descent into babble, but, hey, I was doing all right, wobbling along, talking to Bob Dylan, having a real conversation about something. As we walked, there were other people around, of course, but very few approached us. They must have thought that Christian and I were Bob's minders — we were, after all, flanking him somewhat protectively all the while — but one or two did come up and Bob signed an autograph or two as he walked on, before chivvying other hopefuls away, though quite kindly.

I couldn't live a lie. I had to be honest, up front. I had to tell him about myself, so he'd know just who he was dealing with here. The revelation that I was the guy who edited the fan magazine about him might well have called an immediate halt to the stroll. Dylan might even aim a punch at me for something I'd written. For I knew he knew about *The Telegraph*. I knew that he read it sometimes.

D. A. Pennebaker, whose documentary film *Don't Look Back* preserved the living, breathing, perfectly imperfect 1965 Bob Dylan in timeless black-and-white for ever and ever, once told me of a phone call he'd got from Dylan just a few months previously. 'Hey, Pennebaker,' said Bob, 'you got your *Telegraph* yet?'

'Yes, it came this week.'

'Uh, could I borrow it? Mine's not come yet,' said Bob. Pennebaker swore to me that this really happened, though there was a worryingly mischievous twinkle in his eye as he told the tale. Anyway, here goes. . .

'Er, Bob, I should tell you, I'm the guy who does the fan magazine, *The Telegraph*, about you.'

Suddenly, abruptly, Dylan stopped dead in his tracks, turned for the first time squarely towards me, and slowly lifted up his shades, squinting slightly as if to fix my moon-faced, awestruck expression forever in his memory.

'Is that you? You do that?' he asked.

'Yes,' I said, half proud, half apologetic, ready to duck. 'Is it OK?' Then we were off again, loping onward into the night.

'Yeah, I seen a few issues of that. It's pretty interesting.'

The whimsical essence of the reply wasn't lost on me, even then. For Bob Dylan to find a magazine all about himself 'pretty interesting' was, and is, pretty funny. He knew it, and I knew it too. It was OK. I was OK. We were OK. Me and Bob. Christian, up to now, hadn't said anything at all. Then, unexpectedly, he piped up with his carefully considered opening gambit.

'Where do you think I'm from?' asked Christian, who always prided himself on his 'perfect' American/English (but obviously foreign) accent.

'Hmm, let me see,' pondered Bob, who obviously had no idea whatsoever, 'where do I think you're from? Hmmm. . .'

'I'm from Germany,' Christian announced.

'Germany!' Bob exclaimed. 'I got a lot of friends in Germany.'

'How do you make friends in Germany?' asked Christian.

'Uh, you don't,' Bob replied.

This was the first example in the conversation thus far of Bob Dylan's famously oblique – some might say impenetrable – way of thinking, and speaking.

'So what are you guys doing here?' asked Bob.

'Well, we're here for the shows,' I answered.

'All the way from Germany? Why do you want to come and see me? Aren't there any bands in Germany?'

'Not like you, there aren't. Anyway, I'm not from Germany.'

'You sound like you're from Quebec, or South Africa or something,' said Bob.

'No, I'm from England. *The Telegraph*'s an English magazine.'

'Oh yeah.'

Suddenly Bob adopted a graver, more serious tone.

'Make sure you tell the truth about me,' he said. 'A lot of people tell lies about me. Make sure you tell the truth.'

And as if he couldn't reinforce the point enough, he added, just for good measure: 'Don't forget now – check your sources!'

We wandered on, talking briefly about the shows – Bob insisted that his favourite shows had been the ones with The Grateful Dead, which neither Christian nor I liked very much at all – and then he asked:

'Hey! You guys gonna be in New York?'

'Yes, we are.'

'OK,' he said. 'Make sure you come see me. At the pier. We'll have a party, right? You gonna see the shows there?'

'Yes, of course.'

'Yeah. I'm pretty sure they'll be real good shows there. I don't know why that is.'

'Maybe because you'll have your birthday when you get there,' I said, knowingly.

Unfortunately, I was the only person who seemed to know what the hell I was jabbering about. Christian looked blank and vaguely embarrassed; Bob just looked bewildered. But only a couple of months previously, he'd been on a birthday special radio programme, telling New York listeners he was waiting until he got to the city to celebrate – that his birthday was going to be a little late this year. I tried to explain that that's what I was talking about when I mentioned the delayed birthday. Extraordinarily, Bob began to jump up and down like a little kid.

'I did say that! I did say that! When did I say it? Hee hee!'

It was a priceless moment.

But what was this stuff about meeting him at the pier? Unfortunately, we never pressed the point. Bob was just rambling, probably. How on earth could we be expected to find him at some pier? Several weeks later, all became clear. I heard someone talking about New York hotels – The Plaza, The Waldorf, The Pierre, but this last was pronounced 'pier'. Had we known, if we'd turned up at The Pierre, would Bob have welcomed his mates from Hartford with open arms? We'll never know, of course, but part of me thinks, well, you know, just maybe . . . if only . . .

What else can I tell you? We must have been walking for twenty-five minutes or so, dribbling on about this and that. Inevitably, the conversation took a slightly surreal turn just before it ended. Bob had begun to ask me about what I did, and then asked Christian what he did.

'I'm a student,' said Christian.

'What are you studying?' asked Bob.

'Law,' said Christian.

'Lawwwrrre!' slurred Bob, in the most outrageously Bob Dylan imitative voice you ever heard.

'That's what you should have studied, Bob,' I joshed weakly. 'You could have got yourself a proper job.'

'You gonna get a job in law?' Bob asked Christian.

'Well, my father has a scaffolding business. You know about scaffolding, Bob?'

Unfortunately, we'll never know just how extensive Bob Dylan's knowledge of scaffolding is. It wouldn't have surprised us if Bob had kept us entertained for hours with tales of scaffolders and great pieces of scaffolding he had known, but just as the subject was broached, Bob's big tour bus hove into view, and a minder skipped out and hustled Bob brusquely towards the bus. He was about to say goodbye, but all he could manage was a half-turn and a wave. And then he was gone.

It was a funny way to end the adventure, but then somehow, it seemed right, even though it was slightly unsettling to watch him as he was frog-marched ever more quickly away, almost as if it were against his will. Ah well. . .

The only souvenir I have of the episode is a photograph, taken without flash, of three dark shapes. They might be bushes, or ink blots, or just vaguely shaped smudges, but they are positively identified by a little Post-it note that's attached to the photo, upon which, above three little arrows, are written three words – 'Christian, Bob, John'. It's one of my favourite photographs.

White Riot

DANNY KELLY

Joe Strummer was a pub rocker of the merely competent kind, stuck in a rut with The 101ers, when, in 1976, he was seduced by a bunch of punks into joining The Clash. Their self-titled debut album was a revelation and, by some distance, the finest punk album, brim full of angry lyrics, bloody livid tunes and – heresy! – a dip into reggae. They quickly shed the bondage trousers and hired American heavy metal producer Sandy Pearlman for their second album, *Give 'Em Enough Rope*, another wonderful record.

The third album, *London Calling*, was voted best record of the decade by *Rolling Stone*, and it's quite possibly the best record ever. *Sandinista!* was a sprawling triple-set. Incredible fare. *Combat Rock* broke them in America but wasn't quite so earth-shattering as its predecessors. They split soon afterwards and Strummer's rump half produced *Cut the Crap*, which deserves partial rehabilitation for the magnificent 'This is England', if nothing else. There are always rumours of a Clash re-formation.

So much of what we are and what we do relies on luck, and geography. I blame my teenage addiction to music, and eventual enslavement to The Clash, on a combination of strange fortune and the simple fact of having been brought up in Islington. Then, over a quarter of a century ago, the Central London borough wasn't the gentrified media honey-pot it's now become, but a comfortable working-class area, whole tracts of it dominated by immigrants from Ireland, Italy and the Caribbean. One of my earliest memories is of a bombsite that, fully fifteen years after the war, lay at the end of our street; now it's a fancy arcade of hilariously expensive antique emporia. That's Islington for you.

As a teenager in the early seventies, I became lost in music; not the rock and pop that filled the heads of my schoolmates, but reggae and soul. The reggae was easy to find, because it was all around. Our street was full of West Indian families who never slept. Instead, they left their windows and doors open and had parties that lasted till the sun came up the next day. Lying in my bed, and turning down the little black tranny I usually had pressed to my ear beneath the blankets, I could hear the booming disjointed sounds with which they filled the night air. The only music in our house was my uncle's handful of Dubliners LPs (unappreciated at the time, but since rescued from twenty years of neglectful unemployment); the stuff I heard in the street, though, seemed like it came from another, marvellous, planet. The black kids next door told me it was 'old people's music' and it was called reggae.

Suddenly my mother found herself being accompanied on her Saturday shopping expeditions to Ridley Road market in Dalston. But what she took to be an unexpected attack of filial duty had an altogether more selfish motive. Ridley Road, she failed to grasp, had not one, not two, but *three* music shacks, wooden hutches which blasted out the latest sounds from Jamaica. While mum struggled through the heaving crowds, weighed down with the amount of potatoes and bacon it takes to feed a family of eight, I'd give her the slip and make for the biggest bass bin. Standing a respectful distance away (the people at these stalls had no problem intimidating a freckled oik) I'd bask, amazed, in the deliciously alien sound. Later, plucking up courage, I'd discover that these records were made by people with names like King Stitt, Big Youth, Dr Kitsch, Dennis Alcapone and The Clarendonians. The air of exotica only cemented my captivation.

The next step was to get hold of some of these discs, no simple task on a pocket-money budget that barely covered the equally necessary packets of football-star picture cards (complete with rectangular slab of pink gum that shattered into gum-shreddingly sharp shards on contact with saliva).

Enter Michael Courtney. Michael's parents ran the Arundel Arms, a local pub whose juke-box accurately reflected its half-Irish, half-West Indian clientele. Once a month a man would come and update the reggae and country records; the old ones, my greedy eyes widened to discover, were just thrown away. I can't remember what deal was contrived with Michael – a Charlie George or Peter Marinello must have been involved, those cards being the only currency to which I had ready access – but I'll never forget the first fruits of our bargain. A fair-to-good copy of 'Peeping Tom' (backed with 'Peeping Tom Version') by The Maytals on the beautiful old pink, blue and purple Summit label. It was the first of many such one-careless-owner-only gems that came my way via this convoluted conduit, and I treasure it to this day.

Others began, with a mixture of scepticism and bewilderment, to deal with my new-found needs. At first, present-buying relatives didn't believe I really wanted LPs that cost half the price of normal records (at a time when the new Zeppelin set you back £2, reggae albums, being mono, came in at precisely 19s 11d). Relentless pleading changed their minds. Trojan's *Reggae Chartbusters Volumes One & Two*, as well as some *Tighten Up* compilations, were the happy result, and I still occasionally smile at the thought of my maiden aunt Betty asking some phonographic vendor for 'the LP called *Double Barrel* by Dave and Ansil Collins'.

My adolescent friends, bless them, caught on too. At Christmas 1973, about a dozen of us each put £2 into a central kitty; the idea being that each person would then receive an LP from the group, so we'd all effectively have given each other a gift. At the great communal unwrapping I held back, fearful that the new Rods or Roxys that were causing such joy among my mates would leave me looking dischuffed and ungrateful.

Eventually I fretfully tore away the cheap bright paper to reveal The Wailers' *Catch a Fire*, smart almost beyond endurance in its now-famous flip-top Zippo sleeve. No, they said, they didn't want to hear it, but they were happy that I did. Sweet people. I cried.

Getting hooked on American soul music was achieved by an altogether different route – the bath. Every Saturday evening in those teenage years was much the same for me. Watch the football results chattering through on the teleprinter (in those days, Spurs always seemed to win, usually against Leicester City), then the weekly ablutions in time for Mass the next morning. Risking, I now realize, electrocution by PP3 battery, my two-hour soak to advanced prunery was always accompanied by the little black tranny. It opened a world of previously unimagined wonder for me.

At that time, Radio 1 – in the person of Stuart Henry or Johnnie Walker, I'm not sure which, the Matey fumes having softened the memory – had a marvellous Saturday-night soul show. The highlight was when they rang two 'Stateside' radio stations, one north of something called 'the Matron Dixon line', the other south. These stations would then run down their respective, and inevitably different, Top 10s. It was through these interludes that I first heard Marvin Gaye, Curtis Mayfield, Sly & The Family Stone, Bobby Womack, Isaac Hayes and the rest. And it was also the first place I heard 'A Million to One' by The Manhattans, a record that was to haunt me and, along with the smell of Palmolive, to remind me of those bath-times for twenty years to come.

The Manhattans were popular in the sixties, then disappeared, then had a string of mid-seventies hits on CBS. It was in the AWOL years that they cut 'A Million to One'. A yearning ballad of *triomphe d'amour* in the face of frankly unlikely odds ('a million to one, that was my chances'), the song, complete with the close male harmonies that have always parted me from my hard-earned, was just the loveliest thing I'd ever heard.

They never played it again on the radio and it never got released in this country; for almost two decades my only contact with it was a memory of the tune and a chunk of the chorus. Sometimes I'd forget about it for years on end, then something would pull it back up from the musty corners of a mind full of such unmarked clutter, covered in mental dust. I'd pretend to myself that I was actively trying to find it, but the truth, as time wore on, was that I couldn't be sure if I'd ever really heard the wretched thing. And if I had, did it bear any relation to the mellifluous classic I carted around in my head?

And then, one day in the early nineties, I was browsing through the soul section of a second-hand shop, like I've done a million times before. The usual dust-crusted clutch of over-priced James Brown, crumbling-cellophane Motown, sequinned has-beens and Afroed never-weres whisked by beneath practised fingers and gaze. Then, without warning, I saw it: a muddy grey-brown sleeve; a black and white photo of a quintet of dudes in hats that would once have been described (depending on the hipness of the narrator) as Superfly or Donny Osmond, and Afghan coats; and a legend that read 'The Manhattans: A Million To One'. The sticky label, top right, read 'VG – £4'. It wouldn't have mattered if it had said 'Unplayable – £All The Money in the World and Your Soul and Your Children's Souls, Forever'. With sweating palms I rushed to the counter, drinking in the few details I could glean from the sleeve. DeLuxe Records out of Nashville. How can foreign, especially American and Jamaican, record labels and place names be so evocative, so damn wonderful? Neptune Records of Philadelphia, Pennsylvania ... Studio 1 Records of Brentford Road, Kingston ... Volt Records of Memphis, Tennessee ... Burning Spear Records of Ocho Rios, JA ...

Amazingly, 'A Million to One' turned out, after all those years, to be every bit as good as I remembered it, every sparkling bit as good as the other sounds that transport me back to that bathtub: '(If Loving You is Wrong) I Don't Want to be

Right' by Luther Ingram; 'In the Rain' by The Dramatics ...
'Tottenham four, Leicester City one – a hat-trick for Greaves'.
And the name of the bazaar where I'd finally tracked down my
long-lost companion? Reckless Records in Upper Street, N1.
Islington.

Not all my memories of my soul boy years are quite so rosy;
one incident left scars as yet unhealed. I remember plucking up
the courage one day to take my new copy of Curtis Mayfield's
Roots (purchased from the princely stipend Sainsbury's saw fit to
pay fifteen-year-olds for filling their cheese and bacon counters
on Saturdays) to school. During the lunch hour, I proudly
placed it on the deck of the Pye record player in the fourth-
form common room. I'd show this lot – with their ELP, their T.
Rex and their Wings – some real music. The opening track,
'Get Down', was ninety deeply funky, hugely socially significant, seconds old when Chez Arquati intervened.

Chez. He wasn't in my class but I knew four vital things
about him. He never used his real Christian name because it
was, rumour insisted, too Italian and girlie. His family were all
butchers. He was the first kid in the school to sport the much-
coveted Solatio basket-weave shoes. And he was The Best
Fighter in Our Year. This latter title was seldom fully tested
(playground pugilism is rather less endemic than the writers of
comics and television scripts would have us believe), and he
lost it some months later when the gigantic Reginald Obicheri
arrived, presumably in some kind of crate, from Nigeria.

The latter comeuppance, however, still lay in the future as
Chez Arquati sauntered slowly over to the Pye. I guessed – just
call it coward's intuition – that my afternoon was not about to
improve, but decided not to argue the toss with a man/boy who
had a hard Christian name, a family who were all butchers and
great, if noisy, shoes. Without looking at me, Chez placed the
backs of four outstretched fingers under the edge of my precious
33 and, with one flick of his muscled wrist (his family were all
butchers, you know), flipped it, in a graceful, slow-motion

parabola, across the room. Bastard. Big, hard, bastard. 'Shit!' he muttered to himself as he carefully slid his own record on to the still-spinning turntable. *Machine Head* by Deep Purple. Even today, I occasionally gaze at the scuff marks on my copy of *Roots*, and thank God for the enormous, pummelling, fists of Reginald Obicheri.

So how does a fan of black music start getting into rock and end up knowing, before most other people, certainly before the music press, that punk, and the mighty Clash, were coming? The answer, rather tediously, lies once again with our old friends, fortune and geography.

In the mid-seventies, Islington, you'll be unsurprised to learn, was the centre of the rock universe. From my home off the Essex Road, I could walk to the Hope and Anchor, Merlin's Cave and the Lord Nelson (where I once saw Kilburn & The High Roads supporting Dr Feelgood); a 4p bus ride got you to the Rainbow, where Dave Kelly – no relation – let us in through the fire-exit doors to see everyone from Stevie Wonder to Kevin Coyne; another tuppence got you to the Roundhouse in Chalk Farm, or the alleged glamour of the West End. Even *Sounds*, then in its heyday, had its offices in Benwell Road, near the Arsenal.

In the midst of all this, it was impossible for me to maintain my musical purity. Like the Likely Lads trying to avoid that football result, there was nowhere for me to hide. My friends began to make me go and see rock groups. It seems surreal now, but I steadfastly refused to join them on their regular jaunts to the Sundown in Edmonton to see Rod Stewart & The Faces, and I bitterly regretted a trip to the Empire Pool, Wembley, to see The Rolling Stones (I only went because Trevor Lawrence, who'd played the saxes on 'What's Going On', was in their horn section). But The Who were great, I saw Springsteen at Hammersmith and became attached for a couple of years to a now long-forgotten post-Free blues rock quartet called The Sharks, for whom Chris Spedding played guitar. Inevitably too, we saw some just plain awful rubbish: Procol Harum at the Rainbow, Isotope (the British Mahavishnu Orchestra) at the LSE, Heads, Hands and Feet at the Roundhouse; we even endured Principal Edward's Magic Theatre.

And so, by the simple, if unscientific, expedient of Hanging Around Loads of Gigs, one got a sense, by the mid-seventies, that something was about to happen. Music, weighed down by the twin anchors of virtuosity and poetry, had slowed down to a crawl, yet the most fun seemed to be had at the gigs by the handful of bands who played fast. The first generation of London punks all paid lip service to The Stooges and MC5, but the part played in the rise of punk by Dr Feelgood and Eddie & The Hot Rods should not be allowed to be written out of the histories. Such was the state of rock at this time, that the simple act of being a half-decent rock band who gave it some welly was revolutionary, inspirational.

I also knew punk was coming because I had the vaguest of connections with one of its inventors: John Lydon went to the same primary school as me. He was a year above me, so I had little reason to know him, yet I remember him well. Our Lady of the Sacred Heart has a playground separated from the main school by a road, and in the corner of this large yard is a tree beneath whose branches would gather the kids who didn't want to be part of the everyday playground rough and tumble, the gigantic, skill-free games of football (at Sacred Heart, Ireland versus Italy could involve anything up to forty-a-side and last for several weeks). John Lydon always had his back to that tree. His main source of recreation seemed to be staring.

At eleven, he went on to Sir William of York down the Caledonian Road and ultimately banishment for crimes against coiffure, while I qualified for the posher St Aloysius College in Highgate and the meaty mercies of Chez Arquati. But our paths wouldn't quite split. The Lydon family lived in the Honeyfield block of the Six Acres estate on Moray Road, Finsbury Park, precisely opposite the Rainbow and one of the less appalling of Islington's many newly built council utopias. They lived, to be microscopically accurate, on the floor above my cousin Maria. My aunt Eileen and Mrs Lydon were friends.

I used to spend a lot of bored teenage time on the Six Acres. We'd sit in the communal launderette talking bollocks and admiring the bottle and prowess of those who'd dared master the latest time-wasting amusement. This – we're pre-Game Boy here – consisted of someone filling their mouth with lighter fluid (Ronsonol was the Dom Perignon of ignition liquids), spitting it out in a steady fine spray, then lighting the resultant mist as far away from their face as possible. The flame would make steady progress towards their lips; the real artists would wait until there seemed no possibility of avoiding a labial inferno, then gob the whole fireball across the room. The big tumble dryers bore the singe-marks of several direct hits.

But mostly we just talked bollocks. About music, about football and, inevitably, about the other people we knew from the estate. The antics of the Connolly family (all butchers; one of them, John, had got married in the only horse-drawn carriage ever seen on the Six Acres) were one source of endless conversation; the moves of the Lydons (John's brother Jimmy, later mainstay of The 4-Be-2s, lost an eye in an incident shrouded in mystery) were another. So I knew about The Sex Pistols.

And I saw them at the Screen on the Green. Not because I was particularly keen to experience what people had suddenly started to call punk, but because of yet another coincidence of fortune and location. The simple, unglamorous truth is that I was a member at the Screen and supported most everything they put on.

The Screen on the Green (so named because it's on, oh dear, Islington Green) was a hundred yards from my home. I first remember it as a flea-pit that showed Greek films. A chap of Mediterranean persuasion would stand outside it all day wondering if passers-by would 'like to see good cowboy film'; he somehow failed to reveal that the equipment required for full enjoyment of 'good cowboy film' included a thorough grounding in the Hellenic language.

Later, taken over and refurbished, the Screen became the best, and hippest, cinema in London. Its refreshment kiosk was the first place I ever saw quiche, and if all the seats in the auditorium were full, they'd let punters sit in the aisles, any-where. I once saw *Five Easy Pieces* lying flat out between the front row and the screen. But best of all were the weekend all-nighters. All-night Clint Eastwood, all-night Marlon Brando, all-night Fellini, all-night Rock, great programmes made all the more exciting for an over-sensitive sixteen-year-old by the fact that you'd emerge, like someone in a novel, blinking and disoriented, into the Sunday morning light.

There was, and still is, a Wimpy bar a few doors down from the Screen, and in the middle of the night during these mara-thons, a woman would come round with dozens of the beefy little fellows on a tray. No wonder the place always seemed packed.

I don't remember The Sex Pistols being as good as those burgers, but the atmosphere was like nothing I'd ever experi-enced before. Strange, bizarrely dressed people (they probably thought the same about my Marks-&-Spencers-but-can't-quite-forget-skinhead look), megawatt expectation and livid, almost uncontrolled, excitement. The recruiting sergeants for the Punk Rock Wars were on the door; I wasn't sure about the music, but I signed up anyway.

During the next couple of months, two life-altering, two life-turned-on-its-head-and-shaken-till-it-screamed, things hap-pened to me. I went to university. And I saw The Clash. The university was Leicester; I did law for a year until I failed, then arts for a year till they threw me out. The Clash played at the Screen, then the ICA.

They played with an intensity that was truly terrifying and a velocity that endlessly threatened cardiac arrest. I'd never even heard of, never mind used, amphetamine sulphate, and frankly didn't much care where the energy was coming from, just as long as it didn't stop. All my notions about how music should sound, what music could do, were shredded forever by this agonized white-boy tower-block blues. The day he quit his pub rock band The 101ers, Joe Strummer said: 'Yesterday I thought I was a crud, then I saw The Sex Pistols and I became a king. . .' I can't claim that level of revelation or inspiration, but in the days following those early Clash gigs, something inside of me had changed.

I'd never seen anything so beautiful, so unquestionably right, as The Clash. I loved *everything* about them. I loved their name, its onomatopoeic violence so at odds with the curly-perm cosiness of the mid seventies, so portentous of the Thatcherite assault on the whole post-war consensus to come. The Clash. The Clash. The Clash. The Clash. The Clash. The Clash. The Clash. The Clash. No band was ever better labelled.

I loved the way they looked. Those cheap military fatigues covered in spray-painted and stencilled words – song titles, slogans, stuff snatched from other musics and arts – gave them the appearance of some kind of living propaganda, of crazed guerrillas. They knew how to use images too, how to throw a pose. The sleeve of their first single (the earth-moving 'White Riot'/'1977') showed them with their hands above their heads, spread-eagled, faces to the wall. It was a scary image, redolent of police states, SUS searches and infringed humanity. All very clever, and all very stolen: from the cover of a dub album (The Clash, like Lydon, were obsessed with reggae, something else about them that I loved) by Joe Gibbs & The Professionals.

I loved the way they sounded and what they said. Their songs seemed to be newsflashes, handouts, calls to arms. They were about things I'd never before heard addressed by pop music. The mighty first album cut its ferocious swathe through TV detectives, anti-Americanism, local councils, record compa-nies, race riots, police brutality, condoms, prostitutes, geriatric politicians, unemployment, letter bombs, racism, drugs, corruption, brainwashing, pickpockets and the wonders of West London flyovers. It was weird, but though Joe Strummer delivered his words like a victim of some South American torture squad, he seemed the most articulate, most eloquent man on the planet.

In Leicester, I was part of a tiny cell that set out to convert the world (actually just the university, which in the minds of students pretty much amounts to the same thing) to punk. My first mission – to look the part – would be pleased to be characterized as a fiasco. I abandoned flared denim for scratchy green battle fatigues. I bought some badges. Unfortunately, grey Marks & Spencer crew-neck jumpers (of which my upper body wardrobe seemed entirely to consist) just don't convert well to the cutting edge of nihilistic style. I encouraged a small hole in one of my sleeves to unravel (on a visit home, my mum darned it).

The barnet was another problem. Ignorant of the tools of tonsorial sculpture, I employed a kind of dry setting lotion to achieve the necessary verticality and stiffness. A combination of the white powder that formed as a result of the spray (no manufacturer's note on the tin – Attention Would-Be Punk Rockers: This product turns to Home Pride on contact with air) and what they used to call flyaway – i.e. shite – hair left me looking like one of those explosion-victims that populate Chuck Jones cartoons. I abandoned the fashion and decided to concentrate on the music.

Me and my punk rock mates (dour, northern Pog, who made 'no concessions' and so still wore his flyaway hair down to his arse; big Micky, a twenty-stone git whose father was a colonel and ran the Chelsea Pensioners; and Bernie – Sly You Old Cunt to his friends – who had a moustache but owned a motor, and so had to be cultivated) became something like evangelists. Pissed evangelists. Micky got himself elected manager of the bar in our hall of residence; we drank cider, so Olde English cost 19 pence a pint. Later we took to mixing OE with Cherry B, a vile liqueur of the purple variety. Girls called the resultant electric soup 'leg-opener', and when it made you sick – and you were *always* sick after the first seven or eight – your vomit was pink. Cherry B and cider was 19 pence a pint too. Like I said, evangelists.

One day we heard that a soul shop in Cambridge had several copies of the hard-to-get 'Anarchy in the UK' single languishing in its remaindered bin. We drove Sly's powder-blue Vauxhall Viva 1100 out to the fens, bought the precious cargo and distributed them to the masses. Equally, when 'God Save the Queen' came out, and there seemed, in those Jubilee-maddened times, some danger that it might be banned, we ordered forty copies of it from Ainley's record shop in Leicester city centre. (The only other half-decent store was Revolver, opposite a fruit and veg stall owned, apparently, by the parents of one Gary Lineker.) We only wanted them, we told Mr Ainley, 'if they had the picture sleeve'; the discs duly arrived, suitably adorned; we distributed them to the masses.

I, addled by The Clash, spent the day of the release of their first album in a mad froth of enthusiasm and mendacity on London's busy Oxford Street. The first ten thousand copies of the record came with a small red sticker on the inner sleeve; this proof-of-purchase device entitled the lucky holder to send off to the *NME* for an exclusive Clash 45 that consisted of two songs ('Capital Radio' and 'Listen') and Tony Parsons interviewing the band on an Underground train.

My plan was time-consuming but foolproof. I bought a copy of the album at the HMV shop by Bond Street station, went outside, took the sticker off the bag, went back into the shop, told a different assistant to the one from whom I just purchased the record that it was faulty, got given a replacement. Then I went outside, took the sticker off the bag ... The HMV store was then the biggest in London, so there were plenty of assistants on whom to pull this stunt. When I'd exhausted them in the morning, I took a couple of hours off, then started on the afternoon shift. By the end of the day I'd acquired a dozen or so of the gold-dust stickers (crime of the century!), and when the commensurate *NME* discs eventually arrived in Leicester, I distributed them to the masses.

Then, from just trying to get people to listen to punk, the ante was suddenly upped, with, eventually, farcically disastrous results. A combination of gerrymandering, typical student indifference and the heavyweight influence of big Micky saw me follow his election triumph with my own, gaining control over the entertainment budget for our poor hall of residence. The kids, I proclaimed, would have punk rock! Whether they wanted it or not. . .

Each term the hall would have A Ball. Like all student events in those pre-AIDS days, it was organized mainly to promote and facilitate the exchange of bodily fluids. These balls, though, were a throwback to more genteel days and maintained some semblance of formality. Studes were expected to 'make an effort' (long velvet dresses and chokers for the ladies, underarm deodorant for the gents) and a dance band, or, at worst, respectable disco, would provide the musical accompaniment. Not any more; first I arranged for The Tom Robinson Band to play, and, when that had proved a reasonable success, decided to really push the boat out. The invitation cards read: 'Clare Hall Easter Ball, 1977. Formal dress. Musical entertainment to be provided by . . . Generation X'. Seemed like a cracking idea at the time.

I never saw Billy Idol and his lads' set. As befits the organizer of such a momentous event, and to my utter amazement, I pulled early. Those days, straight-legged trousers and grey crew-neck jumpers evidently did it for the girls. The unlucky lady and I were just snuggling down to a night of advanced sexual ignorance when frantic poundings began on the door of her room. 'Danny! Danny! You'd better get out of there, and down to the dining room. . .' Jealous bastards, I assured the bemused paramour, trying to get me down to help with the clearing up. As if I hadn't done enough already.

But the pounding and pleading kept going until I was forced

to rise, dress and make my way down to the dining room/gig. There I was greeted by a scene of devastation. People were crying and holding their heads; the bits of Generation X who weren't in Leicester Royal Infirmary were talking to a clutch of policemen; the wooden floor was a mess of broken glass and blood. The rugby club – ever the arbiters of all cultural taste in further-education establishments – had apparently taken a dim view of this new-fangled punk rock music and showered the X with pint jugs. One of these had split guitarist Mark Laff's head open, splashing claret everywhere. He'd gone to get a dozen or so stitches, but not before the band had taken revenge by smashing up the dressing room (actually the staff common room), destroying one of the few colour televisions in the hall. The fracas made the front page of the sensation-starved *Leicester Mercury* and the news section of the *NME*; punk was banned from all university premises. Worse was to follow.

The following week, me, Micky, Pog and a few other cronies went to see Eddie & The Hot Rods at the poly, where punk (The Hot Rods were lumped in with the real thing) was still unproscribed. Now, I was aware that Micky, who had pretensions to being a drummer, had decided to start his own band (he'd already had a few badges made up; big, ugly orange things with The Incident on them) but nobody told me that this gig was crucial to the next phase of his group's development.

The gig was well and raucously underway – us pogoing away at the front as usual – when I noticed Micky starting to remove various portable items of the Rods' equipment from the stage. In the wings, the roadies eyed his gigantic, beardy frame with a mixture of bemusement and concern as he filched first a stray lead or two, then the odd discarded plectrum. Then, without warning (without, some would say, the sense he was born with), Micky suddenly reached up one of his pit-prop arms and dragged a *whole monitor* off the stage. The Incident, it finally occurred to me, were to be entirely equipped with gear once belonging to Southend's finest.

In seconds the majority of hell broke loose. In pursuit of their employers' property, the roadies ran across the stage and hurled themselves into the crowd; we were forced to defend our pal; punches were swapped; noses bled; the concert broke up in chaos. Next morning, Leicester City Council met in emergency session and by noon the *Mercury* had its headline: PUNK ROCK BANNED FROM LEICESTER FOR A YEAR. The first victims of the draconian edict were The Jam, whose imminent show at the De Montfort Hall was cancelled. My plans to bring the white heat of musical and artistic revolution to the East Midlands' biggest city had gone horribly pear-shaped.

Never mind, there was always the mighty Clash, and another happy accident of topography. Leicester is pretty much the centre of the country and so, when the band set out on their nationwide White Riot Tour, we were able, thanks to that 1100 Viva, to see a high percentage of the dates. It was the spring of 1977, The Clash had played less than thirty gigs, but they were, during that string of incandescent shows, the greatest rock'n'roll band I ever saw.

Supported by The Buzzcocks and The Slits, The Clash rolled from town to town, playing with what seemed an un-quenchable sun-hot anger. Neck muscles steel-taut, Strummer, Mick Jones, Paul Simenon and Topper Headon slammed their music into the audience like men possessed; it was nothing less than a sonic war. For me, each gig was a wonderful, if physically harrowing, catharsis; a reckless, spendthrift, joyful expense of energy and emotion.

Having decided to confront the grey crew neck problem once and for all, I'd invested in a navy blue, vaguely militaristic shirt which I wore to every gig. We'd always make our way down to the fearful stagefront bear-pit, keen to take part in, if necessary to start, the heedless bouts of insane slam-dancing the music encouraged, even demanded. For the entire length of The Clash's set, mayhem, often veering into straightforward violence, reigned in the crowd. Bodies sprang, jack-knifed and battered into one another; people fell, clothes sundered, blood flowed. After each gig, I'd get home to Leicester and, after wringing the cold sweat and warm cider out of the blue shirt, assess the damage; ears-ringing deafness that lasted up to two days was inevitable, a selection of livid purple bruises usual.

If the tour was taking it out of me, what chance did the poor band have? As it turned out, not much. I remember one night – Nottingham Palais I think – when, a few minutes prior to show time, I stumbled across a wretched lanky form slumped coughing over a lavatory washbasin. Glutinous strings of vomit and mucus hung limply from his nose; his eyes rolled sightlessly. It was Mick Jones. Two hours later, out the back of the theatre, I saw a bag-of-rags figure draped, steaming and still, on the fire escape. He looked at death's door; it was Joe Strummer. Oddly, that was as near as I ever got to any member of the band during the whole White Riot craziness, and sure enough, a few days later Joe's health gave out. He contracted hepatitis, the result of someone gobbing directly down his throat. I don't know about the lads, but I welcomed the break.

Unlike some, I never believed that punk was going to change the world, but that The Clash had come to have an almost unhealthy influence over me was proved on 17 August 1977. Elvis Presley, the news flashed around the world, had been found dead in his gilded bathroom. I was so besotted with The Clash's 'no Elvis, Beatles or The Rolling Stones in 1977' line that I organized a celebratory pub crawl. That same night at the Vortex Club in London, Danny Baker, hearing the cheers at the news of Presley's demise, jumped on to the stage and berated the punk crowd for their idiocy, reminding them that without Elvis there'd have been no rock'n'roll, never mind punk. By his actions Baker guaranteed himself his place in Heaven; I know that my pub crawl has condemned me to spend eternity in an altogether more frightful place. The irony is that now, all these years later, when I arrive home after one of those days that make you wonder why you ever got involved in this nonsense in the first place, the CD I reach for to soothe my ruffled soul and remind me of the healing beauty of music is Elvis Presley's *Sun Collection* ...

Live at least, The Clash never again reached the heights they'd achieved on the White Riot Tour. That's not to say that there weren't still memorable gigs (they played the Camden Music Machine, for instance, and I was so drunk that next day I remembered neither Jimmy Pursey nor Steve Jones coming on as special guests), but nobody could maintain that inhuman level of passion and commitment. The memory of it, though, still causes a glow in me today; I can't believe what they did, and I can't believe what I did either.

The lasting influence they had over me was illustrated one day in 1988. Joe Strummer, long, and probably quite happily, in the wilderness, had formed a new band (Latino Rockabilly War!) and enjoyed a small hit with the whizzbang 'Trash City'. He was about to play a big gig for Amnesty International and I was told to go and interview him for the *NME*. I rang him to make the arrangements and told him just what a huge thing it was for me to get to talk to him. With charming modesty he told me he was no big deal anymore. Remembering how, when The Clash had been at their phosphorescent pinnacle, the press had fawned over him, endlessly putting him on their front covers, he said, 'These days, I'm a page 14 sort of guy.'

We agreed to meet in a pub in Lloyd Baker Street (Islington!). I was cool; I'd met plenty of big names and most of my heroes (George Michael, Geldof, Morrissey, Lee Perry, Costello and the rest); never been a problem. But the second I swung open the door to that pub – Joe was already there, courteously early – something snapped. I walked up to him, pumped his hand and, face grin-split from ear to ear, announced, 'You, sir, are Joe Strummer, and I'm going to get drunk in front of you.' The look he shot me suggested he didn't believe me, but he was wrong. For four hours I bought him drinks, bored him titless about The Clash and their every nuance, and never once produced my tape-recorder.

When they threw us out of the pub, I dragged him to a garish loud club and just carried on. Sometime just before dawn, Joe leaned across to me and whispered, 'Hadn't we better do this interview; you do know I'm leaving for New York first thing this morning?' If I'd been in a condition to think, I'd have thought 'Cripes!'; the story was due in about forty-eight hours' time, but right now I couldn't have operated a tape-measure, never mind a tape-recorder. We agreed that Joe would ring me from America and I'd do the interview over the phone. The man, and all that his band had meant to me, had reduced me to hopeless professional incompetence. Like I cared! As good as his word, Joe did ring me, waking me up at four in the morning; he later reported to a mutual acquaintance that I'd been 'grumpy'.

The story was no Pulitzer candidate, but it went on the cover of the *NME*, I made sure of that. Joe Strummer was never a 'page 14 kind of guy' and, for me, The Clash always were, and always will be, front-page news. I thank God for the confluences of luck and geography that brought us together.

All of Me Loves All of You

SHERYL GARRATT

In 1974, The Bay City Rollers had been struggling away for seven years with only one Top 10 hit, 'Keep on Dancing', to their name. Then manager Tam Paton, later to serve three years in jail for indecent acts with underage boys, enlisted pop songwriters Phil Coulter and Bill Martin, dressed his Rollers in tartan and hinted that Les, Derek, Woody, Alan and Eric were all romantic virgins. A teenage phenomenon was born, and some of the singles – 'Shang-A-Lang', 'Remember (Sha-La-La)' – weren't bad at all. They were critically reviled, of course, and were exclusively a girls' thing, like no band before or since. Two years and a further nine Top 10 hits, plus an American Number 1 ('Saturday Night') later, it was all over: both Alan and Eric would attempt suicide, while Alan's eventual replacement, Ian Mitchell, had a porn-star past. There would be no solo success for any ex-Rollers.

I'm in my thirties now and I don't worry about getting old any more. I'm pretty happy as I am, and it's a long time since I've felt the need to look in my scrapbooks to remind myself that being a teenager was nothing to get misty-eyed about. Yet here they are still, covered in dust. They've moved with me from Birmingham to London, from flat to flat, and now finally found a resting place in that forgotten corner in most journalists' homes: the one full of magazines you really will get round to reading one day, old press cuttings and photos, snippets of information that were once meant to be turned into features and which you don't want to throw away just in case. There are four of them, covered with a patchwork of tartan snipped from magazines (there was a lot of tartan around back then), any references to Scotland I could find, and the logo of the Bell record label. Opening them, I feel heat rising to my cheeks. It's not easy looking at yourself when you were fourteen. It's not a pretty sight. You see, I was a teenage Bay City Rollers fan.

In 1975, I lived in a housing estate on the far fringes of Birmingham, a place known to most people in the city only as the end of the number 90 bus route. It's a nice enough place – my parents still live there – but it lacks, shall we say, excitement. It has a park high up on one hill, a huge comprehensive school perched on another, and in between thousands of well-kept small houses with gardens and porches and carriage lamps and names like Dudropin, plus a library, two churches, three pubs and a Co-op supermarket. I spent a lot of time reading, always somewhere else in my head. I had a reputation as a bit of a daydreamer, which I suppose was true. By choice, I spent a lot of time alone.

I don't really remember becoming a Bay City Rollers fan. The music wasn't ever that important, and I don't think there was a particular tune that turned my head. I remember them having hits with 'Shang-A-Lang', 'Summerlove Sensation' and 'All of Me Loves All of You' in 1974, I remember some girls coming to school wearing BCR badges, and at some point quite late on, certainly in 1975, I must have decided to join them. It was good to feel part of something. This was the year of *Once Upon a Star*, their second LP, an ingeniously designed package that had a row of stars lined up at the top of the sleeve, each bearing the head of a Roller. Tug on the head and Bingo! Out came an album-sized picture of your favourite band member. It was the year they went to Number 1 with 'Bye Bye Baby' and 'Give a Little Love', but none of that mattered much. I'd like to say that we knew even then that the music was terrible, but I'd probably be lying.

'The Bay City Rollers are Britain's top pop group,' I wrote carefully on the opening page of my first BCR scrapbook.

'They are: Derek, Woody, Les, Alan and Eric.' Next to it is a picture, cut from a newspaper, of five rather sheepish-looking young men in ridiculously tight half-mast trousers trimmed with tartan, stripy socks and hideous two-tone platform boots. It must have been taken early on in their career, since they all had their names emblazoned in tartan on their shirts (also too tight) lest any of us had forgotten them.

On other pages there's a series my nan had cut out of the *Weekly News* for me in May 1975 detailing the 'inside story' of their British tour ('The Bay City Rollers are Britain's top rave group,' declared a headline). There's a 'happy Hogmanay' poster from *Jackie*, and their weekly 'letters' page in *Mirabelle* and *Fab 208*:

> I am a fan of the Bay City Rollers but the thing is I'm coloured and I don't know if they like coloured girls. Some of my school friends say they might not because they come from Scotland. Please tell me because I would like to go to one of their concerts but I don't want to be laughed at for going.
>
> Letter from a Birmingham fan, *Fab 208*
>
> (The Rollers replied: 'We love all our fans.')

I collected every other mention I could find, even down to the small ads: 'Rollers fans!' declared one, 'Fashionable new cosmetic transfers featuring the boys. Wear your affections for the Rollers anywhere on your skin: the mind boggles! Ten different colourful designs for 38 pence.'

Alan Longmuir Height 5 feet 10 inches, hair light brown, eyes green, inside leg 31 inches, shoe size 8, age variable (Gemini). Alan is left-handed. His favourite colour is blue, favourite food well-done steak, favourite drink dark rum and peppermint. Listens to The Carpenters, Led Zeppelin, Yes. Toothpaste: Pearl Drops.

Leslie Richard McKeown Height 5 feet 9 inches, hair dark brown, eyes hazel, inside leg 31 inches, shoe size 7, age 19

(Scorpio). Drives a Ford Mustang. Likes cars, fashion, flying, comics. Favourite colour marigold, favourite breakfast Sugar Puffs, favourite food duck. An occasional smoker.

Derek Longmuir Height 5 feet 9 inches, hair fair, eyes green, inside leg 31 inches, shoe size 8, age 24 (Pisces). Likes riding, swimming, fishing, sunshine, animals, Tom & Jerry, walking. Favourite colour blue, favourite drink milk, favourite food extra-hot curries. Has a large goldfish collection.

Stuart Wood (Woody) Height 5 feet 9 inches, hair black, eyes green, inside leg 30 inches, shoe size 8, age 18 (Pisces). Drives a Ferrari, supports Hibernian FC. Favourite colour yellow, favourite singer Doris Day, favourite food steak pie, favourite drink Coke. Suffers from hay fever.

Eric Faulkner Height 5 feet 10 inches, hair brown, eyes blue, age 20 (Libra). Likes swimming, horse riding, football, cooking, Benny Hill. Favourite colours black and white, favourite food omelette made with sausages, favourite drink tea, favourite flower rose, favourite bird dove, favourite band The Bee Gees, favourite singer Barbra Streisand. Carries a copy of Byron's poetry in his suitcase. Aftershave: Aramis.

I took these facts from cuttings in my scrapbooks, but once I knew them by heart. We would test each other on our knowledge. These things were important. What if I met one of them, and they asked me their inside leg measurement, and I didn't know? They'd think I wasn't a true fan. They'd desert me for another. It was crucial that I knew which breakfast cereal to buy, which toothpaste they used, so that, given the chance, I would be able to serve them well.

This was a boom time for girls' magazines, and we bought everything. Unable to afford a copy of each publication, groups of us banded together to share. Some of our parents read the *Sun*, others took the *Mirror*, so we'd swap bits from them. (The only other daily newspaper that existed in our world was the *Birmingham Evening News*, which I wouldn't read because they'd once said that the Rollers were lousy live.) We would meet at each other's houses and sit in our bedrooms playing records, updating our scrapbooks together and talking about the Rollers. Which was really a way of talking about ourselves: our hopes, fears, ambitions, desires were all poured out in these bedroom sessions. I'd never been in a gang before, and it was fun. For me, the Rollers offered a new means of escape.

They looked ridiculous, of course. But it was a clever look, most probably engineered by their manager, Tam Paton, who claimed in interviews that the band was his idea, and that he auditioned the members for looks, rather than musical talent. It was clever because it was easy to imitate, and imitate it we did, with help from fashion spreads in the magazines. 'Feet up, all you Roller fans!' screeched *Mates*. 'Super sox to keep rollin'' in! They come in white with a tartan panel in blue, yellow, pink and green down the outside. They cost 39p a pair from good old Woolworth's.' 1975, the peak year for Rollermania in Britain, must have been a very good year for manufacturers of tartan.

A group of us went together to a haberdashery on the Hawthorne Road and bought ourselves strips of tartan. We embroidered them and gave them fringes and then tied them round our wrists, wearing them as symbols of allegiance. Mine was a white background with a red and green plaid, and I loved it. In fact, I refused to take it off. I tanned easily then, but my right wrist was pale and white. I slept with the scarf, and wore it everywhere in public. The Rollers might drive past in their tour van, you see. They might be lost, and they would see my scarf and ask me for directions, and I would get into the van with them and drive away.

I don't think The Bay City Rollers – all resident in their native Scotland – would ever have been driving through our estate in Birmingham. And since I didn't know my way to anywhere much except the shopping centre where I had a Saturday job and my nan's flat in Smethwick – and only then on the bus – I doubt I'd have been much use if they had asked.

I also know now that the last person a teen group would ask for help would be one of their fans, not unless they were deliberately trying to provoke a mini-riot in the street. But still, this trip in the van was always the starting point for a rich selection of adolescent fantasies. At school, during boring classes, I would daydream that one of the Rollers would walk in to fetch me from class, with all my fellow students gawping and realizing – too late, since I was off to travel the world with my band – just how special I'd been. My teachers wouldn't protest at my departure – how could they, when I was with a pop star? Instead, they too would just gaze in open-mouthed admiration as I drove off with my Roller in an improbably large open-topped sports car. I dreamed of standing in the wings while they played live, the roadies and security staff winking at me because I was one of the team.

There was only Suzi Quatro as a role model then, and few of us girls ever dreamed of being pop stars ourselves. We dreamed of being their girlfriends, of being made important by dating someone famous. That's how you got status, respect. In our fantasies, we didn't install ourselves as the Rollers' new manager, instead we dreamed of being Tam's little helper. We wanted to iron their clothes, unpack their cases in hotels, run their fan club, because that was all our imaginations would allow us to do. Most of the magazines ran slots where you could write letters to the Rollers. Susan Wetherall of Bournemouth in Dorset wrote in offering her services as a housekeeper to Woody and Eric in their new house. Did they need someone to clean up, dust and cook for them? 'Can I please shampoo and blow dry your hair for you?' asked Julie Hatton of Guernsey, who worked in a hair salon at weekends. 'If you have anything that needs mending, I'll gladly do it.'

I didn't like this idea much. My parents were starting to ask me to do housework by then, and my dad kept using this phrase, 'you must get domesticated', as if I was a wild animal about to be caged as a pet. I was lazy and selfish in refusing to help with the chores, of course, but there was something nasty about the notion that this was my future, that I was being trained for it.

There was a series in *Jackie* magazine called 'My name's Jenny, I'm from *Jackie*', and in it this girl Jenny got to do all kinds of things just because she worked for a magazine. Most of them were pretty boring things (I was starting to grow out of *Jackie* – it seemed to me that every single problem on their Cathy & Claire problem page could be solved by joining a youth club. Except I'd never seen a youth club. It being the seventies, not the fifties, I doubt if any of the readers had.) But this one week, she got to join the Rollers' security team. She got to meet the Rollers, but more importantly, she was part of their team. She wasn't just hanging out or screaming, she had a role. I vowed then to become a journalist, because it seemed to me that they had all the fun.

Shortly afterwards, we went on a family outing to Birmingham Airport. My dad had been abroad doing National Service, but the rest of us had been only as far as Wales and Weston-super-Mare for our holidays, so watching planes take off was exciting. I remember looking somewhat scornfully at the holidaymakers lugging huge cases, and admiring the few, better-dressed people carrying small but important-looking briefcases. These were journalists, I decided, travelling around the world on assignment.

When I told my parents and my teachers about my plans, they laughed. Mine was a school where that very English phrase 'too clever by half' was used a lot, and ambition was frowned upon. We were already being given careers advice, and I was told that if I wanted to travel, I should think about banking. You could move from branch to branch in Birmingham, and even around the country. I remained determined. I wanted to be like Jenny. I didn't just want to be a fan or a girlfriend, I wanted to be involved.

But in the meantime, there were the Rollers. Their television show *Shang-A-Lang* was on at 5.20 p.m. on Tuesdays. Made by Granada and directed by Mike Mansfield, it consisted of a couple of guest stars (Alvin Stardust and 'lovely Linda Lewis' one week, plus 'a lively dance routine from Him and Us' – I know this because the entry in the *TV Times* is there, in my scrapbook, along with everything else). In between, the Rollers clowned around in clumsy Monkees-style sketches and performed a few songs of their own. We preferred the songs – we weren't used to accents other than our own, and when they spoke, we didn't really understand much (in my fantasies, they must have all spoken with Brummie accents, since we never seemed to have problems communicating then). Details of the show itself are hazy now, but I still remember feeling anxious all day about the behaviour of my classmates. There were no video machines then, and getting detention on Tuesday evening would be a disaster. If we were kept back an extra period, we'd miss it. As soon as the bell went for end of school, we'd pelt down the hill to Kim's house in time to play a few records, talk Rollers and get ourselves up into the mood before the show came on. Kim lived nearest to school, and she had a colour TV, so she was always very popular on Tuesdays. She also had a kitten which her parents had let her call Roller, which was just the coolest thing I'd ever heard of.

Obviously, we all had our special Roller. I told everyone that drummer Derek Longmuir was my favourite, because I felt sorry for him because he was so ugly. How could such a small mouth hold all those teeth? I also didn't want people thinking I'd set my sights too high, since I didn't think I was much of a looker myself. Secretly, I was in love with the singer, Les McKeown. This involved a certain amount of duplicity. I stuck pin-ups of Derek all over my bedroom walls, and on the outside of my cupboard and wardrobe doors. But on the inside of these doors were pictures of Les. I'd open them all at night so they faced me while I slept, then get up early to close them before my family got up, so no one would know my secret. (In keeping with my fight against being 'domesticated', I didn't clean my room or put my own laundry away, but I must have believed the fairies did it, since it never occurred to me that my mum would see my secret love.)

None of us were particularly mature for our age, but the boys in our class seemed even younger. Older boys were scary. Except in childish jokes, sex wasn't something we ever talked about. Liking the Rollers gave us a chance to explore our sexuality without any risks, without being labelled a 'slag' by our schoolmates. The Rollers were safe because, in the end, we all knew we'd never get to meet them. They'd never make demands. We could be in lust, talk about it, live it, without ever having to do anything about it except attack anyone who attacked our boys. Our energy in this task was impressive. Journalists daring to criticize the Rollers in print were besieged with letters. We called Radio 1 to complain after Johnnie Walker said on air that they had no talent. When each of them was finally forced to back down, I lovingly drew a skull and crossbones in my scrapbooks and drew a V (for 'victory') next to their retractions.

Then there were the Status Quo fans. Quo fans wore denim (often oil-splattered, even though none of us were old enough to drive). Quo fans had long, greasy hair. Quo fans were the enemy. A letter in *Record Mirror*, signed simply 'Quo fan, Medway, Kent', showed their attitude: 'Could you tell me how many of the Rollers are married, or are they gay, or are they mere puppets? I'm curious as to the real reason they don't go out with girls.' (The answer to this was obvious. The Rollers didn't have time for girlfriends, even though they were all incurably romantic.) At school, we attacked the Quo boys constantly, fighting with them in the lunch queue. They were particularly hurtful after Les McKeown killed an elderly pedestrian in a driving accident, but we retaliated with incredibly witty comments about their spots, hair and lack of dancing skills. I realize now why they would hang around, waiting to be insulted some more. They probably fancied us.

The Bay City Rollers came to Birmingham Odeon on Friday 9 May. The ticket is glued lovingly into my scrapbook: centre circle, £1.50. 'This tour is the most controversial one in the history of pop,' I wrote. An exaggeration, certainly, but it's easy now to forget the mass hysteria the Rollers caused in 1975. In the *Sun*, Labour MP Marcus Lipton called for 'tough police action to curb pop show hysteria' after one night in which 600 girls were treated by the St John Ambulance crews at Hammersmith Odeon. 'For calculated commercial reasons the emotions of young girls are exploited by performers and promoters who should be made to pay police and ambulance expenses,' he pontificated. A move within the Musician's Union to expel the group for 'disgusting conduct' also failed. 'I believe their act is a bad influence,' fumed the 22-year-old pianist from Oxford who had proposed the motion. Everyone, it seems, wanted to protect us from ourselves.

Three days after the start of the tour, it was announced that Alan Longmuir, the oldest of the Rollers, was set to quit. He revealed that he'd been lying about his age, and that at twenty-six he felt 'too old' to be in the group. The girls' magazines and the *Sun* urged us to tell him this was not so, and we responded magnificently. At school, we organized ourselves into a disciplined, determined outfit that managed to collect 750 signatures by any means necessary – not all of them were given willingly. Two weeks and – according to the papers – 260,000 letters later, he changed his mind. Only now, as I'm writing this, does the timing of this announcement seem a little suspect. Was it just a publicity stunt for the tour? I don't know, but it helped us work ourselves into a frenzy in the weeks before the Birmingham show. It also showed us how to organize – something that came in very useful later in our school lives when, with more or less the same group of friends, I sold badges for Rock Against Racism and collected signatures protesting against the Corrie

Bill's attempt to limit abortion rights. Something else strikes me about Alan now. Looking now at pictures of him taken around that time, I see that he doesn't look particularly old. What he does look is very embarrassed and uncomfortable.

Despite the build-up, I don't remember much about the concert itself, but I do remember everything else about 9 May 1975. At the start of the year my mum had decided not to buy me clothes any more, instead giving me a monthly allowance that I could go and spend myself. On my first few shopping trips into town, I had bought a yellow tartan bomber jacket from Chelsea Girl, and a pair of C&A jeans that I had turned up and trimmed with tartan ribbon. This is what I wore on 9 May, along with a blue BCR T-shirt, some braces borrowed from my dad, stripy socks and baseball boots (the Rollers had stopped wearing platforms by then, because they'd realized they weren't good for your feet). My hair was in two bunches, tied of course with tartan ribbons.

We changed at my house, putting on our blue and green Rimmel eye shadow carefully, then posed for pictures in my living room. My mum – who seemed to find everything hilarious that day – drove us to the bus stop, where there was already a large group of girls I knew from school. Some of them had a white bed sheet with 'We love the Rollers' painted on it, and we posed for more photographs. One girl in my year, Sue, was particularly well-developed for her age, and you could see clearly that she was wearing a bra. I was annoyed because obviously if we met the Rollers she'd have more chance (my mum preferred me to still wear Marks & Spencers vests, but for special occasions like this I wore my bikini top – alas there was very little to put in it). Luckily, Sue's favourite Rollers were Woody, then Eric, so I was pretty safe.

Our estate was where the bus route terminated, and as the empty bus pulled into the stop, the conductor looked genuinely nervous. We whooped in delight, swarming upstairs so we could hang our scarves out of the window, breaking into

choruses of BCR songs. As the bus progressed along its tortur-
ous route into town, the excitement increased. At each stop,
more and more girls piled on, all of them in uniform and in the
same over-excited mood. I'd never talked to total strangers like
this before. We discussed our favourite Rollers, admired each
other's banners and scarves, and, every so often, someone would
shout out and we'd all join in, at the top of our voices: 'B–A–Y,
B–A–Y, B–A–Y C–I–T–Y, and an R–O double-L E–R–S, Bay
City Rollers are the best!' No one told us to shut up. No one
would dare. There were too many of us.

In the city centre, the bus had been diverted slightly because
New Street, where the Odeon was, had been blocked off to
traffic. We were early, but when we got off we ran anyway,
becoming an ever-bigger crowd as we hurtled towards the
police barrier. As we got closer, I saw something on one of the
policemen's faces I'd never seen before. I saw fear.

Inside, we screamed. We stood on our chairs and screamed.
The Rollers were small, very small, down on the stage, and I
don't remember what they played or even whether I could
hear them over the din. They weren't important by then,
because what this was about was us. I'd never been that loud,
that uninhibited before. Afterwards, I felt euphoric. It was pure
joy. I loved the Rollers, but I also loved my mates and the bus
ride and the running and us all being together in our outfits
with our banners and badges and scarves. It was ace.

I've been to a few women's festivals since, but shouting,
aggression and running about screaming heterosexual lust is not
generally welcomed at such affairs. I've been to see groups like
Bros, but by then I was too old to be part of it all. So 9 May
1975 was the only time I've been part of such a large group of
women (6,000 of us saw the Rollers' two shows that day), all
with one purpose, and seen how mindlessly, joyfully powerful
that can be. This must be the feeling boys get on the stands at
football matches, all cheering for the same team. It must be the
reason they always walk in the middle of the road when

approaching the ground, even if there's plenty of room on the pavements. Because they can.

We never got that high again. I loved the Rollers all summer long, but by the autumn I was starting to grow out of them. My last scrapbook has yellowed cuttings fluttering loose between the pages where I didn't find time to stick them down, recording their trips to America and Australia, Woody's collapse from exhaustion, and the reviews of their third album, which I didn't even buy. We all went through the motions for a while more, reluctant to break up the gang, but real life started to intrude. Some of us got boyfriends, the disco at the church hall became more than just a chance to formation dance to the Rollers and sneer at the Quo fans, and a few of us even started to leave the estate for our entertainment, catching that 90 bus into town. I carried on going to concerts: Mud, T. Rex's comeback tour, then new wave bands like The Radio Stars and Boomtown Rats (punk had become new wave by the time it hit our suburbs, although Johnny Rotten was the first pop singer to inhabit my fantasy life with the same intensity as Les McKeown).

Musically, I transferred my loyalty to an older man with a bog brush haircut and tartan fetish: Rod Stewart. Thrifty to the last, I even recycled the tartan scarf, carefully sewing Rod's name on it in big red letters and taking it to wave the first time I saw him live. By the time of the next tour, my mum liked Rod too, and I said she could come to the concert with me because it was right out at the National Exhibition Centre and I needed a lift. It was OK, but just not the same with mum there. Next time he toured, I gave her the scarf and she went with her friends.

The 2-Tone label, from Coventry, had broken by then, and I produced a Birmingham fanzine with Kim, my friend from the Rollers days, and then started writing for the *NME*, interviewing local bands like UB40 and The Beat. As for The Bay City Rollers, that became the Love That Dare Not Speak Its Name. It wasn't something you boasted about in the *NME* offices. Just before I finished college in London, I did write about the

Rollers and our experiences, however, as part of a book I co-authored about women in pop. I received a batch of grateful letters as a result, from girls who had blocked out that period of their lives: 'It's not something you can talk about in public,' wrote one, 'but it was brilliant, wasn't it?' For a while, women would take me aside and come out of the closet, quietly admitting that their first love was Woody or Eric or Les or Alan.

Two final BCR memories. The first is from Volonte, a club that ran on Sunday nights in Slough in 1992. The house boom was at its height, and this club catered for a crowd who would dance all through Saturday night in London, 'chill' at someone's house for a few hours before driving down to Full Circle in Colnbrook on Sunday afternoon, and then still not be ready to go home. At the end of one particularly debauched and messy weekend, DJ Dave Dorrell was playing at Volonte, and like everyone else was way past his bedtime. Suddenly he dropped the house mix altogether and slapped on the Bay City Rollers single 'Shang-A-Lang'. The place went mad. Everyone knew the old Rollers dance and did it, singing along with their hands in the air. I caught a look in the eyes of some of the older girls present, and I knew they shared my secret.

Then in 1993, *The Face*, the magazine I edit, had its now-traditional New Year party. As usual, even though it's a small event for staff and contributors, we were inundated with requests for tickets. One of them was from a friend of Les McKeown, who was touring colleges with an all-new version of the Rollers and appearing as a kitsch novelty PA at club events like Sign of the Times. Did I want the group to play at the party? No, I said, there's not enough room. But could Les have a ticket? I said yes – I couldn't refuse – but on the night he didn't turn up. I was relieved.

A Kiss in the Dreamhouse

LUCY O'BRIEN

Although she'd been one of punk's founding fathers, as it were, Siouxsie Sioux never really looked like she could last the distance. She's still here of course, a grand old dame of British rock, with a song on the *Batman Returns* soundtrack to keep interest perky. Siouxsie & The Banshees were the first and last band to be signed after a graffiti campaign. Record companies weren't interested in a band whose set comprised a 20-minute version of the Lord's Prayer, so the band would scamper around London spray-painting SIGN THE BANSHEES NOW! on walls visible to major-label offices. Polydor took the bait, and band and company are still together sixteen years later. The *Daily Mirror* took sufficient interest in Siouxsie to suggest she'd had a nose job – the singer sued and won. She and her band seem curiously indestructible.

We were cool. We had our second-hand fifties suede stilettos, fluorescent socks, black drainpipes, Crimplene tops, white stage make-up and blazers disfigured by badges. Five seventeen-year-old girls, we walked into a Siouxsie & The Banshees concert at Southampton Gaumont in 1979 with a look of disdain that disguised fear. 'There's The Catholic Girls,' someone said excitedly. We'd been recognized. We had arrived.

My love – and it was love – for Siouxsie Sioux emerged around the same time that some schoolfriends and I formed an all-girl punk band called The Catholic Girls. We were bored convent-school sixth-formers living in draughty, provincial Southampton, where the most exciting thing that happened was the docking of the QE2. Punk had taken so long to filter through from London that it was now new wave, and a small hardcore, all in and out of each other's bands, used to congregate in the Lord Louis, a run-down pub near the old Hants & Dorset bus station. Then, as always, boys got down to the serious business of playing instruments while girls fulfilled their function as peroxide decoration. Anxious to create our own excitement, and none of us willing to play the role of bass guitarist's floozy, we bought a pair of drumsticks and assembled our own band.

After an early practice we got together to discuss the band 'concept'. In those days you had to have a message – preferably political – a context and an image. Our lead singer Tina, the perfect frontwoman with her black hair, gaunt eyes and angular cheekbones, pulled a record out of a plastic Virgin bag, laid it lovingly on the table, and said that this was the sort of thing she'd like to do. We were sat in a darkened room – for some reason we always seemed to rehearse in a dark room, playing for two hours and then stopping at 9 p.m. for Marmite sand-wiches – so I had to peer at the cover. Across blurred underwater shapes I could make out two words, *The Scream*. It was Siouxsie & The Banshees' debut album.

Tina put the record on, and the thump-heavy basslines and harsh vocals of 'Carcass', 'Helter Skelter' and 'Suburban Relapse' transfixed us for a full fifteen minutes. Our bass player, Judith, immediately began doing the trademark Siouxsie dance, arms like windmills, legs like a kick-boxer. We all studied the lyrics on the inner sleeve. Bored housewife in suburbia lacerating herself with a razor blade, a savage fantasy world where women were the stronger sex, a version of a song dedicated to cult murderer Charles Manson, a butcher falling in love with a slab of meat. Wow. This was heady stuff. At first I wasn't sure: the music was a kind of forbidding funk, the voice alienating in its atonal register. Then Tina showed me a picture – Siouxsie Sioux dressed all in black, her jet hair spiked, her eyes glittering, hard, speaking of a thousand nervous breakdowns, her slash-red lips set in a look of nonchalant defiance – and I was sure.

To me then, an idealistic sixth form innocent, timorous yet aching to enter the wild, strange, androgynous world she and her coterie seemed to signify, Siouxsie was the One Who Knew, a woman who had surely been to the edge, nay, was living on it, study of which would somehow give us access. Although she was a lone woman among men, Siouxsie, to me, symbolized a kind of sisterhood. The evening of our first Catholic Girls gig, played in a back room of a Southampton pub, my steady boyfriend (who once said, 'If you put a safety-pin through your nose I'll pack you up') saw the writing on the wall. 'You're going to meet your perfect punk here,' he said ruefully. 'Oh no, no!' I laughed. A month later I finished with him, but the perfect punk wasn't male – it was a combination of Siouxsie and our band, the ultimate sorority.

At the Gaumont gig, three months later, we stood in silence near the front, while mayhem spewed forth all around us. Siouxsie flew across the stage like a bat, dressed in a raincoat. 'Stop fucking spitting,' she said at one point, and we thought that was bone-crushingly fine. A woman in charge.

Before long we were incorporating The Banshees' cymbal-less drumming into our sound. We had a song called 'Small Talk (Small People)' – a rail against ... well, small talk (we hung around with the intense school of punk and subscribed to its grim credo: if you haven't got anything interesting to say, don't say it) – which featured Tina and me rapping the verse before jumping with Siouxsie-like bark into the chorus, Maddy madly slicing up the drums. We also had a song about anorexia, 'Life on a Lettuce Leaf'. 'I'm so fucking skinny...' it began. When asked by fanzines to give a description of our sound, we said it was a cross between Joy Division and The Banshees.

We became fascinated by what we saw as The Banshees' mysticism and psychic powers. One day after rehearsal we sat in the gathering gloom and decided to hold a seance. Crowding round the coffee table, we put our fingers on an upturned plastic beaker, letting it take us to torn letters of the alphabet, placed in a circle. After contacting someone strange who talked gobbledygook, I spoke to my grandmother who had died the year before.

'Hello,' I said.

'HELLO,' spelt the cup.

'Are you happy?'

'YES.'

'What's the name of your only daughter?' (my mother).

'MAUREEN.'

'And her second daughter?' (me).

'LUCY.'

'Do you remember me?'

Now, with a little hesitation, because she went senile in her old age: 'Y . . . ES.'

'Will The Banshees get a Number 1 hit?'

Further hesitation: 'MAYBE.'

Good old Grandma, always hedging her bets.

By 1980 The Banshees' sound had solidified commercially. Christine became our mantra, the signal, whether at a party, gig or in the sixth-form common room, to abandon ourselves to The Dance. Then there was the bliss of 'Happy House' on *Top of the Pops*. As the strains of John McGeoch's eerily high-pitched guitar sound wafted from the TV, I demanded silence from my brother and sister, before watching Siouxsie's every move with rapt attention. Oh, how she threw the confetti from her pocket on the word 'Happy'! Oh, how ironically joyless she seemed on the despised glitz of the *Top of the Pops* stage! She had the last laugh, she knew the secret mystery. The following morning Tina and I went through a debrief, in those pre-video days analysing what we recalled of her performance.

1980 was Siouxsie's year and our year. My parents had split up when I was fourteen, my father re-marrying less than two years later. For a while I'd gone into coping mode, and, as if with delayed shock, the impact didn't register until I was eighteen. I dyed my hair peroxide blonde, wore an anarchist-feminist badge, trooped off to Anti-Nazi League demonstrations, raided jumble sales, bought a synthesizer and generally rebelled. 'I'm not one of the sheep,' I maintained. 'I'll never end up somebody's slave.' In my world, which always seemed to be on the verge of emotional chaos, Siouxsie presented an admirable picture of control.

It was the year The Catholic Girls truly took off. We played concerts in pubs and colleges all over the south. When we finally got a gig in London we hired a Bedford van, and taped a notice on the back that read Catholic Girls on Tour. The gig turned out to be in a pub on a Kingston housing estate supporting a skinhead band, whose followers detested us and pelted us with bottles before chasing us out to the van and beating us up. There was no protocol about gentlemen not hitting ladies. By the time the police arrived we were hiding in the van with fifteen skins trying to push it over. After our escape, we became homecoming heroines. That frightening night eventually became part of Catholic Girls mythology.

Punk was about being hard, tough, politicized and wearing my late grandmother's clothes. I read Germaine Greer's *The Female Eunuch* and made a trip up to London to the *Spare Rib* offices to meet the collective. There was I, the next generation, with my anarchist-feminist badge and spiked hair, severely disappointed with the hippy haircuts and seventies grow-your-own-hi-fi ethos that prevailed there. What made it memorable though was meeting writer Jill Nichols, because she had actually met Siouxsie Sioux.

'What was she like?' I badgered.

'Very cool,' Jill said. 'She didn't want to be interviewed on her own, she had to be with the rest of the guys in the band.'

I sucked up every available fragment, every observation she

could give me, as if by talking to someone who'd been in direct contact with Her, something could be transferred, osmosis-like, to me. That was when Siouxsie had to explain to a Rock Against Racism crowd why she'd started out wearing Nazi swastikas. 'It was all a desire to shock ... an anti-Nazi gesture,' she claimed. Although she was on shaky ideological ground, that added to the mystique – the fact that she would deliberately risk her political cred for some higher purpose. Then I still believed that punks were privy to some eternal sussed truth that the rest of us were too desperately safe and unhip to see.

Our band continued its ferocious activity, A levels or no A levels. I would translate Virgil at home before hiking bass drums on the train to Bournemouth for a gig at Capone's. We'd finish late, maybe stay over in a punk squat in New Milton, before catching the train back to Southampton in the morning to go to lessons. The school part was always a difficult one to live down. Although I found out that Siouxsie was convent-educated too, I felt sure she would never have done anything so mundane and naff as going to school the morning after a gig.

As Southampton punks began the drift to London, the brief, vibrant scene at home broke up. University beckoned and I left the band amid momentary heartache and recrimination. It's true, we were just starting to get good at our instruments, we'd been promised a support slot with Bauhaus, we were learning about verses, bridges and choruses – but I was on course for Leeds, home of The Gang of Four, Delta 5 and a healthy music scene with Soft Cell at the helm. Leeds in late 1980 was on the turn, suitably bleak and industrial with a plethora of home-grown bands, a post-punk groundswell that would develop into Goth with – after the *A Kiss in the Dreamhouse* album – Siouxsie as its figurehead, fossilized in a black clad, Krazy Kolor, patchouli-oiled world. In 1980, though, she was still a cutting-edge heroine.

My big chance arrived when The Banshees came to play Leeds University at the height of their early fame. *Kaleidoscope*, their third album, had just been released. A masterful mix of punk and eighties pop psychedelia, it blasted out of the tinny cassette-recorder I had in my dark purple student bedroom. Its brooding tones were a fitting soundtrack to the chill Yorkshire winter and the sense of an embattled city. Some weeks previously, Peter Sutcliffe had murdered Jaqueline Hill, a girl in my English department, and all women were subject to an after-dark curfew. The atmosphere hung like an intense, explosive black cloud, while erupting from the dark were moments of surreal hysteria; male students escorting women like they were Victorian ladies with a case of the vapours, alongside radical feminists reclaiming the night and throwing red paint on porn cinema screens.

I had started writing music reviews for the *Leeds Student* paper, so the Banshees concert was the opportunity to interview my idol as well as get a lucky break. Commissioned first to do a preview I sat down excitedly to write it, then realized that apart from the image and the music I didn't know the first thing about her. How embarrassing.

I raced down to the hall phone, madly fed in ten pences and rang our lead singer Tina. Good ole Tina. 'Tell me about Siouxsie,' I gasped, panic stricken.

'She was one of the Bromley Contingent. She was on the Bill Grundy *Today* programme with The Sex Pistols when they swore...'

Yes, yes! Phone cradled to my ear, a crackling line.

'...and her first gig was at the 100 Club with Sid Vicious on drums. They did a twenty-minute version of the Lord's Prayer...'

Students behind me, 'Come on, we want to use the phone...'

'...and got signed up after a huge A&R war.'

I made a few more notes, scrawled on scrap paper, and hung up. My journalistic career was born.

Next stop was securing the interview. Belting up my long, enigmatic mac, I strode purposefully into the Union the next day, and went upstairs to the Entertainments Office. Andy Kershaw, later to become a London-based motorcycling Radio 1

DJ, was then Ents Sec. I sat opposite him while he spoke to someone on one phone, barked to someone else on another, writing notes, closing deals and drinking tea in between. I was impressed.

'Now, what can I do for you?' he asked, putting a phone down and looking at me directly. Better get it in quick, I thought, and explained my status as a lowly reporter planning to interview Siouxsie. 'No problem,' he declared, sorting me out a backstage pass. 'See me after the gig, I'll take you to her.' I was shocked. It was that simple. We chatted further; he gave me a poster advertising the Banshees gig (it went straight on my purple bedroom wall) and talked about how much he loved Leeds. 'I'll never go down to London,' he said in his thick Yorkshire accent. 'They're all bastards down there.'

Now, no one could touch me. I was a journalist with an important assignment. When Saturday came I went to the Union with camera, notebook and my Mancunian friend Sara in tow, pushing through the audience to get to the front. We waited a long time for the band to come on, beating and clapping impatiently. Finally the lights went down, dark figures walked on and picked up guitars, then a spotlight focused on the Goddess. With her black, beautifully coiffured spikes, dark plum lipstick, clothes of bright silk and intense glare, she was so cool it hurt. My throat tightened, my heart went numb, I realized I was truly in love. What was I to do? How could I even speak to her? What would I say? My busy, burgeoning journalistic self retreated and once more I was the awestruck fan.

After the gig – Electric! Charged! Magnificent! Etc! – Sara tugged my sleeve. 'Come on,' she implored, 'we'd better get backstage.' I nervously looked round for Andy, found him talking to roadies by the stage and got him to lead me round the back. Trestle tables were lined up, with a gaggle of fans crowded at the door holding autograph books and photos. After a long wait, they walked in. Steve Severin, John McGeoch,

Budgie and then, ah!, the Queen herself, smiling shyly. They sat down at the tables, and the fans (by now in an orderly queue) came up one by one to get memorabilia signed. After a word in Siouxsie's ear, Andy motioned to me. Trembling, I shoved my camera into Sara's hand hissing, 'Take a picture of this,' and walked over.

Siouxsie pulled out a chair next to her. 'Hello, pleased to meet you,' she said, politely shaking my hand. I'd fully expected her to be gruff and impossibly cold, but she was being nice to me! At first my voice was so quiet she had to bend close to hear me, but as we chatted about the gig, the album, her clothes, I started to relax. She was a gal! We could talk!

'I'd like to star in a film with Bette Davis,' she confided. 'I see myself like a light with music shining through me.'

I thought that was so profound I underlined it in my notebook right there and then. At one point she explained that the reason she sometimes appeared aggressive was because she hated people who were insincere.

'I'm not insincere,' I gushed.

'I know, that's why I'm talking to you.'

Oh, heaven!

As she spoke, she signed autographs, but we talked for so long that the crowd at the door dwindled to nothing and we were alone, apart from Sara clicking my camera, the band and Andy Kershaw.

'We're going to have to wind things up,' he said.

'Just one more question,' I pleaded.

He nodded, diplomatically shifting attention to the guys.

'What's it like being the only woman on the road with so many men?' I asked her. She looked into my eyes, and for a moment it was as if there was no one in our world apart from us and this quietly spoken confidence.

'Sometimes I get so lonely,' she said.

Our intimate second was broken by Budgie tapping her arm. 'Are you ready?'

She introduced me to him, and we all chatted for a while about bands and drum kits. It was like joshing with friends, and it seemed like none of it would end, but she was the star, and she had to go. She shook my hand again before wrapping up warm and leaving. I looked behind me and smiled at her, deeply moved. I wanted to get her address, tell her I'd write to her, tell her that she could run away with me and never be lonely again, but of course I didn't.

'I got a great picture of you and her talking,' said Sara, as we bounced out into the freezing winter night.

Meeting Siouxsie gave me confidence, a great interview and the spur to consolidate my identity. That year I went to the University Ball, but with a difference. Instead of wearing an unflattering Richard Shops' ballgown, I hired a smart bow tie and tails. Together with white gloves, black trousers and hair teased impossibly high, Siouxsie-style, I was the proud punk Belle of the Ball. Like her, I was learning how to spin my own myth, to become somebody.

I didn't meet Siouxsie again for six years. By then I was a cocksure young writer on the *NME* and a soul girl to boot. I had an attitude, and trashing old idols was one of them. At the end of 1986, punk was well and truly dead, rock was wavering, and dance music was in the ascendant. Punk to me then was a distant memory, a brief, chaotic, embarrassing interruption in my true calling – seventies disco queen and eighties dance fan. In the ardour of my early twenties, the past was meaningless, the only way seemed to be ahead.

I'd been summoned by *The Tube*, Channel 4's groundbreaking youth TV programme, to talk about women in rock. I was wearing a black Fred Perry, black Levis, regulation white socks and DMs, and had my blonde hair slicked back. I did a brief spitfire piece to camera, slagging Alison Moyet for going air-brushed (poor woman, she was only trying to look nice), and retired to the Green Room with Jools Holland and Paula Yates.

An apparition in black and bright silks came tottering in, hair black and jagged, face coated with thick foundation, lips red. For a second my heart stopped as I recognized Siouxsie. Then I closed up again. I looked at her for a while before approaching, with a kind of detached curiosity.

'Hello,' I said, 'you might not remember me, but I interviewed you when I was a student in Leeds, many years ago.'

She looked at me, distracted. She was shaking, ravaged and monosyllabic, a ghost of her former self. She didn't recognize me, even though she said hello. I felt disturbed at the way fame, stardom and the inevitable temptations had taken their toll. Typical pop star, I thought, cynicism hiding my disappointment. By then she had become that despised thing, a Goth. She was part of my past, like David Cassidy and blue eye-shadow and pixie boots and Subway Sect and rock riffs and caterwauling vocals, the jumble of memories that got stuffed in a mental cupboard and taken out every so often to laugh at.

The conversation with Siouxsie was brief. She had to go on stage and perform numbers from *Tinderbox*, their new album that I had trashed the previous week in a review. 'Tired old Goths,' I'd written, enthusiasm for the new millennium making me cruel. I went upstairs to watch The Banshees on the monitors, crashing through their paces, guitars jangling, drums dark and moody.

'Yawn, same old thing,' I said to Gaynor, the researcher. On the train back from Newcastle to London though, I felt vaguely depressed. As I stared out through the rain-streaked windows, the image of Siouxsie's nervous, foundation-piled face kept returning to haunt me.

Two years later, I was Music Editor on the London listings magazine *City Limits*, feeling jaded with overwork, surrounded by a pile of records to be reviewed and a phone that never stopped ringing. To combat the stress my colleague Andy Darling and I would compile the rock listings with a certain amount of bravado: nothing, repeat nothing, was to be taken seriously. So when Polydor rang saying that there would be a launch for The Banshees' new album *Peep Show*, we thought we'd go along for some free beer and an opportunity to wind up other journalists. At that point the music business for me had lost its spark, I was beginning to feel like the last cog in a factory assembly line, with product arriving daily through my door that I had to process and serve before the public. Buy this record, buy that, go to this concert, whatever you do don't go to that.

When we arrived at the venue (an unusual place for a record launch – a plush house in Central London that had the early-evening sun slanting through tall windows), the second floor was packed with journalists, marketing people and the entire Polydor promotions department. Video screens displayed their latest state of the art video, while *Peep Show*, a return to pop form after the dull ache of *Tinderbox*, played through speakers. Much had been made of the new-look Siouxsie, with unkind rumours that she'd had a nose job.

Siouxsie entered, entourage in tow, and I was shocked at how slim, healthy and bright-eyed she looked. Her hairstyle, in a sleek, black bob, had completely changed. Approaching thirty years old, she'd decided it was time to give up the bad tour food and alcohol and get into shape. People immediately surrounded her, some sycophantic, some asking questions. Mindful of the last time I'd met her, I decided to hang back. Andy and I were chatting away in a corner, when suddenly Siouxsie looked up from the group of people and waved at me. My reflex action was to look behind me. Who's she smiling at? 'You,' said Andy, 'I think she wants to talk to you!'

With that she detached herself from the throng and swooped down on me, hand outstretched. 'Hello,' she said kindly. 'I met you at *The Tube*, didn't I? And you also interviewed me for a student paper in Leeds.'

All eyes were upon us. 'Wh-why, yes,' I stuttered. 'It's nice to see you again!' Whether or not she was just playing gracious hostess, I felt flattered, special and remembered. Weary scepticism dropped from my eyes. 'Everyone says I've had a nose job,' she giggled girlishly. 'I haven't you know.'

'No, of course not.'

In years to come I worked things out, partially at least. Somehow star and fan had gone on a shared journey, our parallel paths meaning that at certain points we collided, and at each convergence, something in the dynamic between us altered. The final time we met was for the grown-up interview. It was 1990: I was working on a biography of Annie Lennox, and interviewing Siouxsie for the *Guardian*. She had recorded *Boomerang*, the second album by The Creatures, Siouxsie and Budgie's part-time band. It was another chance to explore pared down percussion and vocals outside the band format.

'When you've been doing anything for a long time you gather a lot of excess,' she told me. 'Rather than get rid of people in the band it was easier to pause and take a new direction.'

Because no intimate interview suites were free, we were ushered into the record-company boardroom, joking that we had finally made it to the board. My Walkman had packed up, so I was making notes, just as in our first interview. It was as if we'd come full circle, a decade on. No longer in awe of her, I saw Siouxsie as an equal, one of the few women from the punk era to still have a high profile in the mainstream.

'I feel more confident now,' she reasoned. 'In the beginning mine was a protest voice, shouting as loud as possible over other people. Now it's more playful. Before, everything felt so uptight and tense. It was abrasive, missiles were thrown at you on stage, your head was on the block, and you had to survive within that.'

I agreed, recalling The Catholic Girls' gig in Kingston where we had been forced off stage. No longer revering her, I could see that Siouxsie was as I'd first thought – a gal: normal, jokey, salty, straightforward even, ten years on from the swastikas, the aloof, icy image, the searing vocals. Here she sat several floors up overlooking Hammersmith Broadway, calm, collected, dressed in black, a back-to-basics feminist. She was talking about the single, 'Standing There', which told a typical tale of street harassment.

'Every girl despises the fact that she's screamed at from idle loafers. Men together are very ugly in a bar or the street. What do you do? Go round the block to avoid them? I fantasize about being the man with a gun in *Taxi Driver* and blowing their stupid faces off.'

The Siouxsie who once spoke of feeling alone surrounded by men now recognized the force of women in pop music.

'Women are a lot more exciting now – from Salt'n'Pepa to Bjork and Sinead O'Connor – they're trying to do a lot more with their voices. Men are either very deep or sound like their balls are squeezed very hard. There's little interplay.'

Our conversation was professional. But then a shard of the former charisma suddenly resurfaced. She recalled the trip she'd made to Moorish Spain with Budgie, recording songs on a 16-track mobile and driving through dry, arid, cruel countryside where no one spoke English. 'We stayed in an eleventh-century convent which had the original cells: thick walls with narrow windows. In one I had a strong feeling of a nun facing her own demons, as if she was there like an afterprint.'

The ghost that had haunted us, the dark mysticism that infused our band and gave The Banshees their sharp edge, wailed a little behind the framed gold records on the boardroom wall. Once again, for a minute, I felt as if the world had telescoped around us. Then it widened out again; the press officer bustled in, I finished my mug of tea, shook Siouxsie's hand goodbye and made my way out into the bright daylight of Queen Caroline Street. There was something satisfying in my step, as if a connection had finally been completed.

Beast of Burden

DAVID SINCLAIR

Everybody knows about Mick Jagger. He has thick lips, sings with The Rolling Stones, may or may not be married to Jerry Hall and has had a less-than-successful solo career.

Anyway, he was born in Dartford in 1943 and by the time he attended the London School of Economics was a committed blues buff. He met an old acquaintance and fellow music freak, Keith Richards, on a train in 1960. Three years later The Rollin' Stones had added a 'g', signed with manager Andrew Oldham and seen their first single, 'Come On', reach the Top 30. Jagger was an effective spokesman for The Stones, all quotable middle-class sophistication (until he became a Cockney) and snappy put-downs.

By the seventies, Jagger was a wealthy man, a failed, divorced actor, and The Stones were perhaps the biggest rock band ever. The eighties were a blur of Jagger solo activity, moderately received Stones albums and a few stadium tours. Today another stadium tour beckons, the latest Rolling Stones album is produced by Don Was and Mick Jagger is one of the most famous men in the world.

My earliest recollection of The Rolling Stones was being told about them by my friend John Summers. The year was 1963, and we were kicking a football about in the road outside the front of my house in Sidcup. A budding pair of ten-year-old suburbanite louts, we were at about the Beavis & Butt-Head stage emotionally, but without the intellectual pretensions.

'Saw this great new programme on TV last night,' John enthused as he hoisted the ball high over my head. 'Called *Top of the Pops.* They had this amazing group on. Really hard and sort of shaggy.'

Bouncing awkwardly off the pavement the ball began rolling down the garden path of the house opposite, heading straight towards a neat little cluster of milk bottles with the kind of devastating precision that we rarely mustered on our occasional visits to the bowling alley.

'What were they called?'

'The Broken Stones, I think.'

As if by coincidence, it was at about this time that The Stones actually played at my annual school dance. The place was called Eltham College, in South London, and doubtless the only reason the group condescended to do the gig was because Mick Jagger's younger brother Chris was a pupil there.

Chris Jagger was several years older than me. He looked a lot like Mick and became quite a celebrity in the school after The Stones made it big. I never had the temerity to speak to him, of course, but you'd often see him swaggering along the corridors, humming a tune, his mouth puckered into that supercilious expression – half-smile, half-leer – which he'd obviously picked up from his brother. His (and Mick's) dad used to come and help out on Sports Day. Mr Jagger was a wiry, physical education instructor, bald as a coot. I remember him supervising the high jump event with a rather endearingly distracted manner.

The contribution of Mick's group to the social life of the school was less benign. I was much too young to go to the dance myself, but apparently The Stones' reputation was already sufficient to attract a bunch of teddy boys from the town who gatecrashed the event. There were several scuffles, some coats got nicked from the cloakroom and the school chapel was graffitied. It was many years before another dance of any sort was permitted at the school.

Thus were laid the early foundations of my special affection for The Rolling Stones. They were a local legend, personal to me, and heroes in a way that no other group of that time was – the home team, to use a football analogy.

But as I progressed into my teens, my interest in The Stones was far from consuming. They were obviously a vastly superior group to The Beatles, a point which I found myself arguing with the headmaster's wife at the lunch-table one day. She was an unbelievably pretentious old bag called Cloonis (Latin for 'vagina', or so it was fondly supposed), which hardly excused the aggressive and frankly rather vulgar way in which I responded to her lame attempts at conversation. This was around the time of 'Jumping Jack Flash' and the utterly cool promo film of Jagger with his stripes of war-paint looming into the camera, flanked by Brian Jones wearing a pair of impossibly massive shades, his face painted bronze.

'I've always thought The Beatles were preferable to some of the others that you see,' she said with that pinched look of distaste on her face.

'Well, that just shows how plumb ignorant you are,' I responded cheerfully. 'The Stones could piss over The Beatles any day of the week.' These were the days when teachers were called 'Sir' and caning was still considered an improving punishment for boys who 'cheeked' the masters, let alone the headmaster's wife. As usual I took my strokes like a wimp, but considered the marks a badge of pride.

Despite such occasional acts of heroism under enemy fire, I really wasn't that bothered about The Stones at school. I liked their music and what they were about, and I sometimes bought their records. But at that time I exhibited more traditional signs of fan worship in relation to John Mayall's Bluesbreakers, Cream and especially The Jimi Hendrix Experience, whose records I religiously dashed out to buy on the day of release and played, ceaselessly, from start to finish until I had memorized every nuance of every note played and every word sung.

It wasn't until I got to university that I began to develop a Rolling Stones fixation. Over a four-year-period – from roughly *Exile On Main Street* in 1972 to *Black and Blue* in 1976 – it gradually dawned on me just what a vital link with my disappeared childhood and rapidly fading adolescence the group was. While most people seem to grow out of their hero worship, I grew into it. Hendrix was dead. Clapton had gone soft. The Who were already an embarrassment. There were lots of great new acts around – Mott the Hoople, David Bowie, Free, the young Thin Lizzy – and I loved them all. But in my heart of hearts I thought they were lightweights compared to The Stones. The Stones had emerged unbowed from the maelstrom of the 1960s, which, I liked to think, in my own modest way I had too. They were living proof that you didn't *have* to lose your outlaw chic just because you got older (just like me, I thought, now that my hair and beard had grown as long as they were ever going to). And if anything, The Stones were in their prime, still just as arrogant and wild, and to my ears making some of their best records ever.

Since Barbara Charone wrote *Keith Richards*, her incredibly candid, groundbreaking biography of the guitarist, in 1979 it's been cool to cite him as the key man in The Stones. People admire Richards's spirit, his down and dirty soulfulness, his essence-of-rock'n'roll personality. I do too. But to me Jagger was always the smart one. He took a few drugs and had a good time, but he had a weather eye on the future and kept himself in incredible shape. He somehow baited the establishment and courted it at the same time. He kept his options open. He was incredibly resilient, and still is; able to ride out the roughest situations without losing his smirk. How many of today's tortured young stars would have been able to walk off the Altamont stage and carry on without taking six months off to have a nervous breakdown about it first? Jagger didn't worry about being rich and successful. He enjoyed it. He didn't analyse life, he made the most of it. People have always disliked him for his arrogance, his lack of concern, his apparent lack of any weakness. I've always found all that rather inspiring.

For me, leaving university was an awkward period; that time when you're old enough to know you should be doing something with your life and young enough to be trying as hard as possible to avoid whatever it was you should be doing. To that end I'd joined a music-theatre group, a half-arsed singing, dancing, playing, drinking troupe of post-graduate misfits who lived in a castle in a village called Hanwell, near Banbury. I played drums, which excused me from the worst of the nonsense that went on there, much of it promulgated by the guitarist in the group and writer-to-be Tom Hibbert.

There was no question of trying to interest any of that lot in The Rolling Stones, who even by then were regarded as hopelessly old hat, and it was here that I first realized that my continuing passion for the group was likely to prove a social handicap. Little Feat and Genesis dominated the communal turntable. I sometimes managed to sneak a Be Bop Deluxe record under the wire, but I only ever got to hear *Black and Blue* in the privacy of my own room. I used to sit there for hours listening to 'Hot Stuff', 'Hand of Fate' and 'Memory Motel', looking at the cover photograph and marvelling at the years of incredible experiences that lay stored behind the dumb insolence of Jagger's stare.

But that was nothing compared to the shame of still being a Stones fan during punk. As anyone who lived through those times will doubtless recall, it was a musical era defined by its ugly intolerance of anything or anyone who didn't conform to certain rigid guidelines as laid down by the fashion police in the weekly music papers. By the time *Some Girls* came out in 1978, I'd drifted down to London and was playing drums in a pseudo-punk band called Blunt Instrument led by Robert Sandall, a singer and rhythm guitarist who is now rock critic of the *Sunday Times*. True to form I'd been the last in the group to get my hair cut, and the last to get rid of my flared jeans. Punk for me was the ideal conduit for a fairly rudimentary drumming style, but I was less sure about the ideology of the movement as a whole. Just as well we had Robert on board, who could be very fierce about keeping us up to the mark. The Only Ones

and Gang of Four were fine to listen to, but I remember
him telling me off, in no uncertain terms, for admitting that I
quite liked Tom Robinson.

With nowhere to go and with no one to share my enthusiasm
for *Some Girls* – surely one of The Stones' finest albums – I
turned, in quiet desperation, to pen and paper. I hadn't written
anything more ambitious than a letter since leaving university,
and had certainly never contemplated a job as a writer. But this
was plainly a period in my life when I had more time on my
hands than was healthy. So, inspired partly by the best track on
the album, 'Beast of Burden' – still my favourite Stones song – I
wrote a short story.

My pride in the finished product can be gauged by the fact
that until now I have never even mentioned its existence, let
alone shown it, to another soul (who knew me). Some time after
writing it, however, I did vaguely feel I should try and do
something with it, so I posted it to the *NME*. I was genuinely
too embarrassed to put my own name to it so, in the highly
unlikely event of it being published, I sent it in under the
pseudonym of Gordon Bennett.

Here, then, with profuse apologies to anyone who will accept
them, and reproduced *exactly* as it was presented to the *NME* is
my fan's fantasy about Mick Jagger.

BEAST OF BURDEN

'The first shall be last and the last shall be first ... Blessed are
the meek for they shall be trampled underfoot.' Joseph Bailey
worked this notion around his head for a while as he set off on
his way to work one sunny morning. He certainly didn't feel as if
he was about to inherit the earth; just another day at the bank.

In a recording studio half way across the world Mick Jagger
was kicking a few ideas around with Charlie Watts. Keith and

Ronnie had headed an expedition to a club nearby and had swept most of the other musicians, engineers and various on-lookers along in their wake of bourbon and laughter. Their harmonica player, Sugar Blue, was sulking, slumped in a chair upstairs watching some old videos. Bill had never even turned up.

'OK, Charlie,' Jagger idly ran his fingers over the slightly out of tune Stratocaster. 'When I hit that chord, try the hi-hat chop and then move into the reggae pulse – see if it works.' Charlie nodded, a look which would have denoted resigned boredom to the rest of the world, but indicated to Jagger that he was concentrating and ready. They worked through the sequence, Jagger squawking and yelping various ad lib words and catch-phrases. It always helped to run through a lick with Charlie.

At about this time The Audience swept into our corner of the galaxy. As always they rode in on a wave of babbling frivolity. A self-appointed roving court of mischief-makers, they nevertheless retained some vestiges of their original function. Eons before, they had been a seriously dedicated court of redress, touring the countless galaxies and addressing themselves to the issues of balance. They attempted in those days, centuries ago, to uphold the law of averages – to try and ensure, if you like, that the wheel of fortune was turning freely, that the dice at the very least weren't loaded. They'd discovered of course, gradually over the generations, the impossibility of the task, but nevertheless were still compelled to keep journeying. But now instead of worrying and fretting over their work, they laughed and joked about it, regarding it as a stimulus to their thinking, and addressed themselves to the possibilities of balance.

'What we need,' Asap communicated to the assembly, 'is a test period before committing the ruling to a final course.'

'I agree,' replied Alban, soundlessly ingesting a large piece of fruit. 'If we're going to make these decisions of balance then we ourselves must retain a sense of proportion or else we run the risk of missing the target and creating an imbalance that is difficult to rectify.'

'My point precisely,' returned Asap. 'It's all very well throwing a spanner in the works, but look what happened with that Kennedy business.'

'They're still trying to sort that one out to this day.'

There were some mute giggles.

'Sure, but he shouldn't have been killed. In that instance we over-stepped the mark.'

The laughter stopped.

'A test,' Alban mused. 'A day of grace. Well there's always The Room . . .'

Jagger woke as if from a light doze and found himself slumped on the floor against one wall of a perfect white room. It was a strange sensation; he hadn't really been aware that he'd been asleep, nor could he think straight off where he was or how he'd got there. But then he'd long been adept at shrugging off situations of disorientation and moments of uncertainty – his pragmatic arrogance assured him that whatever had happened he was in a position to deal with it.

He looked at the room. It was a complete cube about twenty square feet, and absolutely white. There was no furniture – nothing. Not even a window. No obvious light source and yet it was bathed in a very clean antiseptic white light. He didn't care for it much – a feeling confirmed by the realization that there was no door. Where was he? Certainly not in a recording studio. Slumped against the wall opposite Jagger was Joseph Bailey.

Perhaps it was an interview. The guy opposite him looked a bit like that bloke who'd interviewed him before from *New Music News*. But hadn't he read somewhere that *New Music News* had closed down? He couldn't remember. The singer's brow creased in a frown as he thought and looked at the other man.

Meanwhile, Bailey was also stirring as if from a brief, light sleep. Fleetingly he took in his new unaccustomed surroundings and then 'Christ – that's Mick Jagger.' The realization hit him with some force as his eyes met the quizzical gaze of the performer.

Now Bailey had always lived a fairly humdrum life and had never had occasion to use 'mind-expanding' drugs or face down disorientating situations. He was the kind of person who had trouble attracting the attention of people serving behind bars. 'Two pints of lager and a packet of crisps *please*.' In contrast to Jagger's rather lazy musings about their present situation, his mind and his life seemed to be whirling around him. Of all people, Mick Jagger.

All his adolescent life and till now, Bailey had been infatuated with rock music. He sometimes felt that all of his life's important emotional and intellectual moments had been experienced or at least reflected through music. He recognized this as a rather naïve and romantic idea, but even so ... A mass of images crowded his mind. His first bitter argument with his father and The Who crunching through 'My Generation'; the strains of Jimi Hendrix singing 'Angel' as a backdrop to his love affair with Julie; David Bowie, the Starman of his college days. Of course, through all this strode The Rolling Stones, somehow infinitely more massive than The Beatles (just a fading memory and a store of riffs for The Jam to plunder) or Dylan, who he'd lost interest in long ago. The new stars were – well – new; you couldn't really make meaningful comparisons with The Stones. Current musical merits aside, The Stones had been there, which the new guys hadn't.

Further than this, Joseph had always felt a peculiar affinity with Mick Jagger. Of course he would have liked to play guitar like Jimi Hendrix, to be as wealthy as Paul McCartney, to look like Sting, to write songs like John Lennon; but Mick Jagger was the only person in the world he actually would have wanted to be.

'Right, we've got them there. So far so good. Let's introduce the first random factor. Give them both an equal glimpse of what's on the cards.'

*

Jagger found himself wondering less idly about the other man.

'Who are you? What the fuck am I doing here?' he asked, a slight note of impatience in his voice.

'My name's Joseph,' said Joseph. 'And I haven't a clue where we are or. . .' He was about to say 'why we're here', but caught himself. Because although it wouldn't register in his consciousness, like an elusive name on the tip of his tongue, he did have an idea why they were there. Instead, he blurted . . . 'You're Mick Jagger aren't you?' Stupid question, he thought.

Jagger smiled very slightly and nodded briefly. Ordinarily, he supposed he would have got up and thought about leaving the room or at least looking it over. But there didn't seem any point. It was almost as if he wasn't really there. He felt very detached from it all.

'Are you in music?' he asked Joseph.

'Well no actually. I work in a bank in South Kensington.'

For some reason the words conveyed more to Jagger than they should. As if they were made of real substance, they crossed the few feet between him and Joseph, and he glimpsed a life of ordered monotony. A bus journey in the morning, a cup of coffee at 11.00, a systematic day's work, back home in the evening, a few drinks, see a band or a film. It was as if a veil had lifted from his eyes. Naturally he'd never lived like that. He'd known on an intellectual level that that's how people live, but he'd never come across the thought as vividly as this before. It was the difference between someone explaining what it's like to be cold, and actually being cold. He felt a mite uncomfortable, but curious.

'Good job?' Jagger said. A fatuous question, but again thoughts seemed to flow like electrical impulses from the other man's brain. He could actually feel a wad of £10 notes between his hands, the gummy texture of his thumb against paper as he methodically counted through – 18, 19, 20. He could see a line of washed-out grey faces, the foremost one pressed up against a little window, breath making a slight film on the glass; could hear the low murmur of subdued voices, the rattle of change, the tinkling voice of a girl advising a customer at foreign securities on the current rate of exchange for Deutschmarks.

'Not bad,' replied Joseph. 'A bit dull.'

'Got a girl?' said Jagger. Now why had he asked that?

'Well, yes; on and off.' This time a sense of well-being mixed with insecurity. A small person, with hopes and dreams, fears and lusts that existed in a tiny little world – a broom cupboard compared to his Buckingham Palace. The answer took him through a string of tiny shared intimacies, fleeting sensations of warmth, moments of resentment and despair; an instant of pride, a twitch of self-loathing.

The Audience sat hunched round. This was the best bit really. What happened afterwards, though interesting, was never as absorbing as the actual moment. 'O.K. Let's whack it up to Stage Two. Try the physicals.'

Joseph now felt calm. He still couldn't quite put his finger on what was happening, but it was getting clearer. He composed himself. There was really only one sensible question to ask.

'What's it like to be Mick Jagger?'

He thought he was going to pass out. The first sensation was as if every adrenalin gate in his body had been blown off its hinges. There was a surging rush of speed and blood through his veins. He stood on a stage in front of 20,000 people; he walked down a street and everyone looked at him, tugged their neighbour's arms and pointed at him; he saw Brian Jones face down, glassy eyed on the bottom of a swimming pool and Keith Richards propped up in a hotel bathroom gasping for breath, turning slightly blue. This was fear. Then the drugs hit him. In the flash of an instant he took in the combined experiences of nicotine, hash, cocaine, LSD, valium, uppers, downers, speed, morphine, heroin. Judged by the standards of some of his contemporaries, Jagger had never done much of any of these things. It was enough for Joseph.

'Should we stop it now?' Asap cast a worried look to his left.

'No. There may be complications later, but as long as he's in the room he can take it.'

Joseph looked out on a world bigger than anything he'd ever dreamed possible. Horizons opened and then opened again. He took in America, South America, Japan, Australia, China. He took in parties of glamorous people, yachts, aeroplanes, vast tracts of oceans and deserts. Strangely they all seemed to look similar. He realized that the images were bouncing off a mind's eye that made them look much the same. Although to him they were fantastically new and exciting, he caught an undercurrent of nonchalance and even boredom that tinged the experience; as if a paintbrush was subtly adding a uniform tint to the catalogue of pictures.

'Well,' mumbled Jagger as he thought about it, 'I get by.' He felt tired.

I get by ... I GET BY. The words leapt into focus and hammered themselves against the insides of Joseph's head. He felt the brush of a hand against his cheek, and recognized the passing figure of Bianca Jagger, for some reason a ridiculous, sad sight. Then he saw and heard the voices of other women, one or two he recognized, most he didn't. Lastly there was a warmth and a love embodied in a small blonde girl. Pretty, like the others, but this one reminded him a bit of Julie. Then it was snatched away and he felt lonely again.

More parties, a moment of quiet reflection with Bill Wyman, an upsurge of activity. Anger, frustration, boredom all thrust themselves forward, and all hit him in a much sharper way than he'd been used to. Finally another strange image: a wad of £10 notes, counting them with his thumb – but they were all his and he didn't really care if he got the sum right. It was purely academic.

Suddenly he knew what was going to happen, was already

happening. Jagger got the idea at the same moment and was galvanized into action. He leapt to his feet and looked around. There wasn't much to look at. His eyes locked on Joseph's. The two men stared at each other.

'Right. All the way?'
  'No. Hang on. They know. Give them a chance to work it through.'

Jagger, in a sense, had more to lose if the exchange went ahead. Jospeh still sat looking dazed and bewildered. The singer took command.

  'Listen, do you want this to happen? Think about it.'
  'I don't know,' replied Joseph. 'Do we have any choice?'
  This was a worrying moment. Joseph pondered the dilemma. One essential difference between him and Jagger stood out above all others: achievement. To be Mick Jagger was to have achieved. He'd stamped his mark indelibly and forcefully on the world. People made way for him, deferred to him, stood in awe of him. Few people even noticed Joseph Bailey. In that instant he made his decision.

'Here we go.'

Six months later, Bailey sat on a bench in Hyde Park reading a copy of the *Financial Times*. To the surprise of his friends he'd started investing in stocks and shares and had already made a healthy profit on his first two major deals. 'Time to diversify,' he told himself as he applied his attention to the lists of words and figures. Since leaving his job at the bank he'd earned more money reading these newspapers than he had the whole year before. He gave a wry smile; one of a series of new expressions that his previously passive face had begun to adopt recently. He'd been lucky. If he spread it round carefully now, with a bit more luck, in a couple of years he'd be poised to really make some headway.

  He glanced across at the person on the next bench. He was reading a copy of *Melody Maker*. On the cover in large letters he read JAGGER TO QUIT STONES SPLIT RUMOURED.

'Hmph,' he muttered to himself. 'Kid like that thinking he could boss The Rolling Stones. Must've been mad.'

The sun was shining and there were lots of pretty girls.

The response from *NME* was prompt. The typescript was returned, second class, in a plain brown envelope with an accompanying letter.

4.9.80

Dear Gordon,

  Thank you for your application and the enclosed copy. Unfortunately, we cannot use it, but thank you for your interest.

Best wishes,
(illegible scrawl)
EDITOR'S SECRETARY

At the time I suppose I may have been disappointed, but reading the story over again now, I can only marvel at the great reserves of sympathy and tact on which the writer of that simple letter must have drawn, given the woeful unsuitability of the item. It has lain in my bottom drawer, hidden, all but forgotten until now.

As a piece of narrative fiction it plainly leaves much to be desired, and apart from taking a certain grim satisfaction in finally placing the wretched thing where it will earn a bob or two, it gives me no pleasure, whatsoever, to put it on public display now.

But the writing of it undoubtedly functioned as a sort of exorcism. Fan worship is an essentially juvenile preoccupation, one of the rites of passage in our godless, multi-media culture, and something which most people get over, sooner or later. I'd given voice to my vague imaginings as to what it might be like to be Mick Jagger, and frankly it had come as rather a relief to find that no one else had wanted to hear about it. My fondness for the group remained, but the spell was broken.

The story also triggered the idea of writing. Within a few months I had penned a piece about the problems of practising the drums when sharing a basement flat in Shepherd's Bush. I sent it to a technical magazine called *One Two Testing* who published it and later sent me a cheque. I didn't realize it then, but the door to my adult life had just opened a crack. My days of being a 'real' fan were about to end.

I eventually met Mick Jagger in London on 24 August 1987, at about 1 p.m. I was to interview him for a piece in *The Times*. He was late, of course, and if I hadn't already read a hundred times that he is smaller in person than you'd expect, I would have been surprised at how short he was. I can't remember what he was wearing, but he was rail-thin. I'd recently given up playing the drums, bought a car and got married, a combination of lifestyle changes that had had the net effect of adding about two stone to my weight. Next to him I felt flabby and out-of-condition; unworthy, which is surely how every fan should feel in the presence of their hero. What made it worse was that when a coffee tray was produced, he proceeded to scoff all the biscuits.

As anyone in this game will tell you, there's nothing worse than interviewing a star who also happens to be one of your genuine, personal favourites. Professional and emotional instincts get tangled up and you end up with the worst of all worlds. Small talk degenerates into ingratiating platitudes, while innocent lines of questioning are pursued with a need-to-know intensity that is unlikely to unsettle the most secure of egos. And of course you always end up disillusioned in some way or other.

Jagger was promoting his second solo album, *Primitive Cool*, and I suppose I asked him the standard questions. He played a neat game of one-upmanship throughout. Two moments stick in my mind. It was around the time he had fallen out with Keith Richards about pursuing his solo projects to the detriment of The Stones. I asked him a couple of questions about Richards and was just framing a third when Jagger butted in with something like, '...and I don't want to spend the whole of this interview talking about Keith,' fixing me with a look that would have turned Joseph Bailey to stone. Frankly, this was as much of the steely side of him as I cared to see.

The other defining point was when I asked him about Ronnie Wood. I'd long had this theory that Wood's arrival at the time of *Black and Blue* had had a beneficial effect on The Stones out of all proportion to his modest musical abilities. At a time when the core line-up could easily have started crumbling and a succession of hired hands might have begun to pass through the ranks, dissipating their magic as a group, Wood shored up The Stones in a way that no one else could have done. For one thing, it seemed as if he had always been a Stone. He was Richards's big mate, but he was also friends with Wyman and Watts and happy to play the role of Jagger's stooge. It was very much a fan's theory about the group and of no real relevance to an interview with Jagger about his solo album.

Anyway, I think I asked Jagger if he thought The Stones had been lucky to recruit Wood when they did. Jagger seemed to take it as an insult that I should ask him about something as insignificant as Ronnie Wood's place in the scheme of things, and seized on the question with a kind of exaggerated, incredulous glee, indulging himself in a little roughhouse humour at my expense.

'Ronnie Wood? You're asking *me* about Ronnie Wood?' he roared in his most disbelieving cockney–American drawl. 'You'd better ask 'im yourself. I'll give you 'is phone number.' He leaned out of his chair and yelled to the press officer down the corridor. 'There's a bloke 'ere wants to know about Ronnie Wood. Give 'im Ron's number when you're showing him the door.' It was a real performance. Not really cruel, but designed to be crushing, and I could certainly see why so many people who meet Jagger end up hating his guts.

I was suitably crushed, but suffered no lasting ill-effects.

The funny thing was that Jagger was, ultimately, too smart for his own good. Although the interview was set up as an 'exclusive' (i.e. on the understanding that he didn't do any interviews with direct rivals of *The Times*), unbeknown to me he foolishly went and did an interview with the *Independent* the same day. They ran their piece two days later, and back then there really was a strict policy at *The Times* that forbade us running articles of a similar nature to those that appeared in the *Independent*. In a decade of writing for *The Times*, the only interview I have ever done which didn't get published was with Mick Jagger. He blew it, not me, but what a spooky outcome.

It all seems a very long time ago, now. But Jagger and The Stones are still going strong. More than strong. They're still pretty much the biggest touring attraction in the world. I'm still ticking over too and who knows, I might meet Jagger again. In which case, I'll just have to hope that he hasn't read this.

It's funny though how old loyalties refuse to die. Us critics are popularly supposed to affect a worldly, informed and rational veneer, and yet it is those fiercely subjective formative influences that continue to dictate our opinions to an alarming extent.

I can see as much as the next person what a preening old ham Jagger has become, and sense the faint air of desperation with which he has clung on to the trappings of his youth. And of course there's something faintly sad and silly about a bunch of millionaires closing in on pensionable age still affecting to live the life of rock'n'roll outlaws. But it's not a view I'm capable of expressing. Perhaps The Stones should have called it a day years ago, but I'm still extraordinarily glad they didn't.

In May 1994, the group held a press conference in New York to announce the American dates of their massive Voodoo Lounge world tour of 1994–5. I was invited into the Sky Television studios in London to pass comment, and as is usually the case with anything to do with The Stones, I could sense the anchor man willing me to dish the dirt.

'Are you going to give them a hard time?' he asked me, eagerly, before we went on air.

'Surely they're too old? Can they still have any relevance?' he enquired sternly, once we were filming. (This when Sky TV had booked a live feed from the press conference at £200 a minute, paid me £50 for my three minutes on screen and given over a big chunk of their 6 p.m. news slot to the story.) Much to his disappointment, I defended the group to the hilt. What else can a poor boy do?

Titanic Motives

SEAN HUGHES

Julian Cope has never written a song called 'Titanic Motives'. He was, however, leader of The Teardrop Explodes until he split them after two albums in 1982, allegedly in frustration at the state of pop after hearing a Blancmange record. They were managed for a time by Bill Drummond, later of The KLF, and had a Top 10 hit with 'Reward' in 1981.

The Welshman's solo career has seen flirtations with pop, incomprehensible psychedelia, naked ambience and some of the most inspiring music of recent years. He has many aliases, including Sqwubbsy (a six-foot alien) and Rabbi Joseph Gordan. Island Records dropped him fairly recently, but nothing, it seems, could deter him from making more records. Julian Cope has the firmest handshake in pop.

'More by luck than judgement, here am I.' So goes one of Julian Cope's theories on life. A fifteen-year career has seen him in many guises. Fifteen years of being a fan has seen me in many guises. Remarkably, I love him now more than ever. Usually somebody will come along at just the right time and say all the things you wanted to say, you share the moment but slowly drift apart. I somehow don't think that if The Bay City Rollers were still going strong I'd share the same enthusiasm for their next release, and yet at the time I would have killed for them or at the very least supplied the weapons. Julian Cope is destined, probably in death, to be given his place in music's hall of fame. As far as the media is concerned, he has been continually in and out of favour, never really put up on a pedestal, more given a soft spot in most comprehensive record collections.

And why is that so? Music is oft written about, a band is championed in the weeklies, given space in the monthlies and becomes mass culture when the qualities eventually pick up on it. The problem being, a tired and trying media are continually looking for new trends, even going to the extent of making one up if the situation calls for it. It seems to be that you get your one chance to shine before being relegated to the 'we've heard that before' section. On the other hand, a band with one song and the right image is given preference. I find the short-sighted-ness frightening. I don't understand that a culture of so little quality still feels the need to dish music up, chew it about and spit it back out so quickly. Where the great often go unnoticed, Oasis Get Up This Morning or Suede Go Shopping may soon be worthy of a front cover. Don't laugh, Morrissey got one for signing some autographs.

This is the inherent problem of music journalism. The writers are obsessed by music, they feel a need to write about it, start to earn a living from it, it becomes a job, they rub shoulders with pop stars. The magic goes. It stands to reason. The kid waiting eight months for OMD to come to Dublin or the person making the last-minute phone call to be added to the guest list – who's the most excited?

I've always had a massive appreciation of music; it's probably *too* important to me. Julian Cope stands for everything good about music – ever moving, continually challenging, in short, a visionary. In interviews I'm often asked the question, 'Did you really want to become a pop star?' The answer is always no. I love music too much. After years of playing the air guitar I found I never improved. On three occasions I even went as far as trying to learn to play the real thing. It takes perseverance, time and hard skin on your fingertips. I figure anyone can learn guitar, with the possible exception of Sid Vicious. I'm not saying anyone can become a virtuoso, but the basics can be grasped at. What stopped me? I wanted to retain that mystery, to see somebody on stage making beautiful sounds from such a simple instrument without having to think that was A followed by C# minor bridging to an E.

The first band I really adored was The Bay City Rollers. Me and a bunch of girls would go all woozy at the very mention of Woody. My next obsession, unfortunately, was Gillan. Thankfully, this only lasted six days. At the time every drain-piped jean-wearing macho man was into heavy metal. Every Friday night was spent trying to make our hair look longer and then strutting down to the local disco, forming a circle and head banging the night away. I haven't been able to dance in public since.

The Sex Pistols came along at just the right time. I bought 'God Save the Queen' without hearing it. There wasn't much option as our local radio stations had smoochy songs on heavy rotation. 'This one goes out to Tomo, Zem, Jocko, Mayhem and The Clontarf Posse. Here's Chicago.' I broached punk fully, I even had two Crass singles imported from England. Like most punks I had more badges than records. If the truth be told, I was a tad too young for punk and it was only when Dexys Midnight Runners came along that I could sigh with relief. At last a band I could call my own, whose very conception I was there for. *Searching for the Young Soul Rebels* was released and out we went searching. A cliché usually comes into play at this point, the one that goes 'it became the soundtrack to my life', but it wasn't, it was the soundtrack to Kevin Rowland's life. This was the first time I became aware of the fact that you could like more than one style of music. You didn't have to be just a Mod or just a New Romantic. Around this time, I was aware of two cracking tunes – 'Treason' and 'Reward' from a band called The Teardrop Explodes. I also knew the singer wore a ridiculous flying jacket and had a wayout haircut. During this period I found music liberating and I used to hang out at second-hand record shops constantly looking for bargains. On one such occasion, 14 September 1983, I bought *Wilder* by

The Teardrop Explodes and a record by a Christian band called After the Fire for a fiver. After one play the After the Fire record was put in the section I called Dodgy Mistakes. I was initially disappointed with *Wilder* when I noticed the singles weren't on it, but I was intrigued by the sleeve notes. The album is a classic. The Teardrop Explodes were a pop group, and being a naïve seventeen-year-old I saw album tracks as songs not good enough to be singles. *Wilder* blew this theory to bits as every track was bliss to my ears. I was beginning to doubt whether the best-selling songs were actually the best. Obvious maybe, but an insight to me. With *Wilder* I was haunted by the sadness of it arriving in a second-hand shop; the idea that somebody had heard it and then decided to sell it mortified me.

Julian was my springboard into what music could mean. I gobbled up the first Teardrops album, *Kilimanjaro*, and although it contained the two aforementioned singles I still preferred *Wilder*. What's that they say about first love? I soon started collecting any Teardrops stuff the shops could throw at me, I even had the French version of 'Treason'. This was the wrong time to start following Julian as he had just split up the band and was in hiding. Nevertheless, I busied myself with all the tittle-tattle that goes on between releases. I found that one of the unwritten laws of the era was that if you liked the Teardrops you weren't allowed to like Echo & The Bunnymen, although secretly we all liked both bands. The 'all' being me and my mate, as my local area was still witnessing a frenzied obsession with heavy metal.

As my life stretched beyond the thousand-metre mark that bounded my existence, I found other Cope devotees. This was strange in itself, as Julian has what can only be described as the most English of accents. Not the most popular accent to the youth of Ireland, who were reading history at school every day which went something like – Page 1: The English came over, raped, pillaged and murdered the Irish. Page 2: See page 1. On top of this, Julian had a habit of singing in a very whimsical, nursery-rhyme style. I had this vision of a Republican march going through Dublin shouting 'Brits Out' with ten of us at the back holding banners stating 'Except Julian'.

Awaiting the next release, I would spend time studying the lyrics more deeply. Where others often wonder what their heroes are like in real life, I was always happy just to hear his output. Why spoil the magic? Julian's lyrics, although never simple, have this terrible habit of popping into my head at any given time to make sense of a situation. The line that kept recurring then was 'Secret dreams of Melanie and Melanie knows who I mean'. Unfortunately I took this to be a starting gun for me to embark on writing the most incomprehensible poetry I could muster. These were the kind of poems you show to a few baffled friends, then go on to explain them word for word, waiting for them to crown you a genius. Julian's lyrics have always puzzled me, but from them you get a general feeling that you're in safe hands. From the first track I heard – 'Passionate Friend' – comes the line, 'Celebrate the great escape and carry my soul away'. On reflection, probably about the divorce he was going through, but to me it was about the discovery of this music. Anyway, it beats 'I want to move it, move it' every time.

At this stage of his career he was taking his pop-star hat off and trying on assorted others. This was a risk, as I doubt he was aware how good he could be. So out faded the Teardrops, losing the fame with the hope of gaining the recognition. Julian probably realized he was too intelligent to battle for the pop stakes, and there wasn't much chance with that haircut. He decided to traipse off into the unknown alone, and I suspect he knew there were a lot of us out there ready to man the barricades for him.

It wasn't the case that I spent every minute of my life thinking about Julian, but nostalgia will always heighten the tiny moments. Music is there essentially for us to relax to, to enjoy, dare I say, to make us happy, but at its most powerful it's there to relate to. When you meet someone new you chit-chat, find common ground. We also do this through music. If somebody likes the same music as you there's a fair chance that you'll be on the same wave-length. How many times have you heard a song wishing that the person you loved was listening to it with you, so you could claim the sentiment behind the lyric as yours? Inevitably this thought only occurs when you're alone. Music is best listened to by yourself; when you're with others you're always too conscious of whether they're enjoying it or not. One of the worst feelings is when you play something to a friend which you think is awe-inspiring only to be told to turn it down. The best discoveries are always found alone, you can't force your taste on others. Mind you, it doesn't stop me trying. I would love to strap people into a chair and make them listen to Julian's entire back catalogue. They'd thank me for it eventually. My proudest achievement to date is getting everybody I know in Australia crazy about him.

It never rains, it pours, and out I ran into the drizzle when I heard Julian was playing a gig in Dublin. He was here to plug his first solo album, *World Shut Your Mouth*. For some reason the record stores didn't share my enthusiasm, and with the concert only a day away I finally managed to track it down. I couldn't understand why it hadn't made the national news: 'Julian Cope's album is available in Freebird Records'. But there it was, and on the cover Julian had surpassed himself on the hair front. With the crap reviews it was getting I knew it must be good. I got home and played it sixty times. I had this system for new records: the first time I tried to get a general feel for it whilst coping with the anxiety that my crap record player gave me with its tendency to skip. The second airing was with the lyric sheet in front of me, sussing out the content. After ten plays one song usually stood out, and I'd play that continually for an hour. I loved the album, but it did seem the work of a man fighting his corner, not so much depressing, more a man in isolation. At times it gave me the creeps.

At the gig itself I figured I knew the album better than Julian himself. I was walking around, cocksure, name-dropping tracks off the album. 'I hope he does "Pussyface". Oh, you've not heard it yet?' I know it was an asshole thing to do, but this was my moment. It got to the extent that I felt nobody was allowed to enjoy the gig as much as me, and I demanded they give full concentration while he was on. I was probably too nervous to really enjoy it, much like a parent watching their child on stage for the first time. He eventually appeared after midnight. To this day I don't understand why groups keep us waiting. I can just picture the scenario in the dressing room. 'Are you ready?' 'Yeah.' 'Okay, give it another half an hour.' I'd heard many bootlegs of Julian playing live, and I knew he was keen to interact with an audience. It was a bit of an anti-climax when he walked on in a white shirt and went straight into 'Greatness and Perfection'. He'd finish a song, put down the guitar and walk over to the piano. There were others in the audience trying to impress Julian as well: people started calling out for B-sides. This became the game for the night. The more obscure the song, the more brownie points awarded. I won hands down when I started making them up – 'Do "Titanic Motives"!' I'd shout with my knowing look. It wasn't a great show and he seemed troubled, but I was satisfied and anyway we were at that stage of the relationship where anything was forgivable. The second I got home I played the album again, recollecting the live versions of the songs. A week later in London he ripped his stomach open during 'Reynard the Fox'. I thought this was the beginning of the end.

We only had to wait another eight months for *Fried* to appear. He was spoiling us. There he was on the cover again, this time photographed under a turtle shell while his contemporaries donned shell-suits for their record sleeves. This came as no surprise to me but of course the thoughtless media picked up on Mad Julian. I don't understand this when all it was was merely a man expressing himself without fear of others' opinions being catered for. On the strength of the cover I expected him to be at his most experimental, and *Fried* went on the turntable with some trepidation. There was always that worry that he had gone too far the other way and it would become one of those albums that you say you like but very rarely play. Does My Bloody Valentine ring a bell? Yes, there were some very introspective songs, but in the main it was tunes, tunes, tunes, in fact some of my all-time favourites. In the press it would be called an uneven album, meaning that there isn't a band's trade-mark style filling every groove. The importance of Julian can be seen in his wanting to take you on a journey where various moods are encountered. It was never going to be an easy ride.

In all the arts we are looking for entertainment, a desire to escape from the humdrum. But where most want to escape in a cosy, nice, let's-forget-our-troubles sort of way, there are others who want knowledge and a gathering of new thoughts and to be taken to some scary places along the way. Julian is there for the latter. Again, it's very easy to say Julian makes very acid-indulged records. This belittles him in every sense. It's a basic requirement of any artist to view life from different angles. You never create on the drugs themselves, it's the being in various states of mind which makes you question the norm. You don't need to take drugs to be able to relate, in fact at the time I was extremely frightened of them. I don't like the feeling of being out of control, but I was glad somebody was taking those journeys for me and coming back with the news.

Julian's next LP, *Saint Julian*, didn't appear for three years. I did most of my growing up during this period and music wasn't as important. I moved to London for a start, leaving behind most of my record collection bar a few tapes. I felt I'd outgrown them. Julian was like an old friend who you grow apart from as the regimen of your life changes. One day, shortly after I'd moved, I was walking aimlessly down the tube station when I saw a guy with shades on who looked the spitting image of

Julian. It *was* him. I ran up one escalator and down the other in a blind panic as this utter compulsion had me running towards him. With my heart leaping I tapped him on the shoulder with my shaky hand. 'Julian, I love you, what are you up to?' He looked heavenly and he is the only person who can say, 'Wow man, far out, cool' and get away with it. I feel these words were invented for his use. He told me he was doing a gig next week and had a new album coming out. London, I thought, was paved with pop icons.

The gig itself was upstairs in the Boston Arms in Tufnell Park, North London. It was sold out. I was squatting with a scouser named Dave and were both on the dole. We decided to chance our arm. We arrived at the pub at three, just as it was closing, but with our bad-smelling clothes the barmaid mistook us for part of the group. 'Straight up those stairs, guys,' and on opening up the pearly gates there was Julian dressed in leather on his now legendary mike stand doing a soundcheck. It was an odd feeling, listening to this beautiful voice when just outside there were tramps swigging Special Brew, kebab shops offering off-cuts and single mothers walking the routed daily walk. This was magic realism. We approached his then-manager Cally and lied that I'd come over especially from Dublin, Dave pretending he'd come from Liverpool and how he used to see them all the time at Eric's (a club that helped start the late-seventies Liverpool scene). Cally said there was nothing he could do for us, but as we were about to leave he handed us two backstage passes and told us we could sell T-shirts at the back of the hall. I asked Julian if he remembered me from the tube station. He pretended he did, God bless him.

As the crowd came in we sold the T-shirts in a matter of minutes, and suddenly we had £600 in our possession. It was very tempting just to do a bunk, and we agreed that if we didn't like the first three songs we'd do a runner. Julian came on unaware he was singing for his supper. It was breathtaking, but after the three songs we split with the money. Only joking. We kept smiling inanely at each other all night, just happy to be there. The enjoyment was added to by the fact that we were part of the team. Cally took the money at the end, offering us his thanks. We were having none of it. It was back to the hotel for us, transported there in a little minibus, sitting next to Julian, no less. Of course, none of our friends believed us, but me and Dave have life-long memories.

'Trampoline' and 'World Shut Your Mouth' had Julian playing the pop star once again. This couldn't last long. All of a sudden everyone was excited, and I remember one review of 'World Shut Your Mouth' going as far as to say that one day this would become a football anthem. I'm afraid to report that down at the Palace they still favour 'Glad All Over'. It was with certain pride that we saw Julian back in the charts, but it felt uncomfortable rubbing shoulders with fourteen-year-old girls again.

Album-tour-album-tour has never really suited Julian, but he played along with it. Unfortunately, the rigours of time and success brought about his weakest album, *My Nation Underground*. Julian was never going to have Number 1s, and to play in the pop arena he'd have to work harder than most. To sell tickets and records you have to do much publicity, and being continually asked the same questions by people who don't really care becomes very frustrating. With *My Nation Underground* there is a feeling of Julian wanting both worlds. It was a concept album without the concept. As a loyal fan I bought the record and went to the concert but felt he was passing me by. It was depressing thinking he was losing it. The sole shining light coming from the confusion was 'Charlotte Anne', which can only be described as a Julian Cope song.

I wasn't to know that a new cycle was appearing, two stabs at the pop world and two fingers up to it. But maybe the album title was prophetic, as he went underground again. I thought he might do a Syd Barrett and spend the rest of his days playing with his Dinky toys at the back of the garden. 1990 saw two official bootlegs, *Droolian* and *Skellington*, both extremely extreme but still containing gems like 'Jelly Pop Perky Jean', which I had the good fortune to have a bash at on *Sean's Show*. I was delighted to hear he liked it and had it on tape.

Peggy Suicide appeared, much like the corn circles, in March 1991, and to say Julian had reinvented himself is again to belittle his genius, because this is what he was aiming for from day one. The sleeve notes alone were worth the price of the record. Where *My Nation Underground* let you know you could go through a dull patch and it not mean the end, *Peggy Suicide* made you aware of what we are all capable of. This went beyond fandom; after fifteen years he'd been hiding this from us, the cheeky pup. When you talk of the great songwriters, Lennon and McCartney, Richards and Jagger, Morrissey and Marr, this was Cope and Cope. The musicianship had never been stronger. This will go down as one of the all time great records, it's the sort of album that aliens will land for. I thought it couldn't be surpassed. Then in 1992 he released *JehovahKill*. This is the sort of record aliens *did* land for, and helped out in the studio no doubt. This is the masterpiece that Island Records dropped him over. He might have been disappointed but I was delighted. Never again would he play at being a pop star. You can keep your record industry, we want Julian to ourselves, we'll pay the wages.

A reason for writing this is to get across the importance of music, the importance of being a fan. When we go through our record collection it's the newest ones we rush to play, but it's those records like Julian's that you go back to time and again. It's not that Julian is unknown, he has been praised, but when the media praise him there's always that footnote – he's mad, you know. I'll accept this if madness means not being frightened, not frightened to grow, of wearing his weaknesses, showing us his loves, his new discoveries, but most importantly not being frightened of being frightened. And if that's what it means, I want to be certified now. It should also be pointed out that this madman is happily married with two children.

The importance of Julian Cope can never be overstated. As a teenager you want music to hit you in the face. In your early twenties you want a more thoughtful groove, and as you turn twenty-eight you want an intelligent, fulfilling sound to accompany you as you walk your dog. For any person to influence even a tiny part of your life they should be bowed to; for somebody to continually excite you throughout your various states of mind is mystifying.

I've met Julian on many occasions. I like to keep it to a quick hello, I feel no need to bore him with my chit-chat. I respect the man too much. Let's just be happy he exists and thank God that he still has the ego to keep on sharing his thoughts with us.

Just Like Gene Autry: A Foxtrot

TOM HIBBERT

The Byrds formed in 1964 when Jim (later Roger) McGuinn, a Dylan-obsessed folkie from San Francisco, saw *A Hard Day's Night*. He decided there and then to try to create a sound which would merge Dylan with The Beatles. He ran the two miles home and began to work on a new group. The Byrds' debut single, a Beatly version of Dylan's 'Mr Tambourine Man' (on which they didn't play), was Number 1 in both Britain and America, and they once did a version of 'We'll Meet Again'. Two years later, after another American Number 1, 'Turn! Turn! Turn!', and the controversial 'Eight Miles High', leading songwriter Gene Clark left, partly because he was scared of flying. In 1967, Gram Parsons joined and The Byrds took a more country direction, before slowly, to all intents and purposes, petering out.

San Francisco's Moby Grape were damned by their own hype before they'd had a chance to establish any sort of mark for themselves. However, their stature has grown since their ill-fated late-sixties non-career. Their songs are poppy beyond the call of duty, their harmonies are almost perfect, and there's a feeling that their true re-assessment is yet to come. It's begun already – right now they're a hip name to drop.

It was, I suppose, the sunglasses that did it. My first term at a minor public school (Quaker, i.e. no corporal punishment so lots of mental torture by Latin masters instead), and while searching for cheap sweets in the high-street branch of F. W. Woolworth (contrary to popular belief, not *all* public schools had tuck shops in the mid-sixties) I came across the box of sunglasses. Not any old sunglasses, you understand, but Ben

Franklin-type sunglasses, all rectangular slits and all *cool* because they looked just like the glasses that *Jim McGuinn out of The Byrds wore*. There was no sign above the box saying SUNGLASSES! AS WORN BY JIM MCGUINN OUT OF THE BYRDS — AS SEEN ON TV!, and goodness knows what these superb fashion accessories were doing in the crumby shop at all, but, of course, I had to have a pair, even though they cost a florin (that's 10p in modern money), which was quite a lot for a boy on an allowance of a bob (that's 5p in modern money) a week. Even though the blinkers were fashioned entirely from cheap plastics from the Orient, I *had* to have a pair. So I nicked them. My first ever brush with true crime. God, how scared I felt and how guilty but, you see, this theft was *essential* — 'It was a matter of life and death, Your Honour, I throw myself upon the mercy of the Court' — for Jim McGuinn had been my lifetime hero, much much more than a schoolboy crush, for more than a week now.

You know that hoary old chestnut about everyone remembering where they were and exactly what they were doing when they heard that Kennedy had been shot. It's probably true. Sadly, I am old enough to remember. I was eleven years old and watching the exciting quiz show *Take Your Pick* downstairs while my parents were upstairs taking a bath. (They didn't quite approve of their children watching *Take Your Pick*, so I snuck it on while they were otherwise engaged.) Quite annoyed, I was, I can tell you, when my sinful entertainment was interrupted by a newsflash from Dallas just as Mr Miles was to open Box 13 wherein lay, quite possibly, a hilarious booby prize such as a floormop for one of the evening's common contestants. Yes, I remember it well, the death of the President: but the memory pales into monochrome insignificance when compared with the recollection of where I was and what I was doing when I first heard The Byrds' 'Mr Tambourine Man'. *That* I can rewind and replay in all its technicolor glory. It even comes with smells. The smells of schoolboy piss and schoolboy sweat and schoolboy cabbage and schoolboy liver dinners, the kind of

liver that comes with grotesque tubes in and is only ever served
to schoolboys, wafting in through the windows – for it was in
the changing rooms, after my first ever experience of rugby
football, that I heard The Byrds' 'Mr Tambourine Man'.

I hated rugby and I still do. What a cloddish, graceless game.
Some master had run around shouting at me (and *only* me, it
seemed) to do things that I didn't understand because nobody
had bothered to explain the rules of the cloddish, graceless
game to me. I'd made a forward pass and my team 'mates' had
laughed (Why? What was wrong with passing forward? That
was what we had *tried* to do at my prep school where we had
played footer) and someone had stamped on my hand. It hurt,
and here I was in the changing room not wanting to take a
shower and trying very hard not to blub when a muddy-booted,
jock-strapped (what were jock-straps *for?*) sixth-former came in,
took a transistor radio from his locker and switched it, loudly,
on. '*Da-da-da-da-da-da-da-da-da-da-da ... da-da-da ... Hey Mr
Tambourine Man, play a song for me...*' My mouth dropped open,
I stopped my whimpering. My eyes dropped open. Suddenly,
the world didn't seem such a disgracefully cruel and heartless
place after all. With sweet music such as this playing in the
world, there was hope for humanity. My courage knew no
bounds. Throwing caution to the winds, I approached the
swaggering sixth-former.

'I say, What is that you're listening to?' I chirped.

He turned on me, towered over me, with a withering sneer,
'What does it *look* like, you horrid little oik. It's a radio. Ever
heard of a radio?'

Undeterred by his amazingly brilliant sarcasm, I pressed on.
'No, no, you see, I meant what *group* is it? It doesn't sound like
The Beatles. I wondered if you, er...'

'What's your name?'

'Hibbert.'

'Well, *Hibbert*,' he sneered menacingly, snapping off the transistor just as the twelve-string guitar was starting to sing. 'You

can take two marks for cheek!' (If you got six marks in any one week, you were 'gated', had to do detention, polish floors and stairs or other such delightful punishments.) Then he cuffed me round the ear and swaggered into the showers. That sixth-former is now a Conservative MP. Not a Byrds fan, I gather . . .

Fortunately, the school wasn't *quite* as *Tom Brown's Schooldays* as I have painted it. We were allowed to watch the telly sometimes – albeit sitting squashed up next to one another in our ties and blazers and shiny grey trousers on long benches that reeked of furniture polish. We were allowed to watch sports sometimes (*encouraged* to do so if the sport in question was bloody rugger), and, for some reason that, looking back on the atmosphere of the place, I cannot fathom, we were allowed to watch *Top of the Pops*. And that's where I saw them. The sunglasses of Jim McGuinn. His twelve-string guitar and non-Jaggeresque nonchalance. (Even at that age, I didn't like Jagger, silly fat-lipped show-off, and despite the fact that I'd seen *A Hard Day's Night* at Reading's Glendale Cinema – nowadays a church of foreign sorts – twice on the same day, The Beatles left much to be desired to my ears and sensibilities. The Byrds were simply *it* and life would never be the same again: Michael Clarke, the drummer, with longer hair even than Brian Jones; David Crosby, long before he turned to fat, looking thoroughly groovy in a cape; Gene Clark – who *was* that man with the tambourine, seemingly doing nothing? Obviously a brainbox and genius of sorts.

The sixth-formers on the whiffy benches tutted and said sixth-form things about this assortment of strummers looking like 'bloody girls'. But a majority of the little boys, the thirteen-year-olds, the chaps in my dorm who didn't much like rugger either, seemed to understand. John Patey, who was only a day boy (day boys went home after nine o'clock at night – how very odd this all seems now), got it. We were the class of 1965, and imagine John Patey's furious jealousy when I showed him my Ben Franklin sunglasses before Latin a few days later.

Patey (I'll never call him John: Christian names were always banned at public school for reasons only perverts and disciplinarians have ever understood) was taking guitar lessons. So was I. QED we would form a pop group just like The Byrds. It would take some time to save up for the equipment, but over the coming months we were never diverted from our ultimate cause. He bought a useless electric guitar. I bought a useless electric guitar. I'd begged 'pater' for a twelve-string electric guitar for Christmas, but as these things cost more than £80 and Barnes & Avis had perfectly respectable models of the six-stringed variety (with impossibly high actions ... cut your little fingers to pieces) for less than a fiver, we settled on that. Patey and Hibbert were joined by some spotty bloke whose name now escapes me on the school drum kit and nobody at all on the bass guitar, because we didn't quite understand how that worked. A (liberal) sixth-former lent us a really crappy ten-watt amplifier into which Patey and I would plug our crappy guitars. We were fair set to change the world of popular music (just like The Byrds had done) as sixth formers knew it. It didn't quite happen.

We'd had an enormous setback already when my housemaster, catching me in my fantastic sunglasses after lights out doing a splendid impersonation of Jim McGuinn performing 'All I Really Want To Do', had confiscated the specs and, to add insult to injury, ordered me to get my hair cut immediately. 'Bit shaggy, Hibbert. You look like a *girl*.' Yes, yes, yes. What's *wrong* with looking like a girl, anyway, you frightful man? (With 'kindness', the housemaster handed the spectacles back to me at the end of term, but they were bent beyond all recognition and rendered redundant. Whatever had he done with them? Weedily, I never dared ask. Anyway, this setback worried us greatly. Who was going to pretend to be McGuinn without the glasses?) The next setback was that, when we plugged in our lousy instruments, we didn't seem to sound anywhere *near* as good as The Byrds, for some unaccountable reason.

The final setback was the name. There was a half-hour free period after prep, when we'd rehearse; but after our first disastrous attempt we didn't rehearse at all, we just argued about what to call this band that would rival The Byrds in cool and quality. I wanted to call it The Eagles – clearly years ahead of my time – because the eagle is a brand of bird. Patey wanted to call it The Zambesi Warriors because, or so he claimed, Zambesi warriors dress as birds with feathers on their arms when in combat. I always got better marks in history but, still, not having the relevant reference books to hand, I could hardly put up an argument. The drummer didn't care what it was called because he had a chance of being in the house rugger team which was far more exciting.

Funny how time slips away. Two or three years later two of the members of this blistering trio would be smoking pot and dropping acid and doing, or attempting to do, things with girls. Additionally I would still be listening to 'Eight Miles High' and still adoring The Byrds. I suppose I owe it all to Jim – by then Roger – McGuinn. But it was as The Zambesi Warriors that we took the stage, right there in front of the pipes of the school organ, at the school dance of 1966. Purple chiffon scarves and the most execrable version of 'Turn! Turn! Turn!' anyone had ever heard in their lives. How can you *dance* to 'Turn! Turn! Turn!' particularly when performed by an out-of-tune trio who can't play for toffee and who are 'singing' through microphones first pressed into service between the wars? You can't.

Before our appearance – we were, unsurprisingly, bottom of the bill (trad jazz band and folk troupe to follow) – the head-master, who prided himself on being up-to-the-minute and conversant with all the current phraseology, had made an announcement. 'No snogging on the dance floor!' The girls from the school down the road had giggled and the sixth-formers had wiggled their eyebrows knowingly. But, to the sound of The Zambesi Warriors, 'snogging' was out of the question.

*

Where had my clearly unhealthy obsession with pop music begun? And why was it always American stars rather than the home-grown variety that gripped me so? I don't know. Ask a shrink or somebody. All I do know is that from the moment I first heard Duane Eddy's 'Because They're Young' at the tender age of eight, I was hooked. For life. From that moment all pocket money and financial gifts from maiden aunts were saved up until the glorious moment when I could afford the four shillings and tenpence for the latest single by the twangy Mr Eddy. 'Shazam!', 'Kommotion', 'Pepe', 'Theme from Dixie', 'Ballad of Paladin'. All would be heard over and over in the listening booth of Hammants, Henley-on-Thames, a bicycle shop with a modest record department up some wooden stairs. The shop assistant, a Cliff Richard fan with an unfortunate complexion and very thick spectacles, was always very patient with me. She knew I'd buy the thing in the end. 'Don't know what you want this rubbish for,' she would mutter as she popped my proud purchase into a brown paper bag. I left the premises with an air of superiority, secure in the knowledge that as Duane Eddy came from Arizona that was somewhere probably exotic in America, he was, perforce, a million times better than Cliff's feeble Shadows.

'Some Kinda Earthquake', 'Ring of Fire', 'Deep in the Heart of Texas' followed. And, glory be, finally a Duane Eddy long-player, *A Million Dollars Worth of Twang*, which spent a happy term in my prep-school desk until the geography master found it there, had the effrontery to laugh at Duane's quiff, and confiscated the miraculous thing (confiscation seems to be a recurring theme of my pop music childhood). I also got into quite a lot of trouble when I removed several boxes of Kellogg's Cornflakes from the school kitchens because they had a competition in which you could win a Burns electric guitar just like Hank B. Marvin's (not that I liked Hank B. Marvin, who could never twang like Duane, but I certainly wanted an electric guitar). I didn't win that guitar – goodness knows what the judges were thinking of because my tie-breaking phrase, 'I would like to win a Burns electric guitar because [in fifteen words or less] ... THE TWANG'S THE THANG!' were words borrowed from the Great Guitar God D. Eddy himself; I won the right to clean the school van, inside and out, instead.

Listening to them now after all these years, Mr Duane Eddy's tunes all sound almost exactly the same and, alas, rather tiresomely jaunty, but my ears were different – wider? – then. But then, in 1962, my hero committed the mortal sin (to my way of thinking, anyway) of including *vocals* on a record. Worse than this, they were *female* vocals. With 'Dance With the Guitar Man', my first love affair came to a messy conclusion and I wouldn't feel the same about anything again – until I heard The Byrds. Now, there is no discernible likeness between the music of Duane Eddy and the chimes of The Byrds, but then three years is a lifetime when you are so very young ...

Although The Zambesi Warriors were to triumph in the re-hearsal room (also known as the chemistry lab) when they managed, on one notable and triumphant occasion, to get all the way through '(So You Want To Be a) Rock and Roll Star' without breaking a single string or arguing once about what the next chord might be, they split up when a) John Patey traitor-ously switched his musical affiliations from The Byrds to The Jimi Hendrix Experience, and b) I managed to persuade my parents to take me away from the public school and send me to a grammar school where they had things called girls.

This was the life. Here I would be able to impress the opposite sex with my growing collection of Byrds LPs. I would show them the cover of *5th Dimension,* upon which McGuinn and Michael Clarke and Chris Hillman and Crosby were perched upon a colourful and mysterious carpet. I would lay out my theory: that the carpet was, in fact, a veiled reference to hashish and other exciting narcotics. Then I'd whip out *The Notorious Byrd Brothers,* upon which McGuinn and Hillman and Clarke were photographed alongside a horse, and tell the girls, who would be quite fascinated, that the horse was a veiled reference to David Crosby, who'd been thrown out of the band because his songs were stupid and McGuinn hated him. Then I would play them The Byrds' strange and beautiful 'Dolphins Smile' and they would be mine for ever (or for a bit, at any rate). For some reason, however, the grammar girls of 1968 were more into The Beatles or The Herd or Marmalade than The Byrds while all the boys were trying to grow moustaches (during holidays only) to make them feel more like Cream, *the* school heroes.

I smoked pot for the first time to the sound of Cream's 'Tales of Brave Ulysses' and I was very sick indeed. If it had been 'Eight Miles High' or 'Why' or 'Dolphins Smile' or anything as lovely by my adored young men from California, it would have been all right, I know. And I first dropped acid while the 'friend' who had supplied it played his copy of Spooky Tooth's *Spooky Two* album over and over again. By the time Luther Grosvenor was playing the grinding guitar solo of 'Evil Woman' for what seemed like the millionth time, I was having something called a bad trip. I badly needed the twelve-stringed soothings of Roger McGuinn to bring me down, man. In the words of Vanilla Fudge (another group who tortured me as migraine rabbits scampered around my head that horrible night), I just hoped the trip gets lighter, but my 'friend' didn't have any Byrds records because he thought The Byrds were nothing more than a 'pop' group.

To be a 'pop' group in the late-sixties was a crime of staggering proportions. 'Pop' groups were for girls who appeared in school productions of *Antigone* and for boys who were still virgins. 'Pop' groups were for girls who did their homework in very neat handwriting and who dotted their i's with little circles and for boys who didn't smoke Number 6. I didn't smoke Number 6 and I was a virgin and I didn't like rock music very much at all. 'Pop' music, as purveyed by The Byrds, was the thing; if the philistines with the John Mayall's Bluesbreakers records and the John Mayall's Bluesbreakers fashion sense could but see it, The Byrds were far druggier, hence far more hip, than John Mayall's Bluesbreakers or Cream or The Nice. Indeed, I felt vastly superior to the common rock hordes. What on earth did they see in Led Zeppelin with that caterwauling twerp singing blues clichés rather badly when they *could* be wallowing in glorious harmonies and wondering why Roger McGuinn was so obsessed with outer space and the sea?

Nobody round here liked The Byrds at all and, really, I preferred it that way. The group were mine – my delight alone, and I imagined that this made me somehow special and strange. It certainly made me a snob. I longed to discover another American band, an American pop band more obscure than The Byrds and just as splendid with which to annoy the Pink Floyd-dotty rabble. *That* would show them. While they were out on their army Cadet Force manoeuvres in their stupid khaki uniforms with their stupid bullet-free guns being barked at by a Sergeant-Major type, I (as one of only two boys at the school who refused to join the Cadet Force, being a 'conscientious objector', hem hem) would be in the sixth-form common-room listening to the magical sounds of this Mystery Group and everyone would think me odder than ever. I just *loved* being odd. God, I was odd, and God, I was witty, but nobody understood the jokes because nobody was clever enough. And everyone would hate my Mystery Group because everyone was so Dumb. They worshipped Cream and Cream's tedious drum solos and they didn't like The Byrds. Dumb, dumb, dumb. How they would *hate* my Mystery Group, hate them because they were ... *afraid* ... and didn't ... *understand*. Ha, ha. The poor, ignorant fools. *Fools!!!!*

The only drawback to this brilliant plan was that I couldn't seem to 'discover' this Mystery Group at all. The radio was no help. John Peel was no help. He played Quicksilver Messenger Service on the wireless once and, on the strength of that, I bought *Happy Trails* which was jolly good but not quite *it*, not the stuff of which blind devotion is made. I tried The Velvet Underground because they came from New York and took lots of drugs, apparently, but try as I might to convince myself otherwise, they weren't my cup of tea at all, even though they had cool sunglasses. No, The Velvet Underground were too gloomy; they wouldn't do at all. Tried Frank Zappa. Hated him. Tried Jefferson Airplane. Liked them, but not nearly enough. Toyed with the idea of appointing Captain Beefheart & The Magic Band my Mystery Group but, no, the Captain was just *too* odd, too deliberately bonkers to serve my purposes – besides which the other grammar-school 'conscientious objector', a fine fellow called Basingstoke though that wasn't his name, had already discovered Captain Beefheart and had taken to coming to school in a battered top hat (soon confiscated, naturally).

It was, astonishingly enough, that most staid and conservative of record retailers, W. H. Smith, that came to my rescue. One day, while buying my weekly copy of *Melody Maker* (how I hated *Melody Maker*: it always contained pictures of Jimmy Page and, worse, Crosby, Stills & Nash. David Crosby had become a major hate figure since his bust up with McGuinn and since he had severely marred the otherwise fabulous *Younger Than Yesterday* album with his pompous song 'Mind Gardens', where the fat one had quoted Shakespeare and sounded very silly indeed. I bought the publication anyway because, well, one just did), I noticed they had a record sale on. It was a rather strange sale: LPs, all on CBS, by people like The Electric Flag and Johnny Winter and my beloved Byrds (I'd already got *Dr Byrds and Mr Hyde*, thank you very much) for 13s 6d. And there were four LPs by some group I had never heard of called Moby Grape. 'What a foolish name,' was my first reaction (it came from the rib-tickling joke 'What's purple and lives at the bottom of the sea?' I later discovered).

Then two things happened. One: I realized, with a blinding flash of adolescent serendipity, that the initials of Moby Grape

were the same as those of Mystery Group. Two: I studied the
cover of one of these four LPs and noticed that the group
looked ... achingly, smokingly, cool. They were five men
standing and sitting outside what looked like an olde American
hardware store, as seen in countless western motion pictures
and *Bonanza*. One of them (Alex 'Skip' Spence, I would soon
learn) was wearing a brilliant fringed jacket and had brilliant
hair and was next to an American flag and looked peculiar.
Standing beside him was a fellow (Peter Lewis) in a blazer and
a white polo neck who looked as if he had just escaped from
The Dave Clark Five: the contrast between these two at the
back could not have been more striking. It got even better.
Sitting at the front was a man (Jerry Miller) with a rifle
propped between his legs. Next to him was another man (Don
Stevenson), and between *his* legs was a washboard upon which
he rested his right hand and formed the rude sign of the finger,
the American equivalent of the British V sign. Next to *him* was
a man (Bob Mosley) with brilliant boots, scowling and handsome. Best of all was the fact that this last person had a frying
pan in his right hand. And even better than *this* was the fact that
both he and the one in the middle were, with their left hands,
holding up a spoon for no apparent reason whatsoever. Cool or
what? Intrigued, beguiled, I bought the album.

It was with some trepidation that I put the record, *Moby
Grape* by Moby Grape, on my parents' radiogram (we hadn't
graduated to hi-fi yet; imagine my wonder when I heard The
Byrds all over again in stereo a couple of years later). It was
bound to be a crushing disappointment and I would have
wasted 13s 6d on a dud. It was not to be. This was glorious.
This was what I had been waiting for. They sang things like 'I
got high this time around, this time round/Everything is upside
down, upside down,' which to a boy flirting with drugs was just
right, and the music was weird and spooky, but not *too* weird
and spooky. This was pop – the longest song on the album was
a mere four minutes, refreshingly brief by the standards of the

day – but it was pop turned on its head, and the guitarists, of which there were three, played beautiful, dizzying pop/rock stuff, especially Jerry Miller, which had me thinking, 'Ha, ha, ha, eat your heart out Eric Clapton, Jeff Beck and Jimmy bloody Page. These guys don't show off and monkey about with violin bows. They don't *need* to. Because they are strange and clever, you see. Ha, ha, ha.' I had discovered my Mystery Group. The Mystery Group even dealt in delicious five-part harmonies, unheard of in these progressive times. Yes, the prancing toy soldiers who were my classmates would really detest *this* lot. And so they did.

The next day, I managed to cadge a couple of quid off Basingstoke, who had a Saturday job in a plastic extrusions factory and was, therefore, rich beyond the dreams of avarice, and went to W. H. Smith. To my relief, but not to my surprise in this town of 'straights', the other three Moby Grape LPs were still there, waiting. I bought them. *Wow* had a strange cover with a huge bunch of grapes and an old ship on the front; on *Moby Grape 69*, they stood looking quite bored against a huge slab of rock, but there were only four of them now (no Spence). *Truly Fine Citizen* just had on its cover a stout and grinning policeman – what could it mean? Some anti-establishment message, no doubt. (Actually, it wasn't a cop at all but a security guard at Columbia's studio in Nashville whom the group had befriended and who had made sure no one got into the studio while the group were smoking dope, but I didn't know this at the time.)

'Get out of my town!' 'It's your town, I'll get out of it.' 'Long-haired creep!', ran a strange piece of dialogue on *Wow*'s 'Rose Colored Eyes'. This became a rallying cry for me and Basingstoke in the weeks to come, a secret message between two like-minded schoolboys soon bound for university and the world proper. There was a track on *Wow* called 'Just Like Gene Autry: A Foxtrot'. You had to play it at 78 rpm, and it had nothing whatsoever to do with pop or rock, being a thing written by Skip Spence featuring a genuine 1930s-style dance orchestra and 'starring Arthur Godfrey, banjo and ukulele'. This was such an unlikely joke, I could not contain my admiration. Skippy was clearly so cracked, I had found a new role model for life. I had fallen in love all over again and even The Byrds didn't get much airplay on our radiogram that summer.

By the time I discovered Moby Grape, the band had already split up. I found this out by buying old copies of *Rolling Stone* lurking in a hippy shop in Reading. Somehow, this made me even more of a fan. Moby Grape had split up and I had all their great albums, the entire collection. Moby Grape had split up so nothing could spoil them now. Moby Grape didn't exist. It was a perfect love affair. Nothing could ever come between us. And nothing ever did.

I lasted just one term at Leeds University. Freedom? In a ghastly hall of residence surrounded by Newcastle Brown-guzzling, rugger-buggering, mechanical-engineering types, I felt more imprisoned than I had at public school. It was *worse* than school. Everyone on my corridor was playing Santana, so I just cranked up the sound of Moby Grape on my cheapest of non-stereo systems as loud as possible. Still, 'Soul Sacrifice' or 'Abraxas' or whatever it was called came sneaking in, swamping the soft bits of 'Indifference' and 'Motorcycle Irene' and 'Seeing' (probably the most gorgeous pop song ever). I couldn't stay here. I would 'drop out', that's what I would do.

I was supposed to be studying history at university. And that's what I did. Unfortunately, it wasn't the history of medieval communications and agricultural systems, as it was supposed to be, but the history of Moby Grape. As they were almost entirely unknown in this country, never mentioned in *Melody Maker* or anywhere like that, this was a time-consuming task, one which I set about with passion. I should have got a degree, anyway, if you ask me. The more I discovered about the group, the more I became infatuated with them, the more I absorbed myself in the recordings. It was such a great pop story, the stuff of which legends are made.

They were signed up to Columbia just before the so-called Summer of Love. They were supposed to be a somewhat tardy answer to The Rolling Stones (because there were five of them and they all had what we now call 'attitude'), but it didn't quite work out like that. The *music* worked, for sure, but everything else went horribly wrong from the start. Apart from the fact that the group's bizarre take on pop sat uneasily beside all the other San Franciscan peace-vibe stuff of the era – Airplane, Grateful Dead et al., the marketing of the debut LP put off potential buyers from the start. It was hyped in days when hype was simply not on. Five singles from that first album were released on the very same day: 'Omaha', 'Hey Grandma', '8:05', 'Fall On You' and 'Sitting By the Window'. What was the point of that? Only 'Omaha' got anywhere near the Hit Parade (Number 88). There were lavish launch parties for the record featuring, among other things, purple balloons and orchid petals dropping down from the ceiling on to the floor, where party-goers promptly slipped on them. For the launch party at The Avalon Ballroom there were 700 bottles of wine with Moby Grape labels – but somebody had forgotten to provide any corkscrews. They even had a purple elephant walking down LA's Sunset Boulevard. Moby Grape. Never knowingly under-sold. The PR wheezes only served to make them seriously unhip, all credibility blown before they'd even started.

It got worse. Miller, Lewis and Spence were charged with contributing to the delinquency of minors. Miller was charged with marijuana possession. The debut LP cover was censored, airbrushed to remove Stevenson's rude finger and the American flag as well (they didn't bother with this censorship in Britain because nobody apart from me bought the damned record anyway). The band were thrown out of hotels everywhere in time-honoured tradition. Spence was taking too many hallucino-genics and hacked down Stevenson's hotel-room door with a fire axe, suffering from the delusion that Stevenson was the Devil. For that, Skippy ended up in Bellevue Hospital, an institution we used to call a loony bin. Finally, Bob Mosley quit to join the Marines because he wanted to go to Vietnam. What??!!! When I learned *that* fact, I was a little bit shocked. Wanting to go to Vietnam wasn't on the rock'n'roll agenda at all, but, in retrospect, just *because* it's so non-rock'n'roll, this seems the coolest crack-up manoeuvre of all. Particularly as Mosley was soon thrown out of the Marines for making a nuisance of himself.

So Moby Grape, a band that should have ruled the world, had split up before we'd even been introduced. 'It took some strange kind of genius to screw it up and screw it up so bad,' said Jerry Miller. How right he was. Genius, it is.

Yes they fucked up royally, on a gargantuan scale, did my music idols. Cruel and callous as it may seem, I like my pop stars to fuck up; it shows they are (or were) of the human scale. I can't tell you much about Duane Eddy, probably doing okay, but at the time of writing, which is May 1994, the roll call of casualty looks like this . . .

Michael Clarke. Dead.

Gene Clark. Dead.

David Crosby. *Should* be dead, the shotgun-toting, drug/drunk-driving, rehab-recovery buffoon, but somehow he survives.

Alex 'Skip' Spence. Living in a residential-care house in San Jose, diagnosed schizophrenic. Panhandles for loose change. Promptly gives his takings away.

Bob Mosley. Itinerant.

Don Stevenson. Sells double-glazing or something.

Six down. Four to go. I choose my heroes well.

It is 1991 and I am on holiday in California with my wife, my sister and my friend William. In Fort Bragg, a small industrial town just to the north of the plush hippy enclave of Mendocino,

I am despatched from the hire car into a package store for some more beer. When I return with my purchases in a brown paper bag, there's a strange atmosphere in the car. William seems to be hiding something under the passenger seat and there's some tense whispering going on.

'What's the matter?' I ask. 'Is everything alright?'

'Yes,' says my wife.

'Yes,' says my sister.

'Um,' says William. I am not convinced and I make this clear.

'You'd better tell him,' says my wife with a sigh, and William digs the local newspaper from its hiding place and shows me the small ad he's found therein. Moby Grape, on one of their sporadic reunions, are playing in some sleazy club in Fort Bragg, it says here. What? No! No. It was last night. It has come to this. I missed them. I am plunged into a dark gloom, just as my travel-mates feared.

And that's my interesting story of how I never got to see Moby Grape, not on stage, not on telly, not anywhere. I saw The Byrds a few times but not the *proper* Byrds, just the McGuinn/Skip Battin/ Clarence White/Gene Parsons Byrds who made *Untitled*. They were *all right*, but I longed for Gene Clarke (no longer with us) and short songs and proper harmonies and no bloody bass guitar solos.

I met McGuinn once in 1978 at the BBC and, overcome with horrid hospitality wine, plucked up the courage to tell him he was my hero. He was singularly unimpressed, downright rude if I remember right. I met him again a couple of years ago when, now a journalist, I interviewed him. It was a less than lovely experience. He was a surly old cuss, short on smiles and charm. This was the man who had driven me to crime, forcing me to shoplift from Woolies because I fancied his spectacles, and he could hardly be bothered to give me the time of day. So, really, I suppose I am quite glad that my path has never crossed with those of the men of Moby Grape. It might just spoil everything. Here is a love affair that has lasted for a quarter of a century – think of it! – a love that endures. It's all rather silly, isn't it?

Hell of a Summer

DAVID CAVANAGH

Hailing from Perth, Western Australia, the five (later six) piece Triffids lived in London for much of 1984–5 and were part of a brief musical wave of Australian pure but angry pop. Close musical cousins of The Go-Betweens, The Triffids released six sterling albums (*Treeless Plain, Raining Pleasure, Born Sandy Devotional, In the Pines, Calenture* and *The Black Swan*) between 1983 and 1989, after which they disbanded. A live album, *Stockholm*, was released posthumously. Singer David McComb's intense brooding songs encompassed country, R&B, folk, rock and an occasionally wacky sense of humour, to little avail despite continued critical respect. The Triffids' most populist moment came when their 'Bury Me Deep in Love' was used in an episode of *Neighbours*.

The scar crosses the upper side of my right wrist like a diagonal watch, and in moments of tension and fear I aggravate it. It's one of the principal symptoms of Endogenous Panophobic Psoriasis – 'Eppy' to its international legions of malingerers – and it means, to swathe through science for a moment, that I'm afraid of all kinds of shit I can't put my finger on. It's very groovy. In hot weather, or in panic, or in supermarkets, I scrape at my legs and my arms and they itch for weeks. One of my few ambitions is to someday rip my own head off.

The wrist-maiming tragedy happened to me at a Monochrome Set gig early in 1984. The Monochrome Set were by no means a happening scene and would soon pack it in for a while, unloved and unable to translate their upper-class toilet humour into acceptable cash-flow or even mild controversy. Back in '84 they would gig intermittently at college venues. It was all very childish. The students would smirk knowingly as the singer, Bid, spooned contempt and derision upon us; it was a bedamned ritual that left neither party particularly thrilled. At one particular under-attended Monochromes symposium at the LSE, I had been shoved out to the right and into the PA, ripping my arm.

Nice one, but ... how to extract the full mileage? Squeezing my wrist to make it bleed more, I pushed back through the crowd, wiping my white T-shirt repeatedly to give the impression of having been brutally stabbed in the heart. My eyes stared deep into strangers' faces and my mouth lolled open.

'There's been an ... accident,' I whispered.

At the porter's office I was given a strip of plaster, which, in a spirit of fun, I replaced the following day with a cumbersome shag-pile bandage that encased my arm from elbow to thumb. I refused to talk of the horrors beneath, preferring instead to wince meaningfully and effect ashen. 'You have good days,' I would explain with a sigh. 'And you have ... bad days.'

At the University – my detestable day-job – my reputation was, I was sure, thoroughly clear-cut. Weirdo; ill; won't make it to thirty; inchoate mutterings mask voluminous hidden agenda of angst. I wasn't conning myself. I knew I was a neurotic and a hypochondriac. The thing was, I also knew that I was suffering from several mysterious terminal illnesses. It made concentrating on the job in hand difficult.

Each morning, I passed the Scientologists' office in Tottenham Court Road. 'Would you like a free personality test?' a well-balanced young canvasser would venture neutrally. Each morning, with a theatrical gesture, I would demur. I didn't realize they asked everybody.

A perpetually drunk, uncool nineteen-year-old, I swivelled up and down the echoing stairs of Senate House ('fear of lifts,' I would explain shakily) and in and out of the University's local pub, ludicrously named The Friend At Hand. For a change of scene, I would patronize my college's own subterranean bar in

Russell Square, where exciting foreign vodkas with names like Bok and Vax were sold for ten pence. Here I would sit, imaginary handkerchief clasped tight to my mouth, knocking back the Vax and looking like I was really getting into *Vanity Of Duluoz* by Jack Kerouac.

My heroes were, as far as I was concerned, secrets, and I worshipped them through a private fug. Representing the jazz world I had Miles Davis, whom I was convinced no one had ever heard of. He was one of my cool discoveries, like the fact that you fall over if you don't sleep very often. Idolizing Davis (a white kid like me would never have called him Miles; it would be like calling your father 'geezer') usually indicates an otherwise shallow and superficial knowledge of jazz. Too bad. I loved all his albums, particularly *In a Silent Way*, and kept Ian Carr's biography of him within browsing distance. Lester Bangs's massive *NME* piece, printed posthumously (for Bangs, that is) in 1983, was actually up on my bedroom wall, its amazingly daring conclusion ('. . .all that's left is the universe') following me around the room like a pair of paranoid eyes.

My other heroes were the equally obscure Beatles, Captain Beefheart, Syd Barrett, The Byrds, Tom Verlaine, Can and a weird Canadian actor named Alexis Kanner who, at fifteen, had lied about his age to land a role in *Softly Softly* in the mid-sixties, and had subsequently acted his arse off in the last three episodes of *The Prisoner*.

Kanner had a hell of a vision. In 1984 I saw a film he'd directed, called *Kings and Desperate Men*, which was edited like a Tango advert but provided me with an important catchphrase: 'Mr Lucas has a grievance'. This you were supposed to say in a curiously high-pitched Shakespearian screech. I do recall it was a bastard trying to manoeuvre it into conversation.

I listened to practically no contemporary music. I had abstained from the 1980s. They were evil. Even their best stuff was rancid and poxy. Their politics, their films, their music, their weather, their football, their eerie emphasis on cash and muscle ... I knew that if I was foolish enough to mix it with the eighties they would fucking bury me. I sort of hibernated.

But, I needed a role model for this one, otherwise I couldn't proceed. I found him in a 1958 British film called *The Man Upstairs*. Richard Attenborough, my main man, played a mousy little lodger who goes mad because society is really evil. He barricades himself in his upstairs room. As the police circle the house (I can't remember why; perhaps he'd murdered a few people) and shout at him to come down, he suddenly throws open the window and screams – really loudly for Attenborough – my all-time favourite cinema line: 'I am not available!' Unavailability was my big thing in 1984. It all got a bit stupid. Then one day in October, looking through *Time Out* for the week's afternoon showings at the Gate, Bloomsbury, I observed that The Monochrome Set had yet another LSE gig pencilled in for that week, supported by a bunch of what the capital's hard-pushed listings directory confidently termed 'quirky, B-52's-influenced Aussies' called The Triffids. The name rang a vague bell. *Melody Maker* had reviewed them the previous week, supporting The Mint Juleps. The *MM* man had made an off-colour reference to Triffids organist Jill (misspelt Gill) Birt and impending blindness. But his gist was that The Triffids were very good, so I went along. By now I was alone in London. I had been left behind by the evacuees.

During my university end-of-term party the previous Easter, a ridiculous altercation over some pâté had finished up with me waving a knife around and being punched into some chairs. It was a small disagreement, soon forgotten, except by me.

In the three or four weeks it took me to calm down, gazing up at my mantra, which, you'll recall, read, '...all that's left is the universe', my understanding of the knifing incident subtly changed. The role of the pâté, particularly, underwent a complete restructuring, shrinking in relevance from its one-time

key role as a sinister, liver-based catalyst or agent, until, like 80
per cent of Dennis Hopper's part in *Apocalypse Now*, it wound up
on the cutting room floor.

In my mind, all that was left was a hard frost, half-way
between waking dream and horrified recollection, that spelled
out my imminent downfall in big scary footprints. I had attempted the cold-blooded murder of a fellow student.

It was laughable and stupid and implausible and it all made
perfect sense. My guilt established, it became difficult to look
him in the eye without immediately visualizing him as a corpse.
Ach! That wretched pallor! Those horrible dead eyes!

There was no way we could carry on as normal. Previously, I
had always sat next to him in tutorials. *God! That pestilent stench!
That fetid aroma!*

Presently, with a murderer's cunning, I began to arrive for
tutorials somewhat on the late side. I would apologize in a faint,
some might say distracted, whisper. All the seats being taken, I
would offer to 'go and get another chair', which I would
ruthlessly position on the opposite side of the room. Then, with
a groovy catatonic stare based on Storm Thorgeson's memories
of Syd Barrett in Rick Sanders's book *The Pink Floyd*, I would
gaze out of the window, looking penitent and full of self-
loathing.

'I know you've said Tolstoy was ... (*shakes head sadly*) ...
immature and glib, David, but perhaps on your next visit to
Earth you could drop in and comment on the principal dispari-
ties Anna Karenina experiences between Levin and Vronsky?'

I would let four seconds elapse, then snap to attention with
an expertly panicked double-take.

'No! I, uh, didn't say he was, uh, immature, I just said he ...
(*voice gets indistinct, eyes start to wander*) ... didn't go far enough.'

'Yes. (*Sigh.*) Well, one tends to find this complaint of Tolstoy,
doesn't one, cropping up in most of the major biographies. That
somehow he just didn't go far enough.'

Irony is wasted on the insane. They just hear the words, not the tone of voice. In the far right-hand corner of my field of vision I could discern the impassive face of my victim. *O putrefying lips, O disjunct brow.* And in my fever, I saw myself standing over him with bloody blade, turning in horror to greet the shadow in the doorway.

'Porfiry Petrovich, it is you. . .'

'My dear fellow, of course it is I. Cannot an official of the Criminal Investigation Department of the Spasskaya District Police Office pop in on his old friend for an informal drink when he wants to? But my dear old chum, you look agitated!' (His eyes drop to the carpet, positively liquid with fresh blood.)

'Look, I don't want you getting the wrong idea here, Porfiry Petrovich. This has never happened before.'

'Hmm. "All that is left is the universe." The phrase intrigues me. Is it yours?'

I'd read *Crime and Punishment* and I knew a slippery slope when I saw one. Then they sent for me. I knew they would.

As a student of Russian, I was up for the big holiday. The second year of the course was traditionally, almost obligatorily, spent in the Soviet Union. The young holidaymakers, if everything went to plan, would return to Britain fluent in the language of Pushkin, or at least Chernenko, and aflame with a craving for zealous learning. Qualified thus, and provided you were prepared to vote Tory, a job at GCHQ was as good as in the bag.

There were three choices. For those who sensed they might respond well to a life of sub-zero penury and Rugby Union-esque male bonding, the university offered a year in Minsk.

Failing that, the travel agents could heartily recommend five months in Leningrad. The advantages of Leningrad were that the tourist came home seven months earlier and was near a useful-looking river, the Neva.

Finally, for the profoundly timid, there was the three-month bucketshop calling at no stations to Voronezh, with no buffet car. Very few people bothered to read the literature on Voronezh, but I did. It was a sobering brochure. Three months in Voronezh would have been extremely similar to three months in the Russell Square bar with no heat and no nearby cashpoint machine. Voronezh, while admittedly being situated in the Soviet Union, had no Soviet people living in it whatsoever. It was a student village. Soviets never went there. Why should they? They didn't need to learn how to speak their own language. The only people the student would meet would be other students.

I wanted to go to Leningrad, and nobody was going to stop me. However, in the light of the murder attempt, the whole tawdry affair became wrapped up in politics and I was expressly told by the Head of Department that I was not yet felt to be ready for serious foreign travel. They offered me Voronezh and I turned it down flat.

In the event, one guy who got a Leningrad place was later arrested on a train, after attempting to hold it up armed with a home-made wooden rifle and a false Cossack beard. When accosted, he was heard to shout, 'Look, my friends, I happen to know this is the Lupin Express.' Meanwhile, a girl from Nottingham was almost instantly raped in Minsk and had to come home eleven months and two weeks early. And two girls from Hull University cried themselves to sleep every night in Voronezh, wrapped in each other's arms and convulsing in unhappy spasm until sleep and their comforting redbrick dreams gently prised them apart.

I stayed in London and was forklifted out of the abyss by five Australians called The Triffids.

To silence, they walked onstage at the LSE in Houghton Street and picked up their guitars, all except for a tiny girl, whom I shrewdly took to be Jill Birt, who held aloft a single drumstick and positioned herself in front of the drum-kit. Not behind it;

they already had a drummer. She stood by one of the cymbals. It looked odd.

They were all youngish, probably a bit older than me, and handsome. But the singer, who had wild black eyes, a complexion like scuffed pink Tarmac and a black leather jacket, was a frowning, prowling vision of the uncomfortable. He didn't bother with introductions. At the back of the stage, by his amp, he suddenly banged out a one-chord reveille, the same frenzied chord over and over, fast and angry. Then he paced menacingly towards his microphone, at which point the rest of the band exploded into a leering, upwardly swooping riff that practically re-booted my aimless existence there and then.

It stuttered and exploded, again and again. As the drummer slashed at his snare and hi-hat, Jill Birt nonchalantly tapped at the crash cymbal, holding down a kind of swinging jazz beat. The singer swung into the lyric – about having no family, friends or life – with a demeanour of totally convincing psychosis. I wasn't to know it, but what they were playing was the most inflammable reconstruction of a Bob Dylan song since Jimi Hendrix poured petrol over 'All Along the Watchtower'. 'I Am a Lonesome Hobo', or at least a weedy blueprint thereof, appears on side two of Dylan's *John Wesley Harding*, and only the most black-eyed, agile minds approaching the end of a feverishly intense bout of sleep deprivation could have re-wired it as recklessly as The Triffids did that night.

As soon as it finished I moved to the front of the stage and stood, tensed and thrilled, as they tore through one magnificent song after another. The next one was a Triffids original, I presumed, that chopped and scythed like a non-cartoonish Birthday Party. The one after that, a rowdy rockabilly thing, made an instant star out of the lead guitarist, whose violent string-bending was totally at odds with his nonchalant appearance.

Four points were buzzing round my mind. One: how could these people look so calm – apart from the singer, who was hospitalizing himself a little more dramatically by the minute – when they were playing explosive, exciting rock music on a par with The Velvet Underground?

Two: they were so tight, so together, so new and fantastic: they pissed all over every other band I'd ever seen live.

Three: did the rest of the band know that the singer had a monstrous drug problem, and, if so, did that mean that they all did too? Even the girl, who had now moved to organ, which she wrenched at like a sluggish iron?

And four: did they have any albums out? They didn't look like the kind of band who would make helpful announcements about this.

When the lead guitarist took up a violin and they played a slow, gorgeous waltz, I was convinced I was hearing the loveliest song ever written. Which one of them wrote the songs? Clearly not the singer. He didn't look like he could be trusted with a pencil. Was it the lead guitarist/violinist? Was it Jill Birt?

Then she sang a song. It was a fragile, aching thing which she sang like a child, eyes wide and alive, not imploring or beguiling like all the other girl singers in all the other bands. She sang not like Nico, but like Deerfrance, the mysteriously named girl who had sung 'Only Time Will Tell' on John Cale's *Sabotage* live album in 1979. Now I was thinking furiously. My impression of Deerfrance had always been of a limpid little *ingénue*, kidnapped by the mad Cale and his band, and forced to sing her song under duress, after which she would be flung back into her dungeon, mewling pitifully, until the next gig. Was this the case with The Triffids? No band could possibly include that black-eyed singer and that girl, other than by the most nefarious of devices. What would conversations between them be like? Could I overhear one someday?

As she finished singing, the forbidding features of the front-man softened and he spoke his first words. 'Jill Birt,' he said, grinning at the crowd and clapping his hands. She got a round of applause. It was the coolest thing I'd ever seen in my life.

They did a song called 'Hell of a Summer', a title which was destined to become a new catchphrase in my life. Whatever happened to me between 1984 and 1985, I would shake my head sadly and repeat, 'It's been a hell of a summer.' It was perfect. And it didn't even have to be summer. It just had to have *been* summer, at some point previously. People who had previously said, 'Shit happens,' or 'God moves in mysterious ways,' well, they all thought, boy, his catchphrase is much better than ours, and started ripping me off.

Meanwhile, the singer was talking about a Triffids album, but I only caught a few words, two of which were 'Rough Trade'. In an instant, I saw the cover: a blurred garage, and monochrome musicians in movement, with just the leads from their guitars in focus. The song titles written in red on the back cover. To finish, they played an endless song which had patterns of The Doors both in Jill Birt's organ playing and in the evangelist-style hollering which the singer employed to get over his message. Even now, as the melody collapsed and they drilled their way through to the heart of all musical chaos, not a flicker of emotion could be detected on the faces of the lead guitarist or the bassist. They just did it. By the time they left the stage, I was absolutely assured that I had discovered the best band in the world. I wanted to talk to them, quickly.

Stupidly, I deliberated too long. I watched too much of The Monochrome Set's feeble performance, and when I collared an LSE doorman he told me The Triffids had left.

'Oh, wow, for Australia?'

He looked at me oddly.

I walked down The Strand to Trafalgar Square and caught a bus. Those songs were making my wrist itch. No junk food for me. I couldn't get my brain out of waltz time.

October at the School of Slavonic and East European Studies was like a quiet day at a snowed-in hotel with Jack Nicholson and Shelley Duvall presiding. Tutorials-for-one were not uncommon. There was a war vibe on. My fellow non-evacuees were either ill or old. We were the infirm; the guys out in Minsk and Voronezh were fighting the real war. Had I done the right thing in staying? It didn't look like it.

Time Out served me well. It told me where this week's obligatory screenings of *Darling* and *The Return of the Secaucus Seven* were happening, and, about a week after the LSE gig, it told me where I might next track down The Triffids. It was at the Rock Garden. Here, wherever the hell it was, I would meet them. I hadn't prepared an introduction, but it was going to be something slavering and epic.

After a quite staggeringly dreadful support band, who used backing tapes of – they claimed – their girlfriends having orgasms, The Triffids singer strolled on stage, dropped to his knees and started fiddling around with leads. I went up to him and suggested non-committedly that his band's gig at the LSE had been the best thing to happen to music in my lifetime, and that all their songs were, as far as genius went, absolutely off the scale.

'Outside of music business people, you know, you're our first real fan,' he grinned charmingly.

His name turned out to be David, too, David McComb. Still in his songwriting infancy, he would later be hailed as one of the great masters of the songwriting art, a visionary, a poet. I bought him a drink and grilled him for information.

They hailed from Perth in Western Australia. Unable to progress there, they had invested all their money in a trip to England and were now living here, just as fellow Australians The Saints, The Birthday Party and The Go-Betweens had before. Money was so tight they had borrowed a drum-kit off Clare Moore from The Moodists. They loved music, it was just a case of getting the English to find out about them.

Yes, yes. And the waltz song?

Embarrassingly, I had to get him to repeat the title three times. I just could not make sense of his accent. Rare *what*? Rare Pining?

Just as he was about to write it down, I twigged it. 'Red Pony'. My favourite song was called 'Red Pony'. How beautiful. Would they do it tonight? Sure. They did it every night. It was, after all, one of their songs. The endless evangelist's song, it transpired, was called 'Field of Glass' and had only recently been added to the set. Jill's song was 'Raining Pleasure'. The rockabilly one was 'Branded'. He listed three or four others: 'Jesus Calling', 'Property is Condemned', 'Bright Lights Big City' and 'Monkey On My Back'. And the album? What was the title of the album? This needed about five or six efforts. I couldn't get it at all. Patiently, he kept saying it, over and over, until eventually . . . Oh! *Treeless Plain*. Did he mean like a plain that didn't have trees on it?

'Er . . . yeah,' he said. 'I guess so.'

Well, if *Treeless Plain* wasn't the best title for an album I had ever heard, I didn't know what was. He told me they had another album, too, called *Raining Pleasure*. Next big point: were they available?

'They're coming out over here on Rough Trade Distribution,' he explained. What the fuck did that mean? Did that mean I could have them tomorrow? He looked amused at my excitement. These were songs The Triffids had been playing live for two years (hence their tightness) and some guy was asking him to say all their names five times. After arranging to go backstage and meet the others when the gig was over (thus showing unbelievable naïvety: you don't have to arrange to go backstage at the Rock Garden, you just go), I retreated about four feet into the small audience.

Now I was ready for all the songs. I recognized each one instantly, noted a new one called 'Embedded', watched every musician in turn, picked out phrases and waited for 'Red Pony'. I learned that my catchphrase had a bit more to it. 'It's been a hell of a summer to be lying so low.' Wow! I thought I knew just the occasion for that one. When they played 'Red Pony' I felt privileged to be there. It was that autumn's big moment.

Hearing them play it was the only thing that could make me stop thinking of Voronezh and all my absent friends and I never wanted it to finish.

My brief chat with McComb hadn't enlightened me much on what other music they liked, other than to confirm that the support band, apart from being truly appalling, were also dickheads of galactic expanse. But when The Triffids came back for an encore, we were given a clue.

The lead guitarist took over on drums and the drummer picked up a guitar. They sang Elvis Presley's 'Can't Help Falling in Love' and McComb and the drummer harmonized like dissolute Everly Brothers. In 1984, Elvis to me was just a big fat dead person, but they sang his song with total commitment and no irony. They sang it with love, basically. Although most of my memories of that era relate to the weather – it was cold, it was colder, it was coldest – those three minutes at the Rock Garden will always be a warm place. It wasn't as complicated an emotion as the one 'Red Pony' triggered off in me. It was a simple, pleasing, womb-like warmth and it had nothing to do with any of the music I ordinarily listened to.

It was, for instance, the precise musical opposite of *Stimmung*, a wintry, nullifying piece of choral experimentation by Stockhausen, which I had taped off Radio 3 and listened to every morning on my Walkman. Fuck knows why. In fact, now that I thought of it, all my favourite music completely alienated me from the people who made it. The idea of following a band was ridiculous, like following a lorry purely because it was on the move. The Triffids were the first band who made me come closer. I clambered across the Rock Garden's stage, downwards and in.

If meeting one of them was tricky, coming face to face with all five was petrifying. In the space of two gigs, these people had turned my life around. Unversed in backstage protocol (rule one: no excessive use of metaphor), I yammered tentative greetings and waxed perilously solemn, manfully struggling to keep the abyss out of it. David McComb wasn't a drug addict or anything of the kind. He didn't even smoke. He was simply an excellent, vivid performer of his own songs. Yes, the songs were his. The lead guitarist was Rob, his brother. At twenty-seven, Rob was the oldest Triffid, an easy-going Bohemian guy who helpfully answered each question as though it were completely fascinating, which, believe me, it wasn't.

The others were about twenty-two or twenty-three. The drummer was Alsy MacDonald, a thoroughly excellent fellow with a dry wit. The bassist, Martyn Casey, seemed even drier, quiet and unfailingly polite. Jill Birt wanted to know if I could understand their accents. I wanted to know if I could move in with them.

Helping them load their van up, I was delighted to be offered a place on the guest list at Dingwalls, their next gig. But again, when, with abundant overuse of adverbs, I brusquely demanded information about their two albums, they shrugged and said they would probably be released in a few weeks, through Rough Trade Distribution. I really hated Rough Trade Distribution now. I hoped they knew what misery they were putting me through. In the following days, I seethed my way through chilly Stockhausen bus rides, affected catalepsy and muteness in tutorials and waited for darkness. Then it got dark.

Ever since I had moved in, I had known I was living in a street with a curse on it. Up around the bend of the L-shaped St James's Lane, just where the hill reared up in near-vertical abruptness to connect with the elevated Muswell Hill Broadway, there was a pub. It was called the Royal Oak. The big murder case of the previous year had introduced the world to Dennis Nielsen, his evil fridge, and his rapidly dwindling cache of neck-ties. In a murdering spree going back some years, Nielsen had picked up young homosexuals, brought them home – at first to Cricklewood, then subsequently to 23 Cranley Gardens, Muswell Hill – where he would drug them, strangle them with one of his many ties, dissect their bodies and dispose of them in instalments via the lavatory system.

An unsatisfactory arrangement at the best of times, the lethargy of his U-bend led inevitably to blocked drains, saucepans cluttered up with bits of torso, and a ferocious odour that stirred plaintive feelings in his neighbours. It was this odour that finally led the police to his door.

What was not widely reported at the time was that one of my fellow students at the School of Slavonic and East European Studies had been a lucky escapee from the dreaded house of Nielsen. Indeed, he had awakened from his drug-induced stupor just in time to monitor the downward momentum of the tie with his name on it. I knew this. I also knew, from my flatmates, that the Royal Oak had been Nielsen's local. He used to sit in there, on his own, drinking 'steadily'.

One of my flatmates, Brendan, reckoned he could speak for the population at large when he said the Royal Oak had a horrible feeling about it. I gave it the full-on swerve. When Brendan left, he was replaced, first by a girl called Heather, then by a guy called Neil, whom I perfunctorily auditioned one afternoon and more or less okayed. He was older than we were – about thirty – and because socializing with my flatmates was way out of my range, Neil began to go for an evening pint in the Royal Oak without checking it over with me. It is quite possible that he sat on his own on these occasions, and it is by no means out of the question that he drank 'steadily'. All I knew about him at this stage was that he came from Tring and he didn't arrive home on certain nights.

Around that time, as if through a thick fog, my subconscious began to take note of a sequence of worrying news stories in the *Evening Standard.* These concerned a highly dangerous criminal nicknamed The Fox, who operated in the Bedfordshire, Hertfordshire and Greater London manors. The reason he was known as The Fox was because he would break into people's houses while they were not there, then, while waiting for their return, he would construct a kind of den, or lair, from pieces of furniture. These he would arrange around the living room's most comfortable armchair and, settled in, he would watch TV and eat beans.

Like a lot of people, I felt uneasy about the beans. Mention of beans can only mean bad news. The beans invariably appeared early on in each Fox-related story in the *Standard*, even before the bit about the lair. It would go: The Fox, struck again, beans, lair, latest ghastly crime, police warn residents. Because when the people returned, The Fox would put the beans down and he would become extremely scary. He raped women. He defiled them. He stripped them of all their dignity. Once, when a married couple returned to find him there, he forced them to have sex while he watched. Then he had sex with her, while the man watched, and the man couldn't do anything about it. The Fox permeated my inner discussions quite listlessly and randomly, rather like the King of Spain had once troubled Poprishchin in Gogol's *Diary of a Madman*.

You could learn a lot from the *Evening Standard* in the autumn of 1984. You could find jobs. You could find out which West Ham players were receiving treatment for hamstring injuries. You could learn that The Fox was now thought by the police to hail from the Tring area.

Further down, and maybe you would be shaking a little now, you could learn that the police urged people to contact them if they knew of a man, about thirty, who was a bit of a loner and who didn't come home on certain nights.

What I did next says a lot about me. I ran to the kitchen and looked in Neil's cupboard for signs of beans. I tell you this, I badly wanted to know what the beans situation was, regarding old Neil. To my fantastic shaking relief, there were no beans.

Ohhh ... I started to laugh uncontrollably and went back to my room. Whoa! Boy! Beans scare over. What a hell of a summer that had been. Then I got very scared again. I had made a dangerous error. I had been looking at it the wrong way

round. Of course there weren't any beans! We'd already established that he liked beans! He'd eaten all the beans! He couldn't
get enough of the fucking things.

I flew back out to the kitchen and emptied out the black bin-
liner. Kicking through the rubbish, I now kept an eye open for
beans-like debris. Tins, labels, even sardines in tomato sauce
might qualify. I didn't need to sift for long. There, grinning up
at me, was an empty tin of Sainsbury's beans. Neil was The
Fox. I was alone in the house. Madly, I decided to search his
room. I was delirious. Just then I decided not to search his
room. Fortunately.

'*What do you think you're doing?*'
'*Oh, hello, The Fox! Ha ha ha ha. Listen, you're not going to believe
this. Ha ha ha. Only, I heard a noise and I thought you were a burglar
coming to steal your Heinz.* (*Pause.*) *Your* stereo. *So I thought I'd hide
in your room behind the beans.* The door. *And kind of pounce, you know,
sort of pounce and, and, and, oh God, don't rape me, The Fox, don't rape
me.*'

Instead, I called my parents and relayed the worrying develop-
ments. Wisely, I kept the beans out of it.

'Are you sure it's him?'
'Absolutely. The Tring connection was the thing that con-
vinced me.'
'You don't know for certain that The Fox is from Tring.'
'Of course I do. The police said so.'
'Maybe you ought to call the police, then.'
'Yes, but what if he isn't The Fox? It would be terrible. I
have to make an important decision here.'
It was OK, in a way. All that was left was the universe.

Every lunchtime, just before slapping on some of that *Stimmung*
and getting the 134 bus home, I would visit the Virgin Megastore, looking for the two Triffids albums. They were never

there. 'Possibly they're in your Antipodean section?' I once suggested to the man at the Information Desk.

Then, one afternoon, things started to happen very fast. Neil left the house, owing a lot of bills. And The Triffids albums arrived in the Megastore. Neither of the records looked like I had imagined. *Treeless Plain* was green, for a start, which really threw me. *Raining Pleasure* was yellow. *Treeless Plain* started with 'Red Pony'. That seemed wrong.

I wanted those albums to be perfect and, for a while, they were. The sound was softer than their live shows. There was even a fruity country number or two. *Treeless Plain* ended with a song sung by Alsy, called 'Nothing Can Take Your Place'. It was sweet and happy, very un-Triffids. It wasn't long before the three music weeklies started raving about the band. Lynden Barber from the *Melody Maker* interviewed David McComb for a full-page feature, which ran under the inevitable headline Day of The Triffids. I read it downstairs in the Wimpy in Tottenham Court Road. The big news was that McComb hated everything. Absolutely detested everything. Nothing about the 1984 music scene brought him any pleasure whatsoever. I munched my hamburger thoughtfully. He and The Triffids were even angrier than I had bargained for.

At my third Triffids gig I began subtly to befriend them for real. Cruising into Dingwalls for the first time ever (come 1988, I would spend every Monday night there for an entire year), I approached them all in turn and got them to sign my *Treeless Plain* lyric sheet. They knew I was Irish so, cutely, Martyn Casey signed his name Martyn O'Casey. At the bottom, one of them wrote the band's communal telephone number in West Kensington.

Yet again, they played magnificently. The stage of Dingwalls was small, with a big pillar in the middle, and they stood cramped, all squeezed together. They looked electrifying. I loved their name. I loved their songs. I loved the way there were five of them.

'Why do you only play for fifty minutes?' I asked David afterwards. 'You should play for two hours – more.'

I was getting pretty cocky. I was now leaving my coat backstage during gigs. Watching the headlining band – I can't remember who – with Casey, I informed him in the most officious voice ever that his bassline on 'Red Pony' was a stroke of Godlike ingenuity. It was. But there are occasions, as a bass player, when you don't need the hassle.

The bills came to about £50. It was obvious what had happened. Neil, sensing that I was on to him, had split for Tring, where he would fling a few possessions into a rucksack – shirts, socks, beans – and go on the run. My other flatmate, Kerry, didn't know about the Fox business. She knew him as Neil, just as Son of Sam was once plain old 'Sam's lad' to his drinking companions. Once or twice she had even stepped into the Royal Oak with Neil for a spot of 'steady' drinking herself. Although this scared me, I didn't want to freak her out.

'Kerry, something really problematic's occurred with Neil,' I explained one night. 'He's left. And there's lots of bills which I've taken care of and now I'm incredibly in debt.'

'Oh no, what a bastard.'

'Yeah, I know. What shall we do?'

I got the job of phoning Neil's father in Tring. I explained who I was, making sure I called his son Neil rather than by, say, a vulpine-style nickname.

'If I see him I'll tell him, mate,' he promised.

The chances of you seeing your son again are pretty remote, you deluded fool, I thought as I disconnected. He's done a moonlight. He's had it away on his toes.

I saw The Triffids play at the Jackson's Lane Community Centre in Archway. Jill Birt was swaying in the bar. She and Alsy told me about Perth. 'It's just like Houston,' Alsy revealed. They had been drinking all day. We painstakingly went through the formalities of establishing that they would play 'Red Pony'. I saw them play upstairs at the Manor House pub, headlining above yet more Australians, The Scientists and a band called, what else, Purple Onion. Martyn's strap broke at the beginning of their newly introduced Otis Redding cover, 'You Don't Miss Your Water', and he had to go back to the dressing-room, where, let us not kid ourselves, I had once again left my coat. He arrived back on stage just in time to hit the song's last note.

The best part of that gig was the first airing of McComb's new Triffids song. David had told me about it and I latched on quickly.

'So does this mean you'll be playing for longer tonight?'

'No, we'll just drop one of the old ones.'

O bitter night, O palsied moon!

It was called 'Lonely Stretch'. For what seemed like about nineteen minutes, but was probably nearer six, McComb reared up over the microphone and bellowed one scintillating metaphor of doom and panic after another:

> I took a wrong turn off of an unmarked track,
> I did seven miles and couldn't find my way back,
> Hit a lonely stretch.
> Must be losing my touch
> I was out of my depth. . .
> Fingering my silver St Christopher and saving my empty shells for her.

I could not believe that this man was not revered throughout the world. These were the best words to a rock song I had yet encountered. I had to let him know, just in case he didn't realize. And unfortunately for Casey, his bassline was tremendous too, which I planned to tell him all about in a head-on effusive backstage tryst.

'Well, I suppose I did write it, yeah, if you can write a bassline. Er . . .?'

That gig had been pleasingly full. The reviews were nothing

less than a thrill to peruse. The *NME* called them 'the best band in the country', which showed real class. I wanted to work for the music press and write things like that too.

In the meantime, they had recorded a session for John Peel. I rang David before it went out, after it went out and, in all probability, while it was going out. 'It's still going out!' he'd helpfully confirm.

On 13 November it went out. I knew in advance what they had recorded: 'Bright Lights Big City', 'Monkey On My Back' and 'Field of Glass'. The evil three. 'You've only done three?' I remarked, crestfallen. 'But you could have done four. Normally, bands do four.'

'Well, "Field of Glass" is really long.'

In an instant, I was revitalized. 'Really long.' That could mean anything. That could mean endless. An aural picture formed in my mind, of Peel bidding his listeners goodnight at 11.27: 'Well, that's it for tonight. I'll leave you with the last number from The Triffids, who, as the *NME* so rightly said, are the best band in the country. If only they'd play for two hours, though. Incidentally, this last song is the most incredible piece of music you will ever hear.'

Alone in the house, alone in London, already over-familiar with *Treeless Plain* and *Raining Pleasure*, I tuned into Peel and finally heard The Triffids as they were meant to sound. 'Bright Lights Big City' was awesomely loud and scary. It also gave me my new pet catchphrase.

The only reason I'd moved to Muswell Hill in the first place was to live within crawling distance of a girl at college whom I adored, but she immediately panicked and fled to Clapham. Hurt, I examined the situation for plus points. Let's see: Muswell Hill, *aaarggh*, Clapham. No, it didn't look too good. There was no chance of getting hold of the wrong end of the stick with that one. It looked quite clear-cut. And yet I needed proof. This, I felt, would only be forthcoming if I were to move to Clapham and she were to commit suicide.

Symbiotically, on 'Bright Lights Big City', McComb screeched the words: 'I followed her round like a lapdog.' This became my tragic new catchphrase, and I had no one to say it to. When 'Monkey On My Back' finished, with a resounding slam, Peel said, 'That was fantastic.' At that precise instant, I felt for Peel a rich, quivering, sexual longing.

'Field of Glass' lasted about ten minutes, which I had to reluctantly admit was quite fair. The chaos bit in the middle sounded shaky and unconvincing – there was a line that went 'What would your little doggie say' that I wished McComb would remove – but the last two minutes ate up the airwaves like a Pacman. The Triffids had done wonders.

'Oh, thanks, Dave,' McComb retorted bashfully.

'No, really, it's absolutely imperative that you appreciate how brilliant it was right now.'

Meanwhile, a letter arrived from Neil. Oh God, would this beast perpetually torment us? Frightened, I ripped it open, expecting a folded-up Heinz label and a card reading, 'There are some areas in which The Triffids cannot help you. Regds, The Fox.' It was a cheque for £50. Reimbursed and light-headed, I headed back to my lair.

My twentieth birthday was scheduled for 7 December, but since my friends were scattered across the Soviet Union, I thought I'd invite The Triffids out for a drink.

'Yeah, come round,' said McComb.

They lived in a block of flats called Welbeck Court, opposite Olympia. There was a pub on the corner called the Hand and Flower, which has since been renamed Harvey Floorbanger's Hammersmith Charivari. It's nowhere near Hammersmith.

I walked down the sedate little residential turning, looking for lonely stretches. It amazed me that David McComb had written a whole song in this sleepy West Kensington side-road. A tiny lift scraped me up to their floor. It was much nicer than the house I lived in – warm, friendly, full of beer and life. There was a settee that beckoned softly to me. They were listening to side two of *Pet Sounds*. It was paradise.

The plan was to eat at a nearby Italian restaurant. I didn't eat much in those days – mad people like to stay thin – but reckoned I could handle this. Again, the restaurant was lovely and warm inside. My cold life rubbed up against the heat and enjoyed the sensation. When you're as hopeless a case as I was, straightforward acts of friendliness seem uncommonly beautiful and harsh words crush you effortlessly. I remember two things about the meal, one of each.

Firstly, they paid, which genuinely threw me. As far as I knew, they had even less money than I had. 'It's your birthday, Dave,' Casey said kindly.

Secondly, David asked me what other bands I liked. 'I really like R.E.M.,' I said. 'Do you?'

'I don't listen to Byrds rip-off bands,' he shot back, cutting me dead. I said nothing for the rest of the meal. This would have worried me all night if he hadn't later given me a birthday present back at Welbeck Court. It was an Australian 7-inch single of 'Beautiful Waste,' one of their prettiest songs, with 'Property is Condemned' on the B-side. The cover was silver and shiny and there, at last, I had my song-titles in red letters.

Later, at home, I studied my gift. 'Beautiful waste,' David sang over perfect drum tattoos and peals of trumpet. 'Terrible fever of love/Stupid feeling, making fools out of us.' I looked up from my map of the Clapham area. Did he know?

Dingwalls was fuller this time, and The Triffids were headlining. Bill Black in *Sounds* had belatedly reviewed *Treeless Plain* and written that 'Red Pony' had the best string arrangement he'd heard in his life. I wanted to know about that life. It sounded like Bill Black could help me. The support band at Dingwalls was Bush Telegraph, led by Kevin Armstrong, later David Bowie's guitarist, and I listened to them at the bar with David McComb. He was saying how frustrated he was by having to play the same set, in the same order, night after night. Already outgrowing their old songs, he was listening to more and more country music. A Triffids set held no more secrets for him.

All I did was suggest they start with 'Monkey On My Back' rather than 'I Am a Lonesome Hobo'. I had always been amazed at the ferocity of the roar in his voice as he sang the first lines of Monkey, 'I have this monkey on my back/I dare not even mention his name.' It was his big demon moment and he always rose to the occasion.

'Do it first,' I said. 'You'll scare the shit out of people.'

'Where would we put "Lonesome Hobo"?'

'After "Field of Glass". You know when it's all chaotic at the end, all white noise and feedback? Just start banging out the chords.'

'Yeah! I could do that, actually. They're both in A.'

I tried to look like I had known that all along, then gave up. He was really happy. He went back to tell the others. Being totally naïve about rock bands, I didn't know that musicians change their sex more regularly than they change their set. It's a very big deal. It's their agenda. It's their life-force, as The La's later proved when they played the same set for four years running. When I went backstage to park my coat, Martyn Casey looked up and said these magical words: 'Looks like we're playing the Dave set tonight.'

I have to be honest, it didn't work as well as I'd intended. McComb's microphone wasn't working when he roared the first lines of 'Monkey'. And the first chords of 'Lonesome Hobo' didn't sound nearly powerful enough after the chaos of 'Field of Glass'. But they tried it. For one night only, they tried it. That was the closest I got to them.

At Christmas I returned to Ireland for a while, and The Triffids moved back to Perth, their London stint complete. They had done everything they could have. Maybe, leaving Heathrow, they experienced some kind of professional satisfaction. Maybe, like The Birthday Party before them, they took their exit with a sackful of stinking contempt. I wrote to McComb in Perth, wished him a happy Christmas and asked him to recommend me a country album, as a first-time buyer. He wrote back suggesting *Grievous Angel* by Gram Parsons. 'It's just perfect,' he wrote, and he was right. The New Year began with me in scared limbo and The Triffids on the cover of the *NME*.

Back to London came the inmates from Voronezh, but we were too estranged to be proper friends again. They had seen things I hadn't.

The Triffids came over to play the University of London Union in the spring. It was a prestige show for them. Martyn Casey spotted me in the bar before the gig and took me backstage; this required official passes and it was obvious that The Triffids were on a new, elevated level. Also, they had added a sixth musician, 'Evil' Graham Lee, on pedal steel. They now had organ, violin, raging drums and pedal steel. The sound they made was thrilling. But afterwards, in an overcrowded dressing room, McComb looked weary and irritated to see me. I said I'd catch him soon, and left for home. *You'll get over it*, a pragmatic inner voice counselled me, *you little loser. Stop snivelling and set to work. It's the beginning of your life.*

I couldn't help but agree with this voice wholeheartedly, beating out a familiar waltz on my pockets and thinking furiously as I ate up the miles.

Goin' Out of My Head

JOHN FORDHAM

Wes Montgomery didn't take up the guitar until 1944, when he was nineteen. Not unreasonably, the neighbours complained about the racket, so he abandoned the plectrum and used the flat part of his thumb instead. A unique sound was born. For four years he wouldn't leave his Indianapolis house and six children until star band-leader Lionel Hampton tempted him on to the road. He recorded a succession of classic jazz albums in the early sixties for Riverside, but with a switch to Verve in 1964 embraced the mainstream and achieved a Top 5 American single with the Grammy winning 'Goin' Out of My Head' in 1966. He died of a heart attack in 1968, aged 43.

Browsing through a shiny piece of coffee-table commodity fetishism known as the *Ultimate Guitar Book*, looking at the pictures of those National Steels and Travis Beans and lean, low-flying Strats and recalling the words of *Wayne's World* ('It will be mine, oh yes...') it all came back to me. How it had all started with the guitar.

It was a sunburst Gibson semi-acoustic single cutaway with pearl inlays that looked as if they'd been personally inserted by five hundred fretworking gnomes sweating night and day for a month. The soundbox glittered with dancing highlights, the tuning nuts shone. But it wasn't in a shop window, or being heaved around a stage by performers who looked like prototypes for Spinal Tap. It was on an imported Riverside Records album sleeve, and it was in the hands of a crop-headed, genial-looking black man too big for his suit. This was the sixties, when most of the pop icons likely to make much sense to a teenager with a personality vacuum were gaunt-looking, scrawny white men not in suits. But it looked great to me. I played guitar a bit, like a lot of kids. But this one, bigger and more traditional-looking than the minimalist, toy-coloured Fenders, seemed to be saying something the others weren't.

The instrument was a Gibson E175. The guitarist was no teenage role model but a man hitting forty, with mouths to feed, who hated leaving his home town, and who looked like a cab-driver. He sat down to play, he had a serene, unaffected smile on his face, as if sunning himself on a porch while he ripped out impossible-sounding lines. He plucked the strings with a bare thumb rather than a pick, and sounded as if he never even used the treble pickup, let alone beat his amp with his guitar for the feedback or gave house room to reverb. His name was Wes Montgomery.

In the past couple of years a young black Briton, Ronny Jordan, has had hit records with a mix of Wes's freewheeling style and a blend of hip-hop and soul grooves, and George Benson has been a big-time, stadium-soul act for years on a foundation built by Wes. Pat Metheny has been a disciple since his teens. But back then, nobody here knew him from a hole in a soundbox.

In 1965, getting interested in a player like Wes as a teenager with no access to any arty Boho circles consigned you to a pretty monastic sphere of cultural discourse. You could drop the name 'Wes Montgomery' into all the coffee-bar conversations and stumbling, acne-inhibited seduction routines you liked, without so much as fluttering your audience's mascara in a flicker of recognition – and from blokes the reaction might be even more actively indifferent, at least where I was living out in the North London suburbs.

The Beatles were just beginning an occupancy of the Number 1 spot from which they would hardly be shifted for the next five years, the Stones and The Who were moving up, and anybody who wanted anything with more integrity pinned on its sleeve was into Bob Dylan. Modern jazz was supposed to be for eggheads – repressed, anti-social, romantic intellectual snobs who walked with stoops and were recognizable by their dog-eared copies of Camus and Kerouac, or the newly launched *Private Eye* poking out of crumpled cord-jackets.

I didn't really know where I belonged in all this. Rock and pop seemed to be the soundtrack to a party that a lot of people were having a ball at but for which I didn't know the address. Folk music seemed to be made by finger-waggers who didn't like jokes, and who sounded like the curate deep in an elaborate deception involving dusty buckskins and a shit-kicking accent. I liked the whiff of existentialist angst of modern jazz fans, descended from the fifties Beats, but there weren't any proper ones at my school because the parents were all branch managers of grocery chains and thus didn't spawn tortured Byronic types. Anyway, I suspected you had to be raised somewhere nearer to Hampstead to meet any. It was a rudderless and mapless existence. But Wes seemed to beckon, as if he knew somewhere worth going to.

I did have one soul-mate who liked Wes too. It was, in fact, my friend Dave who had discovered that precious Riverside album, even if it was by accident. He was a Shadows fan, but had lobbed out the cash equivalent of a 1990s Japanese Blue Note import CD, just because of that picture of the Gibson. Nobody else gave a monkey's.

It wasn't as if I hadn't tried to get where the action was so obviously supposed to be. Not so long before all this I had heard one night, down the single earpiece of a tiny, tinny transistor radio (you had to stick your finger in the other ear), both The Beatles' 'Love Me Do' and the Stones' 'Come On', and felt an eerie tingling deep in the synapses. This was certainly better than The Shadows, my previous connection with pop music. It sounded as if it was coming from somewhere more rugged and real than across the desk of a Denmark Street music publisher's office.

It was all the better for the effort it had taken to get in touch in the first place, of course. In the enterprising build-your-own-British-Empire mode cultivated by fifties boys' magazines like *The Eagle* (techno-fetishism designed to keep your hands off your own or other people's anatomy and get you into grammar school), I had attempted making my own crystal-set radio at first. But it could only get the Light Programme (the forerunner of Radio 2), sounding as if it was being beamed from an outside lavatory somewhere in Millwall in a hailstorm. The crystal-set's mail-order successor wasn't much better, but you could at least get Radio Luxembourg, which was where you stood the faintest chance of hearing any music that didn't resemble the soundtrack to *Come Dancing*. Down into the draughty, stone-flagged basement of our crumbling Gormenghast home came The Beatles and the Stones. But it didn't just make me want to listen, I wanted to join in. They were English for chrissakes. The Stones were on the pub circuit in Richmond, wherever that was.

In common with teenagers throughout those few hot years from the mid fifties to the mid sixties, I discovered that the doors to making music had been flung open. It was as if there was a mass movement, a pilgrimage, a mission, a sense of all being drawn to a Lost Ark by unseen forces. I borrowed a Spanish guitar somebody had bought in Woolworth's for a fiver, and learned a few chords, pretty quickly. I acquired the *Bert Weedon's Play in a Day* manual. It was a wonderful leftover from the showband and danceband era, a phenomenal anachronism featuring a dapper, smiling man in a suit with a bank clerk's haircut proudly disclosing the chords to 'When the Saints Go Marching In', but the new guitar generation hadn't had the time or inclination to rush out the appropriate infrastructural stuff yet. It had the Three Chord Trick and that was enough.

But the Spanish guitar had the wrong shape. It made you look like a folkie, and the school-teachers liked you playing it, so it was definitely out. I abandoned it in favour of a hand-made clone of a Fender Stratocaster that one of the sixth-formers had built and then ditched due to the spinal curvature involved in carrying it around, the guitar being apparently fashioned from Formica-veneered lead, with a finger-board as wide as the Grand Canyon and strings that could have supported a suspension bridge. But it looked right from a safe distance.

We were all on a roll, of course. It wasn't good enough just to be a group of mates who hung around coffee bars, nudged each other at the same girls, dreamed the same dreams and then went home for tea. You had to make music. Everybody seemed to be trying to. The skiffle movement of a few years before, a low-rent offshoot of traditional jazz and country music involving washboards and home-made basses made out of broom handles and string, had sparked off the notion that anybody could do it. The dawn of democratic music-making, no longer the preserve of Archer Street professionals in suits who could read the dots, had come. We had learned the movements The Shadows made on stage before we learned the chords to the tunes. We had bought little sleeveless leather jerkins and narrow knitted ties. We pored over the Selmer and Fender catalogues for details of amps and instruments, we made expeditions to the West End on Saturday mornings to press our noses against the windows of the guitar shops.

I played on the impossible DIY Strat for about a year. First of all, I learned all the instrumental tunes I could that you could play on the open strings, which made it easier, though playing a solid with no amplifier meant you had to crane your neck over the strings a bit. I bought Shadows sheet music and learned tunes like 'Apache' and 'Wonderful Land'. I didn't learn the chords to songs. This wasn't a communal activity godammit, it was a serious private activity, something you could get on with in your bedroom without leaving marks on the sheets. But after a year I was bored. If you weren't physically cut out to be a rock guitar hero, three chords were three chords and blues licks were blues licks. I didn't know then that it wasn't just the notes – I could rip most combinations of those off nearly all the records I heard by this time, from Keith Richards to black guitar masters like Lonnie Mack and Chuck Berry – but the way that you hit them, and I never found that out until years later.

But just when the guitar honeymoon was cooling, just when it seemed there was neither enough to hold on to in the technicalities of the music or the dim promise of stardom, groupies and six-album contracts, Wes appeared.

When Dave and I finally got over staring at the picture of him and his machine and actually played the record, we were awed but faintly disappointed at first. The music operated in a strange time, a kind of ambiguous, undulating flow rather than the cheery thump of Ringo's or Charlie Watts's backbeat. It was very quiet, the guitar sound being soft and blurry like a bass, and there were no big raucous climaxes. Nobody sang, and the tunes were either Tin Pan Alley ballads or fast, jerky themes with notes spraying all over the room. It sounded vibrant but private. That was the way I fondly, and mostly mistakenly, imagined myself to be, only I was nervous most of the time, and Wes didn't look like a man who knew the meaning of the word. But I knew by now that rock'n'roll was too much for me at fifteen. It was clearly all about sex, and I'd read enough D. H. Lawrence and Norman Mailer to know I wasn't ready for that.

This other music was expert, cool, unconcerned with transient fashions or on-stage posing. Some of its exponents, like Miles Davis, even ignored the audience altogether. I had to learn this haughty, mysterious language for myself. It would be like a hobby, it would occupy solitary hours on end, it would be something to be proud of, now that unveiling working models of the Ark Royal wasn't getting the respect it once did.

Trouble was, we knew absolutely nothing about where this stuff had come from, and there were apparently no easy ways to find out, at least not at the northernmost end of the Piccadilly Line. Piccadilly itself seemed an awful long way away, let alone Indianapolis or 52nd Street, and though the runes on distinguishing the subtle nuances between jazz styles were probably written on a stone buried somewhere in W1, prising its whereabouts out of the initiates looked a tough job. The secrets were locked in the black-sweatered bosoms of the bearded, heavy-spectacled cognoscenti who flicked silently and balefully through the record racks in sanctified premises like Dobell's in Charing Cross Road. If you asked them a dumb question, they gave you a look that could freeze your blood.

The only information that was in common currency was a skimpy collection of clichés. There was 'trad' (fat blokes in bowlers and striped shirts waving trombone slides around), which had regularly been in the Hit Parade before the arrival of The Beatles bounced it forever, and 'modern' (thin, nervous-looking blokes in shades and Italian suits apparently playing for their own amusement and trying to stop you figuring out what the tune was), and nothing in between. Wes wasn't thin and nervous-looking, and his music was breezier than much post-war jazz, but it was definitely 'modern'. People hearing it constantly said things like, 'It's all right, this stuff, but I like to hear a bit of a tune.'

Worse still, this quest was throwing up some logistical obstacles which needed a bit of capital investment. The main snag was that I hadn't got a record player or any means of reproducing sounds. This is where my mother comes into it. Her strange relationship to soundwaves was a crucial brick in the wall, or maybe hole in the wall.

I lived alone with my mother and Oedipus. She was a small but powerful, obsessive, mercurial and hilarious individual with a terror of spending money and a paint-blistering temper. When roused she made so much noise and hurled so many blunt objects around the premises that the cat used to hide behind the kitchen boiler and you had to be fast on your feet and hedgehop the furniture to negotiate the trajectories. None the less, she hated most kinds of noise she wasn't personally initiating, including music and the sound of other human beings. (I should say that this is not meant as a vengeful observation.) Sounds meant the airing of the ideas and wills of other inhabitants of the planet, and rival wills made her paranoid. We therefore didn't have any records in the house, or any means of playing any. The television set (a big mahogany box on curly legs like a Queen Anne cabinet – all unhealthy twentieth-century technology had to be disguised as if it derived from something with a classier pedigree, like a gentleman's club) had a radio too, but we never turned it on. Those unfamiliar, declamatory voices made it seem to my mother as if the barricades to our castle had been breached and the human race had got in. It was OK with telly, you could see from the patterns on the armchairs that they were safely having a chat round at their place.

But though my mum was putting off recognizing the implications of my adolescence as long as possible (so was I for that matter, it looked like a can of worms to me), she was at least coming slowly to terms with the possibility that my interests might now stretch to something noisier than tearing the wrapping off a model kit. At Christmas around 1963, after a lot of wheedling, she stumped up the cash for a second-hand Philips reel-to-reel tape recorder, not without the traditional hand-to-hand combat with the shop's staff over the resale price. I went straight to Dave's place with it and taped the Wes disc.

Then came the hard part. Having committed that quietly swinging, breezy music with its dazzling fast runs and soft, nudging chordwork to the tape, I sat for hour after hour playing the same few bars over and over. How did he hit that octave run so fast? How did he sound all those semiquavers so clearly without dropping or muffling any? More to the point, where did he get all this stuff from? People said musicians like him made it up as they went along. How was such a thing possible?

Nobody knew. I started buying more complicated guitar tutors, chordbooks laid out like telephone directories (the more chords they put in the better value for money they thought it was, and the more bewildered you were) and a few handbooks written by practising jazz guitarists I'd never heard of. I wanted Wes to do his own guitar tutor, I was sure he'd make it easy, but since all his sleeve notes repeated stories of how he'd held down a day job while performing in a nightclub for years to feed an apparently vast family, it didn't sound as though he'd find the time. The books I did get were mostly incomprehensible – the only decipherable sentiments were little sentences with screamers at the end saying things like 'follow my method and PLAY JAZZ!!!' – and assumed a working knowledge of scales I'd never had the application to acquire. Dimly though, I began to get some insights. Beginning haltingly to introduce variations on the solos I'd learned note for note, I started to discover that I'd acquired the fundamentals of a good many scales without knowing it. Crucial to many of the tunes and much of the phrasing was the blues, which was at least a common language and as central to what was then in the charts as it was to *Bert Weedon's Play in a Day*. And, though the technical challenge of making a fresh chord change every beat or two was pretty daunting, clearly there were clusters of notes that belonged with certain chords and which were the raw material of jazz improvisation. But the yawning abyss between beginning to wrap the head around this and being able to do it with the freedom and relaxation and panache that Wes did seemed unbridgeable.

I learned this particular fact of life the hard way. Moving from school to university in the North seemed at first to shine a light into some previously darkened corners. The place had a Jazz Society! It took small knots of lip-chewing enthusiasts to the Free Trade Hall in Manchester when big-time American jazz stars came through! The president of this intimate little organization was a schooled piano player with black-rimmed specs and a leather jacket (the kind now only seen on Polish dock-workers), who dropped names like Bud Powell. They wanted anybody who could play to audition for a band. I took my guitar and waited for an opportunity to play my Wes party-pieces. 'The Street, in B flat,' came a voice from somewhere inside the leather jacket, and away he went. What did he mean? Were we supposed to go outside and play? (This turned out to be shorthand for a staple jazz 32-bar chord progression, Green Dolphin Street). But as the pumping chords from the direction of that hunched and forbidding back view swept towards me, and the stalking line of the double-bass seemed to beckon but with notes whose relevance I couldn't fathom, I realized there was no way in without knowing the rules.

Wes might have taught himself, never read a note of music in his life, gone on the road with Lionel Hampton at seventeen after six months playing from scratch, but though I was never reluctant to admit he was a genius, maybe I had to face the fact that I might not be. But then, he had grown up in the homeland of jazz, at a time when the music was commercially big, in a family with a pianist and bassist for brothers, in a neighbourhood where the local nightclub musicians were people you'd been to school with, not at the end of the Piccadilly line. These things couldn't have done him any harm. That was my story.

I stopped playing early in this briefly thrilling episode and let the others blow, crouching concernedly over the guitar and fiddling with the tuning as if professionally fastidious about accuracy. 'Can't you even tune it?' came the voice from the leather jacket. I did go back to the Jazz Society, even heard one of my all-time favourite discs, Miles Davis's *Kind of Blue*, for the first time there, but I never took the guitar again.

The only comfort to be salvaged from this episode was wrapped up with the fact that socially, even in a far more variously populated community like a university, this kind of music was still out to lunch. In other words, none of my friends and none of the women I fancied from near or far would have dreamt of going to the Jazz Society, so this humiliation remained a secret. So indifferent to such vulgarities of life as gossip were the Jazz Society members, that they could be relied on to show no interest whatever in passing the story around. So I kept practising, but by this time I was starting to repeat myself. The big surge of learning new stuff, apparently bursting open a door every few days by how fast I could get my fingers around the woodwork, was ending. Now I had a rough idea of the kind of structural stuff I needed. A year of just practising chords and related scales, not just trying to repeat somebody else's licks, would have cracked it. But I was losing my myopic, Airfix-kit concentration.

The world was getting too distracting. Us baby-boomers, gambolling in the short-lived sunshine of a post-fifties economic upswing, mass-marketing to youth, good employment prospects, the contraceptive pill, soft drugs and overnight meritocratic expansion in education, were beginning to doubt the grey fifties conviction that only diligence earned you the right to a good time, and even then a little of it would go a long way. My mother, an anxious but vigorous hedonist for most of her pre-parental life, never shared this view, but replaced it with the equally inhibiting one that you weren't safe out there for a minute.

Around about this time, my understanding of jazz and a passing knowledge of other significant performers who didn't just play it on guitars blossomed. I met another student piano player, a much less forbidding individual who didn't wear a leather jacket, and he liked some of the guitar/piano discs that the white guitarist Jim Hall – a more private, introverted player than Wes – had made with the great pianist Bill Evans. Not only did we play some of them together, he showed me how Green Dolphin Street worked, and how you could make a jazz blues sound a lot more interesting if you didn't play it all in major chords. He loved Wes Montgomery: 'There are a handful of jazz musicians who can play anything they can think, and he's one.' That was the first piece of considered and insightful analysis I'd ever had from anyone about Wes.

With hindsight, I can see what was happening to me in music then. Way further back down the line, out in the foothills of a mountain I never would climb, I was encountering what most of the middle generation of today's jazz guitar players – John Scofield and Pat Metheny for starters – were going through too. They were hearing soft, scurrying guitar bop like Wes's, but they were hearing The Beatles, The Doors and soon Hendrix too. It was hard to go on playing Wes's way after all these other hurricanes had passed over. Late in my university time, I almost recovered a little of the obsessive midnight woodshedding preoccupations I'd had a few years earlier, but this time with Eric Clapton licks from Cream records. Cream functioned like a jazz trio, trading ideas, playing long improvised instrumental breaks. Jack Bruce and Ginger Baker, the bassist and drummer, were formerly jazz artists.

And what was happening in Wes's life was making it harder on his fans too. One vacation, with some money to spare, I bought my first record player and a new Wes disc to inaugurate it with. It looked great, there he was on the cover again, still clutching the same guitar, this time striding purposefully across the artwork. The disc was called *Movin' Wes*. The record label had changed, but I didn't know that made any odds then. Riverside Records, Verve Records, what was the difference? He was with a big band, that was a departure. But it just showed they were taking him seriously. Wes was worth a little more investment than just four guys and a couple of mikes.

The first track, Ellington's 'Caravan', was a bit brash and glitzy and the brass section did a lot of tight, session-man riffing, and Wes played a lot of chords and octaves rather than tear-it-up single-line runs, but it was OK. Maybe this was just the sweetener, to hook new listeners.

Or maybe not. The whole album was like it. Wes's solos

were shorter, they were mostly restricted to manipulating the textures of his unique soft sound rather than giving him open spaces to blow in, the contributions from the others were mostly straight from the written parts and the material was unremarkable.

This was disappointing, but it was to get worse. Wes expanded his audience so fast by these compromises that he won a Grammy Award in 1966 for the pop adaptation 'Goin' Out of My Head', and *A Day in the Life*, for A&M, was the biggest-selling jazz album of 1967. I didn't buy it. Though history has confirmed that very little of what Wes played on these later records was a patch on his early work improvisationally, it's also true that many of the reasons for my attitude were cultural snobbery. Though I always denied it when challenged, part of the pleasure of being a modern jazz fan then was that most people weren't, and involvement in the music was a badge of indifference to mainstream fashions. The corporate leisure industry was the enemy to a good many students raised on Herbert Marcuse, and Wes's kind of jazz seemed pure – untainted by marketing departments or image-makers because it was of no commercial interest to them. 'Selling out' was a serious crime then. And it wasn't just when jazz went funky or soft that it happened. The first time Bob Dylan played London with the electric Band and himself in a gold suit, a lot of people in duffle coats left the gigs in apoplectic and uncomprehending fury.

You could, however, still be a Pure Guitarist in student social circles, and I worked pretty shrewdly at it as long as I kept the volume and the quantity down, and the atmosphere of cool 'I like to play' understatement up, always stopping just when the other people in the room realized where the music was coming from and modestly admitting that, yes, you had made it all up and, no, it wasn't really as tricky as it sounded. You had to look like someone who had all this music inside you that you wouldn't let out for just anybody, and you didn't take requests. The opening softly caressed melody I'd ripped off from Wes's 'Days of Wine and Roses' would often do the trick, or the lazy swing of 'West Coast Blues'. It was remarkable how many stoned individuals you could jam into those cramped, fetid, chaotic student rooms in which you could pick up the tables by the coffee cups stuck to their surfaces, and just occasionally the blonde curled up on the floor in the haze would wind up letting her head drift against your knee as you kept those silky semiquavers coming, a faraway look in the eye. It was always worth trying to capitalize on this effect as the evening drew to a close, but she'd usually be asleep. Hendrix reputedly didn't share this problem, and I couldn't altogether convince myself it was only because he played louder.

Friends could fall out over Wes too, and it seemed bizarre considering he'd clearly never hurt a fly. When I see the pictures from the former Yugoslavia, a semi-sobering, semi-farcical image comes into my mind of a blazing late sixties day on the beach at Dubrovnik, facing a torrent of abuse from one of four bosom buddies with whom I'd travelled across Europe in a bumpy student train, suitcases optimistically weighed down with condoms, on the assumptions and presumptions of modern jazz. 'It's just for pseuds,' came the complaining litany across the burning sand. 'Wes Montgomery couldn't keep a cocktail lounge awake. It's just so you can patronize people who buy pop records. Look at Miles Davis. He can't play in tune and he can't stand the audience anyway.' And so on. I lurched off for a seething splash around in the glittering blue water, only to be driven back by a shoal of turds drifting rapidly inland. It was that kind of a day.

Then, in 1968, only a few short years after I had discovered him, without ever having seen him work in person, he was gone. A young folkie who was living in my mother's house, who played banjo and guitar and bought the guitar buffs' magazines, told me Wes Montgomery had died of a heart attack back in his home town of Indianapolis. He was forty-three. I couldn't believe it. Even if the passion had lost its urgency a little, I was sure I'd hear him play one day, maybe get to shake that big, reassuring hand, examine that famous contortionist's thumb, perhaps even show him I could play a little 'West Coast Blues'.

Without knowing it or knowing why, Wes had shown me much of what was good, not just about jazz but about all music. How performances of commitment and energy exert a power that transcends the vehicles they travel on. How rhythmic drive is fundamental to jazz improvisation and transforms the most mundane of melodies. How musicians should never seek to camouflage the quirks of their own personalities and histories, or avoid the pull of what seems right to them. Wes's unique methods included the thumb-picking single-note style, which released his right-hand digits to build the armoury of octave clusters and fleeting chordal runs that became his trademark – he did it because nobody told him he couldn't.

I went on celebrating Wes, on and off, long afterwards. I kept my guitar – a half-decent red Harmony semi-acoustic by this time – and though long months went by when broken strings didn't get replaced, I'd get bursts of enthusiasm for it and practise like hell. All the same old pieces mostly, although John McLaughlin's 'Binky's Beam' made it shakily into the repertoire. From time to time I met people with the same preoccupations, and occasionally we'd just play, way into the night. It happened one time on a trans-European train with a Swedish student who couldn't speak any English. It happened once on the second date with someone from whom I'd gleaned the notion after the first that a lot of meaningful communication was still to come. Wes just got in the way with his big smile and his beating right foot. We found ourselves crashing at a guitar player's house at midnight. 'I'll be right up,' I said. Three hours, most of a bottle of malt whisky, and all of the Montgomery repertoire the guitarist and I could remember later, I finally got up to the room. 'Guitar widow' came a voice from under the duvet. This time, though, Wes let me get on with the rest of my life.

*

Me and Dave, the guy who opened the box in the first place by buying that beautiful record, still regularly met for most of the seventies. He'd come round with his guitar and we'd play for hours, him strumming, me whacking off solo lines that now inevitably owed as much to Clapton and John Lee Hooker as well as Wes. Nothing surprising happened, it was like the same commuters meeting on the same bus to have the same chat, but it was always a pleasure. Then we'd talk about it down the pub – always the same order, two halves of Double Diamond twice, two rounds of Scotch & American. I wished sometimes, after I'd started to hear guitar guerrillas like Sonny Sharrock and Derek Bailey, that I could have found an angrier ritual to repeat, in which we tore down these elegant tapestries instead of keeping on rehanging them. But Wes's way was gentle, it was hard to get mad at it.

By the usual string of accidents, something called a career slowly stumbled into existence. In the first few days at University, I had met a couple of guys who also played, and though they weren't crazy about jazz – one preferred The Doors and The Who, the other was a fine acoustic guitarist who liked percussive folk-blues styles like those of Bert Jansch and John Renbourn – they had ears big enough to know something was happening. I had played a lot of folksy stuff with Bob, the guitarist, during my four years in the North. The other one said he was a bass player and that we should form a band, but though I never saw him with a bass in all the four years, we got close and worked on magazines instead. A year before we were due to graduate, he said he was going back to London because he had a great idea for a magazine. Get away, I said, it'll go down the plug and we won't even have any letters after our names. He was Tony Elliott and the magazine was *Time Out*. A couple of years later, after I'd got the letters after my name and was working in a garage, his voice came on the line. 'You like jazz don't you?' he enquired in his usual brisk fashion. 'Wes Montgomery and all that stuff. We need somebody to review jazz for the records pages. You get £1.10 for a fee, or you can keep the record.' Fantastic, I thought. And that was that.

Sometime in the early eighties, and now a regular jazz writer, I interviewed Pat Metheny in London. Metheny was promoting a new record, and we talked about his past and his plans. When time was running out, we somehow got on to the subject of Wes. Metheny, always affable, became euphoric, a fan. He had adored Wes from when he was a kid, he said, that free-rolling relaxation, those long lines, the delicate chord playing, the cherishing of melody. The interview started all over again, and the next time we met, a couple of years later, we picked up where we'd left it.

In the 1990s, the first jazz record to have made it into the British pop charts since the boom for Dave Brubeck and traddies like Kenny Ball and Acker Bilk thirty years before, made Ronny Jordan a hot ticket. There was a backbeat all right, but the guitar sound was pure Wes, gliding octaves, plush chordwork, slinky runs and all. Well, it wasn't pure Wes. Jordan wasn't really an improviser, and his lines didn't make your jaw drop. But it was a gesture of respect, and it made me feel good to be at his gigs. Somehow it was more honest and forthright than the hi-tech tributes of a much more skilful and experienced guitarist like Lee Ritenour, who released an album of Wes pieces at much the same time in which he even sampled The Master and played alongside him on 'West Coast Blues'. Ritenour was doing something I had yearned to do myself, but not once Wes was dead. Still, that was his way of showing he cared. Wes was like a friend we all knew. He'd helped us grow up.

Eat Yourself Whole

STEVE LAMACQ

There are three people in Kingmaker. They hail from Hull, home of The Housemartins, they tour a lot and it was once said they were Wonder Stuff clones. Bespectacled singer Loz Hardy resembles *Alfie*-period Michael Caine. Words like 'guts', 'passion', 'romance' and 'unpleasantness' are bandied around willy-nilly where Kingmaker are concerned, and their debut album, *Eat Yourself Whole*, had artwork which featured sperm. On tour they eat, drink, sleep, soundcheck, travel and sometimes play concerts, just like any other band. They have not broken through to the mainstream quite yet, but hopes remain high.

'So, let's get this straight,' an astonished colleague at the *New Musical Express* once said. 'You're taking a week off to go on tour?' The suggestion in his voice was that a week away is meant for hiking in the Lake District, or decorating the flat, or making that optician's appointment you never usually get round to.

Yet there I was affirming that, yes, indeed I was going away to follow a group around the country for six days. And whatever explanation I came out with at the time to justify my gig-going fixation (ones I've tried in the past include the meek 'I like being on tour' and 'It's a good way of finding out what's happening musically in the rest of the country'), there was no way of curing his disbelief. He had spotted what I'd known for some time: that music is the fixation which became my job, and that following bands on tour is one of its obvious symptoms. It's the tour that's my obsession, not individual bands, although I don't do this kind of thing with anyone.

It is a ritual experience for me, like going to a football match or getting dressed up as a teenager for the local disco. You get the nerves, the hopes, the sudden panic attacks about transport and where you're going to stay afterwards. You get the thrill of Being There, in a crowd, and feeling part of the atmosphere, and you get it every night, away from home, with a band who, in classic fandom terms, you insist relate to every aspect of your life.

In recent grillings, I've taken to quoting from a song by long forgotten early-eighties anarcho-pop group Zoundz as my defence. The lyric, from a single called 'Demystification', goes, 'I'm not looking for escapism, I just want to escape.' And that, in essence, is what following a band across miles of motorway provides.

When I was threatened with the sack from my first job as a junior reporter with the *West Essex Gazette*, I went on tour (Newtown Neurotics); when my first long-term relationship ended, I went on tour (The Moss Poles); and when I was suffering a bout of disillusionment with the music industry while working at the *NME*, I went on tour to rekindle the feelings I once had (Mega City 4).

It's not just that gigs are still the backbone of rock music. My obsession is also accounted for by the fact that you can lose yourself in another world of motorway services, soundchecks and conversations with strangers about the merits of obscure B-sides. I become fidgety at home if I don't get away every few months. Writing this piece unsettled me so much that I had to break off half-way through to see Blur in Nottingham. Okay, it was only one date – not the real thing – but it was outside London, and involved trains, laminates and seeing the new set before any of my friends.

Plus, the bands I've trekked round after have always seemed to mirror different times in my life (as well as the above there was a Soup Dragons/My Bloody Valentine tour in 1987 which summed up a time of optimism in my life and coincided with the rebirth of my fanzine, *A Pack of Lies*). And then there was – and still is – Kingmaker, a three-piece from Hull whose power-driven, passionate and tense pop music has been a source of inspiration since late 1990. Originally I'd dismissed their first demo – recorded under the appalling name of Tombstone Graffiti – as a poor collision of The Wonder Stuff, U2 and retro pub blues (the harmonica solos were enough in themselves to provide the pillars for my conscientious objections to rest upon).

The first EP, *Celebrated Working Man*, didn't do much to reverse the view, yet giving them the benefit of the doubt, I saw them at London's tiny Camden Falcon and was bowled over. Myles Howell looked like a young Joe Strummer, except he was playing bass. Behind him, John Andrew was one of the most competent drummers I'd seen in years and to the other side of the stage, there was Loz Hardy, singer/guitarist, who was a mixture of anger and insecurity, confidence and vulnerability. The trio sparked off each other, just as the lyrics sparked off the music. We did an interview shortly afterwards for the *NME*, which reinforced my view that Loz had a perception and depth lacking in the competition (mostly limp so-called shoe-gazers and sorry Wonder Stuff clones). And it started from there.

The band were to fall foul of the press later in their career, as much because of the politics of the weekly music press as because of their own erratic popularity, but to me there has been a constant challenge inherent in their music and an outlook that has remained absolutely compelling. Another *NME* feature was pencilled, which we conducted at the start of their mammoth fifty-date Eat Yourself Whole tour in Sunderland and Middlesbrough at the end of 1991, and by this time I was hooked. Loz was a fascinating, ambitious young man; Myles shared with myself a similar sense of humour and love of The Clash and John Cleese; and John, while being the older, more educated third of the group, was indulging in a second teenage-hood of his own making.

Their set was a series of emotional explosions which I came to rely on, notably the bit in 'High as a Kite' where Loz starts screaming near the end. Even the harmonica in 'Pockets of St Malachi' had been excused and given its rightful place as the climax to the set. In the end I saw eighteen of the fifty dates, travelled in the van with them for a week (to escape a particularly disturbing, mid-twenties crisis birthday in London), and even determined their set-list for a while as part of a dare, so, selfishly, I made sure they played 'Hard Times', one of the overlooked tracks from their first album. It was a time of naïvety, building audiences and exceeding people's expectations. You could tell, as the autumn tour progressed, that the New Year would provide a breakthrough for them, and sure enough, it came in the second week of January. *The Idiots at the Wheel* EP, featuring lead track 'Really Scrape the Sky', went Top 30, followed by their first Top 20 single, 'Eat Yourself Whole' (though *Eat Yourself Whole* was the title of their first album, the track of the same name wasn't actually written until later on). I missed the next tour because of work commitments, but I was comforted by the knowledge that they were on their way.

By the time the Armchair Anarchist tour started in November 1992, however, the world appeared to have turned upside down. For no real reason, apart from the all-too-obvious lethargy of their record company, the next single, 'Armchair Anarchist' – their best to date – had entered the chart at a disappointing 47. Not only that, but I'd just resigned from the *New Musical Express* and didn't know what the future held. The choice, once again, was simple. Either sit at home worrying, knitting with loose ends, trying sensibly to rebuild my life outside the music press, or make the escape on tour. There was no contest really.

The opening dates of the AA jaunt were in Scotland, which I ruled out because of expense. Instead I took the train to Leicester on a mild Saturday, arriving too early, as always, and spending too much money on a Super Mario pinball machine in a local amusement arcade.

It is Kingmaker whom I blame for my pinball addiction which lasts to this day (although I'm over the worst of it now, honest). When the band you're following disappear to sound-check, you become painfully aware that you are, frankly, a spare part in the operation, and no amount of standing by the sound-desk, nodding sagely as the engineer fiddles with the snare-drum levels is going to alter the fact. You are left to kill time any way you can. On the Eat Yourself Whole tour Loz had challenged me to a game of pinball – Bride of Pinbot, at the Windsor Old Trout to be precise – which he won convincingly. But I stayed on, to offset the pre-gig tedium, ramming £1 coins into the machine for a full hour afterwards, and was lost forever.

Steve Rispin, guitar tech on the tour, later told me he had wasted nearly a term's grant while at college after becoming addicted to pinball. Like an alcoholic and beer, he refuses to play now. And that's why, come soundcheck, you'll find me in the Student Union bar instead of helping with the merchandising, where by rights I ought to be. One day we'll both be on *The Time The Place*, talking to John Stapleton about the horror of our shady other-lives. It won't be pleasant.

Also I was suffering first-night nerves before the Leicester gig. Joining a tour can give you the same mixed emotions as meeting an old schoolfriend you haven't seen for ages. Have you grown apart? Will you still get on? Never mind that by this point I used to speak to Loz quite regularly on the phone and that we'd become friends to the point of swapping tapes and meeting for a drink when he was in London to see the record company. You still become paranoid about intruding on something that ultimately you're not directly part of. So I ambled to Leicester University, rehearsing some nifty entrance lines and hoping that the single's comparative failure hadn't taken the wind out of their sails.

There was nothing to worry about. My magnificent opener, 'All right, how's it going?' worked and we watched some TV in the dressing room, while catching up with the gossip. The first three dates of the tour had gone well and there was no sign of the crowds dropping away, as this Leicester show illustrated. Although an ambitious size, the Union looked fairly full with 500 people in, and the band played well, with Loz in confident mood. When someone in the audience lobbed a jumper on to the stage, he picked it up and proclaimed, 'Which fashion victim threw this?'

After the gig we went to an indie club in the city centre, with Loz still on a roll. 'Pernod and water please barman ... two cubes of ice. Hey, that's tap water! I want bottled water.' Obviously we were welcomed with open arms.

The morning after in the hotel foyer is always a farcical affair. When people talk of the class divide in this country I immediately think of the hotel foyer. It epitomizes the whole Us Them rock'n'roll ethic, which, despite everything, you tumble into.

In one corner you have your typical, perfectly inoffensive, weekend-break residents, taking coffee before a hard day's tourist activity. One of them, you then decide, works in a bank, and therefore is a member of the filthy white-collar rat-race, which stands for everything you have ever tried to avoid in life, and you vow never to get a proper job ever. Obviously your state of mind on tour, deprived of sleep, works on a very basic level.

Round another table, which establishes itself as base-camp, various members of band and crew emerge bleary-eyed, looking dishevelled, tired or hungover. Far from loosely falling into place, most tours have a pattern that is both reassuring and, well, pretty dull. Having agreed a leaving time the previous night, you sit in the lobby; one person (in our case Loz) is always late; the tour manager phones the offender's room and the culprit lies that he'll be down in ten minutes, before finally showing his face half an hour later. There is much muttering about leaving him behind. It never happens.

Then, if you're lucky, you travel in the tour bus or Transit van, the ultimate symbol of being genuinely part of things. How many soccer fans would like to travel away with Arsenal or, in my rather sad case, sit on Colchester United's team coach bound for Darlington? It would, of course, be fantastic beyond human comprehension. It allows an undiluted insight into the individual personalities of the band and the way they tick. It also, helpfully, says that magical phrase, 'I'm with the band.'

At Leicester I was bracing myself for the trip when the routine fell apart. One of the vans had been broken into in the street outside during the night, and two boxes of money-spinning T-shirts had been stolen. Getting your van broken into on tour is an occupational hazard, but that doesn't lessen the anger when it actually happens.

Tour manager Matt led the convoy of two vans and a truck through the unnervingly complex one-way system to the police station so we could report the theft. After about fifteen minutes of sitting in the main mini-bus, agitation levels slowly rising, Myles went in to find out what was happening. He re-appeared five minutes later with a cup of hot chocolate from the police station vending machine. 'I told the guy behind the desk this was the best café in town. He didn't seem amused.' It happens.

You get characters in any office, job or drinking circle, but the music industry is overcrowded with them – especially on the road, where real life is suspended. The cast for the Armchair Anarchist tour included several, notably the group's regular soundman, Bo. Shaven-headed, with a coarse London accent, impish grin and the capacity to out-grumble anyone, he was a dream quote-machine. Already on a previous tour we'd noticed his catchphrase – when arriving at a venue, he'd look at the mixing desk, scratch his chin and say, in no uncertain terms, 'I don't like that.' The cause of his gloom could have been anything from 'I don't like red faders, I like black faders,' to 'I don't like the look of those speakers.'

He played an integral part on the Eat Yourself Whole tour where one night he led a videoed commando raid through the corridors of a hotel in Reading. Stopping at the door of Steve Rispin, he and the rest of the band stuck toilet paper across the entire doorframe, so that when Rispin emerged in the morning, he'd open his door to see himself barricaded in by a wall of Kleenex. Sadly, the proprietor, doing his rounds late at night, tore the paper down – and fined the group £2 for their trouble.

Bo can't go to sleep without the television on either, although whether this is a tactic he's dreamt up to dissuade people from sharing his room on tour or a genuine need is unclear. But he excelled himself even before bedtime in Nottingham. Having managed to persuade the night porter to serve us alcohol after the bar closed, we ordered drinks and settled into a discussion about The Jam and the fact that someone inexplicably wanted to go ten-pin bowling on his day off. Five minutes later the weary porter returned, managing to retain an air of politeness, when all around him social graces were flagging.

'I'm sorry sir,' he said, kneeling next to Bo's chair, 'but I'm afraid we only have one bottle of the white wine you requested. Will that be enough, or would you need some more?'

Bo, in his best brillo-pad accent, suggesting a deportment learnt at Millwall Charm School, thought for a moment and turning round to the rest of us, shouted, 'Oi, how many bottles of plonk do we want?' Perhaps you had to be there to fully appreciate this scene, but here lies another crux of the pro-touring argument. Stories like this are your own; they belong to you and your small group and nobody else will ever get the gist. Nobody else need care (in fact who does?), but it confirms that you are on the inside of the rock business.

This is why there are so many in-jokes on long tours. It separates the diehards from the chancers and part-timers. It sets you apart, when, miserably, your life is just as much a routine as the next man. We are very sad people, but we have a great laugh in the process.

In recent months, since I started DJ-ing around the country in my own right, I've analysed the touring process and honed in on its rituals. My friend and manager Tony drives, and we have the same habits as any band (we have our favourite service stations, stock moans, in-jokes). You begin to understand why groups need to wind down with at least a drink most nights, and why on long tours you have to at least try to look after yourself. It's good experience, but it's not the same as watching a band, it's just not.

The gig at Wolverhampton was being recorded for possible use on B-sides or a live album. Unfortunately, Maz, the all-too-Brummie lighting-rig man, managed to swing his huge lorry round a corner into an alleyway beside the venue and straight into the side of the Manor Mobile Recording Studio, which wasn't probably the best start to the evening. Loz and I were inside meanwhile, marvelling at guitar tech Russ Hunt's pen-knife, which hid within it, among many treasures, a screwdriver, a pen and a pair of pliers.

There are tapes of this gig in existence, and a couple of tracks eventually found their way on to the flipside of the band's single 'Saturday's Not What it Used to Be'. Generally it's agreed that this was one of the best gigs on the tour, starting with 'Everything's Changed' again going straight into 'Eat Yourself Whole', followed by Loz's greeting of 'Nice to see yer, to see yer. . .', which became his traditional opening gambit. I realize that so far I've underplayed the importance of the actual music, which is the climax of the day and in fact the whole reason why you're there, but I've always found it hard explaining why I'm moved by watching bands play live. People often ask me whether I get bored of seeing the same group every night and hearing the same songs, but they're missing the point. No two gigs are ever the same and, after all, why is seeing a band live six times in a week any different from buying a record and playing it over and over again in your own home? The more you hear music you love, the more you like it.

The Wolverhampton show was pretty typical of the set they used for the entire tour, although 'Honesty Kills' – one of the new tracks which they soundchecked with – did make a couple of appearances elsewhere. They played a mixture of old songs and material that would appear on their second album, *Sleepwalking*, including 'Sequinned Thug' and 'Sleepwalking in the 5 o'clock Shadow'. There was a fiery version of 'Lucy's Down' to close and an encore including 'Armchair Anarchist' dedicated to John Lydon, who'd been interviewed in the *Guardian* the previous weekend. 'Even *Guardian* readers can be anarchists,' explained Loz.

I missed the finale to the gig. This was the tour where the band were giving away a free flexidisc to fans at the end of the show, which entailed someone (i.e. me) standing on a table at the exit with a pile of cardboard boxes, dishing out the discs, surrounded by a swarm of punters. When we ran out of stock, I feared for my life.

With a day-off the next day, the band returned home to Hull after the show while I stayed with Bo in Wolverhampton. He fell asleep with the TV on.

To the band, a day off is a blessing. To me, it was simply a gap which reminds you that you're not actually doing anything but escaping from home. I managed to bribe Bo and Steve Rispin into dropping me off in Leeds on their way to re-join the band in Hull. My scrawled notes (always working, me) for the day read, 'Met Sarah [a longtime Kingmaker fan who was at college in Leeds] and went to see Therapy? at Duchess of York. Stayed in Headingley.'

As far as I remember, the gig was sold out. Therapy? were excellent and they played a scorching version of 'Teethgrinder'. Keith Cameron and Ed Sirrs from the *NME* had travelled up to review the show, and we went to a club afterwards where the beer was 80p a pint. It went a bit hazy after that.

If possession is nine tenths of the law, then touring with a group is your way of legally proving the ownership of your favourite band. Again there's an element of snobbery here, not to mention martyrdom, but if I've seen twenty gigs by Band A and you have seen six, then they are my band not yours. Sorry. It's an irrational argument, but one you never fail to draw on, when a drunken student stabs you in the ribs with his elbow as he hurtles out of the mosh-pit, or obscures your view, when you've spent fifteen minutes working out where to stand. The fact that these amateurs (Christ, that *is* snobbish) have every right to enjoy themselves as much as you do, if not more – after all they're only going to see one gig, and you'll be there tomorrow – doesn't come into it. So I apologize to the whole audience at Huddersfield University for my grumpy behaviour and irritated hard stares, but I couldn't get near the front and someone who probably doesn't even buy Kingmaker records knocked my drink over. So there.

The gig, though, was another strong one, despite the 'difficult' sound mix, and I did make it to the dancefloor (initially to take revenge), along with Phil and Gibb, two of Kingmaker's hard-core fans who became their T-shirt sellers. It's been said before, but there is a sort of World War I-type bond between any group's regular followers. You share your cigarettes and buy drinks for each other when one of you is strapped for cash. Anyway, Phil and Gibb's choreographed actions to 'High as a Kite' are worth two pints by anyone's exchange rate.

A few of us stayed up back at the hotel. But the drink was taking its toll. One of our party, tired and emotional, approached the night porter at 2 a.m., demanding his room key, to be told, 'I'm sorry sir, I gave you your key half an hour ago.'

I stayed on Myles's floor and we had a massive, philosophical discussion about life, the band and our ambitions. Unfortunately, just at the interesting, emotional bit, I fell asleep.

*

Staying in hotels on tour is a luxury which should never be underestimated. Many people still manage to follow tours by finding floors to crash on – or, in extreme circumstances, sleeping in railway-station waiting-rooms or service-station toilets. In my younger days, I was lucky enough to have a battered old mini which provided accommodation on tour, although, as is the nature of these things, it didn't guarantee an uninterrupted night's sleep.

After one Newtown Neurotics gig in Sunderland, I'd parked in a lay-by just outside the town, only to be awoken by a loud rapping on the window from a Military Police officer who was scouring the area for a squaddie who'd gone AWOL (I like to think of myself as someone who has the air of never having been in the army, but even after he'd realized that simple truth, he still wanted to search the back seat to make sure nobody was hiding behind me). I've also been accused of being a vagrant in Norwich, where two police officers pulled me from behind the steering wheel, claiming I'd broken into my own car, and been moved on from the car parks of many top motorway services. As a general rule, you can crash out at Watford Gap, but you'll always be moved on at Newport Pagnell.

The hotel also offers you the opportunity of a sociable drink after the gig. After Keele – a disappointing show, in a huge, sparsely populated hall – we adjourned to the hotel, where Myles and I bought two bottles of red wine and sat up talking to support band, the soon-to-be-famous Radiohead, who for once weren't travelling back to their native Oxford. Bands know they've arrived when they can afford a hotel, or even a bed and breakfast, instead of piling back into the van and driving home the same night.

You do things on tour which you would never consider in the cool environs, of say, a London club. That's why my over-riding memories of Cambridge are twofold.

The first is of me and Russ Hunt – brother of Miles from

The Wonder Stuff – dancing openly in public to an Abba record after the gig; and the second is of Russ lecturing a cigarette-handed thirteen-year-old about the perils of smoking. 'Look, I know better, he smokes and he knows better, but you will die of these things.' The kid's probably on heroin now.

For reasons as yet undivined, Cambridge concerts are populated by some of the youngest fans you'll see anywhere in the country. At the end of the gig, there are lines of parents, sometimes three deep, waiting to collect their sweat-sodden offspring. The other highlight of the day occurs in the afternoon when Myles and I spend the dull time before the soundcheck talking about his musical past. He was in a band who once played school assembly; he started off playing Clash covers and he used to be in a group whose drummer had one leg longer than the other. Kingmaker are splendid company. Loz, for instance, talks a terrific argument about music and its history, and most earnestly about his own lyrics, motivations and influences. He's a sensible and creatively inquisitive character and at the same time, he can go likeably mad on occasions, and this is exactly what the tour addict desires. Having stayed off the drink since Leicester and retired to bed early most nights, Loz made a spectacular return to the bar which we thought nothing of until the next morning and the journey to Colchester.

You secretly crave involvement on tour. That's why tasks like manning the T-shirt stall or giving away flexidiscs at the end of the gig become all important. They elevate you from the role of hanger-on or journalist or record company employee to being part of the crew. It is the same reason that tour laminates – the passes that provide 'access all areas' – are so sought after. In a way, it confirms your existence (you become invisible to security guards and fans without one).

It's always occurring to me that if I'd been born a girl I'd be considered a groupie, but because I'm a man I'm simply a moderately eccentric enthusiast. We are all just infatuated with watching the band, and our motives for hanging around them don't change with our sex. But anyway, for the Colchester University gig I got the job of chaperoning the fast-fading Loz. The morning after the Cambridge gig he had telephoned hotel reception to ask advice on how to put his shirt on and things went downhill from there. Still lubricated from the night before, he started drinking in the bus en route to Colchester. On arrival he'd fallen asleep under the glove compartment.

Attempts to revive him with black coffee at the University failed rather dismally (and the rambling phone call he made to his mother from a callbox was probably ill-advised in hindsight). Russ Hunt soundchecked for him and it was decided someone should take Loz back to the hotel, two miles away in the town centre, and watch over him. As the sole person with no other responsibilities, I hove into view like the stooge in an Ealing Comedy.

We were dropped off at the hotel in Colchester High Street and I started to check Loz and myself in, confident in the knowledge that I was performing my task with supreme efficiency. Here was something to tell the grandchildren – the day I roadied for England! The day I saved the entire Kingmaker tour single-handedly! But as I looked round to get Loz to sign his name he had disappeared. I found him holding himself up in the hotel bar.

We eventually made it back to his room, negotiating a difficult staircase on the way, and he promptly fell asleep on his bed, leaving me to watch *Brookside* and *You Bet* while drinking endless cups of coffee for us both. When he woke, I shoved some aspirin at him and we waited for the lift back to the venue. He looked less than sparkling, but despite his condition Kingmaker pulled it off again, even managing a Queen pastiche midway through the set.

Everything else is a blank, except I remember going to bed early – or rather, curling up on the floor of someone's hotel room – and waking up again in the middle of the night, freezing cold, with a set of keys sticking in my rear. The next morning I gathered my gear, and cadged a lift back to London.

And when I finally arrived home, with a bag full of dirty T-shirts and underwear, I began suffering all the coming-down symptoms that have plagued me for years. There is nothing to build up to in the evening (try as I might, I can't get the same excitement about going to gigs in London); all the in-jokes you've mastered over the past week fall flat on your friends, who look at you sympathetically, as if to humour you, while your hilarious hotel stories sound distinctly lacklustre under the microscope of the real world.

It's at this point that you know, whether it be next week, next month, or in a year's time, you'll be back at Leicester Forest services, down to your last five cigarettes, listening to a roadie talking about 'guitar specs', whatever they are, and wondering where your next backstage pass is coming from. It's a dangerous state of affairs. Some roadies remind me of an inmate I once met serving his third sentence in a Glasgow prison. He'd re-offended because he preferred life in jail to the real world outside. He couldn't handle the pressures of bills popping through the letterbox and shopping and signing on. And being on tour, to a certain extent, provides the same sanctuary from your partner, the taxman and problems at home. You can't go on doing it forever, but you can stick your south of France, your Lake District and your DIY. I'll see you down the front.

Halfway to Paradise

MICK HOUGHTON

Billy Fury, Britain's only authentic rock'n'roll singer, wrote most of his own material but had his most outstanding commercial success with big ballads like 'Halfway to Paradise'. This, coupled with what today's tabloids might call 'smouldering good looks', meant he was the first star British women openly screamed at. His big break came in Birkenhead in 1958, while Fury was still working on the Mersey tugboats. Marty Wilde came to town and Fury wangled his way into Wilde's dressing room and started singing. Manager Larry Parnes signed him there and then and shoved him on stage there and then too, just to make sure his investment started earning.

By 1966, after twenty British Top 20 hits (bettered in the sixties only by Elvis, The Beatles and Cliff), Fury's career was winding down and he devoted his time to horse-breeding. Comebacks in 1973 (two years after open-heart surgery) and 1981 proved unsuccessful, although he was always held in high esteem by the rock'n'roll fraternity. He died, on 28 January 1983, of heart failure. He'd been plagued by ill-health all his life.

Born during the final year of that great post-war Labour Government's term of office, I grew up and formed my character under what became known, in Harold Wilson's oft-used phrase, as 'thirteen years of Tory mis-rule'. The Suez crisis, Anthony Eden's great folly of bombing Egyptian airfields, provided me with one of my earliest memories. I was six years old and literate enough to read the full front page, block-type headline of the *Daily Express*: – BRITAIN IS GREAT AGAIN. I may not have understood what it meant but I recognized the hushed tones of the adult voices around me reserved only for talking about bereavement, illness or the war. This was happening now, though. Unbeknownst to me, the Soviets invaded Hungary that same month, the world was on the brink of the unthinkable and, somehow, unbelievable as it seems, this impending doom frightened the life out of me. I was certain that there was going to be another world war and I was convinced I'd be called up into the army. Six years old and haunted by the spectre of National Service.

I did my best to retreat from the outside world. I would have to be forced to go out and play and did so under protest, at least as far as the garden. I could handle going to school but mostly I preferred the safety of home. And above all else, home was my bedroom and the living room, which was dominated by an enormous TV set in one corner and, occupying the far side, beneath the bay window, a gramophone.

It pulled down at the front to reveal the turntable, next to which was a compartment stuffed with 78s. I'd play with them for hours on end, sprawling them over the floor. The labels fascinated me, I'd collect all the same ones together – Decca, Brunswick, Coral, HMV. I'd put them in alphabetical order once I could, a six-year-old anal retentive in the making. Most of all, I loved the names – Alma Cogan, Teresa Brewer, Ruby Murray, Dickie Valentine, Johnnie Ray – and the titles. 'Hernando's Hideaway!', 'Cherry Pink and Apple Blossom White', 'Little White Cloud that Cried'. It was another world and more fun than Matchbox cars and Ludo. Those records even defined the extent of my mischievousness, as I hid the pieces of the ones I broke from time to time.

The following year my dad brought home the family's first long player, Bill Haley's *Rock Around the Clock*. I'd never enjoyed actually listening to the 78s, but I played the LP to death! I knew every song, every word. And I loved the images and this new language: 'Get out in that kitchen and rattle those pots and pans' from 'Shake Rattle and Roll', or just titles like 'Rock-a

Beatin' Boogie', 'Mambo Rock', 'Everybody Razzle Dazzle'. Not romantic and slushy and dull like the 78s. This was rock'n'roll of a kind, even to a seven-year-old's ears.

Over the next few years we acquired more and more records, the new 45s replacing my old childhood toys, as my sisters, Beryl and Sheila, in turn eight and four years older than me, entered their teens. More significantly, Beryl started courting. Lee, her boyfriend, became something of a boyhood hero. As far as I was concerned he was a fully fledged Teddy Boy. They were bad lads, trouble. I knew that from TV reports about fights and stabbings and general bad behaviour. Yet, as shy and quiet as I was, the idea of these rebellious rockers had a strong appeal.

Lee had dark, slicked-back hair and always wore black. Drainpipes, long jackets, black shirts, but with the uniform white tie and white silk scarf. My mum didn't approve, of course. A spiv, she called him. He also loved rock'n'roll: Eddie Cochran, Little Richard, Buddy Holly, Elvis.

Hearing Elvis for the first time made Bill Haley sound like Perry Como. No contest. Elvis was – as would be said many times again – the King. That voice and the way he looked. Not only did Lee have such stirring singles as 'Hound Dog', 'Lawdie Miss Clawdie', 'I'm Left You're Right She's Gone' and 'All Shook Up', but also those classic 10-inch LPs – *Lovin' You*, *King Creole* and *For LP Fans Only* – that my sister had on permanent loan. As soon as Lee and Beryl went out I'd sneak them into my bedroom along with Beryl's portable record player and blast out these pounding, primitive sounds until bedtime, sucked in by something I could not explain. Lee and Beryl are still married today, and whatever Elvis was singing about, he meant it. This was real in a way that chubby Bill Haley, with his silly kiss-curl, could never be.

My younger sister was no slouch either. She favoured the more melodic stuff, the dramatic voices and sweet harmonies of The Everly Brothers, Roy Orbison, Ricky Nelson and Paul Anka. A little later she discovered the trad jazz of The Temperance Seven, Kenny Ball, Acker Bilk and Chris Barber. But I have no complaints: it was the perfect grounding owing to my sisters' remarkably discerning and catholic taste. These days I can forgive them the odd Craig Douglas or Adam Faith single, even Faith's inane 'Lonely Pup (In a Christmas Shop)', that contaminated the household collection. My sisters may have been a constant source of irritation to me (as I most certainly was to them) but they were responsible for my initial pop education. It more than made up for all the squabbling and door-slamming that went on.

By the age of eleven, I was a complete pop fanatic. If any of the other kids at school bought pop records then I didn't want to know about it. Pop was my private world along with a passion for reading, particularly the Bunter and Biggles books. My main aim in life at one sad point was to read all forty-three W. E. Johns books in the library. That they were all jingoistic, stereotyped, heroic escapism didn't matter. I had my football annuals, too. I'd spend hours memorizing the names of all the teams in the league, their grounds, their nicknames. I knew every league champion, every FA Cup winner. It was a constant quest for the trivial. Once I had discovered something, it was all or nothing. I had to learn everything about it.

Unsurprisingly, given my bent for acquiring worthless knowledge, I passed my eleven-plus with no apparent trouble. The following September I'd be attending Shooters Hill Grammar and despite my, for once rational, fear of being bullied by the older kids (I'd recently read *Tom Brown's Schooldays*) this was something to look forward to.

That wet and dismal summer of 1961 saw the space race go into overdrive with the second Soviet and American astronauts competitively orbiting the earth at almost the same time. It also saw the Cold War intensify as the Berlin Wall went up. But what did I care? There was no more conscription. I went to my first Test Match at the Oval, where Wally Grout and Middlesex's John Murray both broke wicket-keeping records for an

Ashes series. Here was a new minefield of statistics to negotiate courtesy of the indispensable *Playfair Cricket Annual*. More
importantly, I had my first pair of grey flannel long trousers in
which to walk into impending adolescent life, and I'd bought
my first pop record, Billy Fury's 'Halfway to Paradise'. I was
ready for anything.

'Halfway to Paradise' had been released in April. By the time
I bought it in July it had reached Number 7 in the Hit Parade.
It was to spend five months on the charts without reaching
Number 1 (it peaked at 4) and was the fourth biggest seller of
1961. None of this mattered, mind. I'd discovered my own
Elvis.

Quite why Billy Fury had slipped through my sisters' net I'll
never know. After all, he'd released his first single, 'Maybe
Tomorrow', early in January 1959. 'Halfway to Paradise' was, in
fact, his ninth. We must have crowded round the TV set and
watched him on pop shows like *Oh Boy!* and *Wham!* or heard him
on *Saturday Club*, even on *Pick of the Pops* (the chart run-down on
Sunday afternoon), since he'd had minor hits before. Curiously,
though, we had none of his records. Maybe they hadn't liked his
earlier rockabilly-style stuff, maybe they thought he was just a
poor Elvis clone, but, for me, discovering him that summer, he
was the only singer about to give Elvis a run for his money.

Not that Elvis could do any wrong. The supposedly neutered,
post-GI Elvis made as great a run of singles as anyone before
or since. From 'Stuck On You' in 1960 through to 'Viva Las
Vegas' in 1964, the Houghton collection remained complete. I
was even buying them myself towards the end. But when Billy
Fury released 'Halfway to Paradise', he bettered even Elvis as a
passionate pop balladeer. Presley's 'Surrender', Number 1 at the
time, was a poor second.

Billy Fury looked the part, too. He had *it*, call it what you
will – attitude, presence and a sex appeal that, remarkably, my
sisters missed. Perhaps my mum was right, he was ugly and his
arms were too long. Like Elvis, Billy Fury had been neutered.

The tall, lean, gangly figure in neat suits I'd now see in photos and on TV was a cleaned-up version of the gold lamé suited rocker who'd been labelled 'indecent' and 'offensively sugges-tive' just as Elvis had before him.

I knew little about my new idol but somehow I gleaned basic biographical details from one source or another. I knew he wasn't born with the name Billy Fury but Ronnie Wycherley. He'd been rechristened, like so many others, by impresario Larry Parnes. Incredibly, though, he was from Liverpool. That he wasn't American was the biggest shock of all. I was instinctively aware that our home-grown rock'n'rollers were pale and poor imit-ators. Cliff Richard, Marty Wilde, Adam Faith, Tommy Steele, they were little better than Ronnie Hilton and Dickie Valentine. I had no time for the skiffle boom either. I'd only come in at the tail end, by which time Lonnie Donegan was making novelty records like 'My Old Man's a Dustman' and 'Does Your Chew-ing Gum Lose its Flavour'. My mum's washboard and thimbles were safe in our house.

The thrill of owning records is still indescribable. Soon I bought a second single, Del Shannon's 'Runaway' (always a sucker for soaring falsettos, me), and I became horribly posses-sive. It was OK that I'd borrowed my sisters' records for years, but would I let them near mine? No way. I was to keep them in special cardboard sleeves, rather than those plastic record racks where they'd warp and get scuffed. Not long after I'd started at Shooters Hill Grammar, Billy Fury released a new single, 'Jealousy'. It had been out for ages before I was aware of it. Alan Freeman played it on *Pick of the Pops* – a new entry.

Once aware, I had to have it. If the thrill of having your own records was a high, the thrill of anticipation was higher yet. 'Jealousy' was no disappointment. What an opening, a tension built up by piercing staccato strings, then Bill's moody intro . . .

Jealousy
Was only through jealousy

>   Our hearts were broken
>   And angry words were spoken.

This was real-life drama, unlike Cliff's latest wimp offering, 'When the Girl in Your Arms is the Girl in Your Heart'. The title said it all. In terms of popularity and chart success, Cliff was streets ahead of Billy Fury, but for the next three years it became a close-run thing. The rivalry only heightened my passion for Billy Fury and loathing for Cliff in the upcoming months.

Travelling to school each day gave me a new sense of freedom. A twenty-minute bus ride away, it also gave me access to the shops and cinemas in Eltham and Woolwich. The Coldharbour Estate in South East London where we lived had no record shop at all. I'd bought those first two singles while shopping at the weekends with my mum and dad. Now I was free to browse the record racks in the big stores, notably the basement of the Co-op in Eltham. Proudly, it was here I did my first solo run and bought Billy Fury's next single, 'I'd Never Find Another You'. I heard it on *Saturday Club* and already knew it was brilliant, but before I'd even got it home I'd learnt something from the label details: it was written, like 'Halfway to Paradise', by Goffin/King. That obsessive, inquisitive part of me now made a true and glaringly obvious discovery. For a mind no longer satisfied by football and cricket facts, there was so much to learn about pop music. Who were Goffin/King? Come to think of it, what did I actually know about Billy Fury?

Christmas came and went with the usual injection of cash to boost my increasingly inadequate pocket money. I was also given my first record token for ten shillings (almost enough for two singles). It was wisely spent on Elvis's 'His Latest Flame'/'Little Sister' (my first Elvis purchase) and Bobby Vee's 'Take Good Care of My Baby'. They were Numbers 1 and 2 at the time. I was hardly ahead of trends.

But how could I learn more? The library had nothing, and

the local bookshops had nothing beyond picture pop annuals. So it was that I began regularly buying either the *New Musical Express* or *Record Mirror*. That spring, *Record Mirror* increased its chart from the Top 30 to the Top 50, and it also had a more comprehensive column for singles reviews and new releases. Now I could find out about records, if not before they were released, then certainly before they entered the charts. I'd pore over the charts, take note of anything that was new to me, scrutinize the news pages – the true grist of the paper. The features and interviews were woefully inadequate, but I'd cut the charts out every week and refer to them constantly.

With my new reference tools and increasing awareness, I became more choosy about radio. There were countless request shows like *Family Favourites* which played the odd gem, and the essential *Pick of the Pops* covered the charts, but above all were the two weekend morning shows, both at that time hosted by Brian Matthew, *Saturday Club* and *Easybeat*. This was the place to hear those new releases I was reading about before they made the Top 20. As for Brian Matthew, he simply knew everything there was to know. He was friends with all the stars and would chat to them on the shows.

Not that 1962 was a vintage year to be making this voyage of discovery. Billy Fury and Elvis Presley presided over proceedings like two transatlantic gods. Elvis had four Number 1s that year, including two of his absolute best, the incredibly sexy 'Can't Help Falling in Love' and 'Return to Sender'. Fury, however, topped and tailed the year with two relative flops, 'Letter Full of Tears' and 'Because of Love'. In *Record Mirror*, Fury said that 'Letter Full of Tears', a Don Covay song recorded by Gladys Knight, was his attempt to record some R&B, and, he continued, he wanted to get back to his roots. The public voted and it scarcely made the Top 20, so he responded with two more big-production ballads, 'Last Night Was Made for Love' and 'Once Upon a Dream', from his debut film *Play it Cool*. The corresponding EP from the film was also enormously successful, and all five were essential acquisitions.

The year was dominated by instrumentals: The Shadows, trad jazz, the stupid twist and other dance-craze songs. Ironically, one of these was Telstar by The Tornados, Fury's backing band. A staggering three months in the Top 10, it was Number 1 for three weeks yet, unjustly, Billy Fury himself never reached the top spot. With hindsight, the appearance of 'Love Me Do' by The Beatles that December was to prove not insignificant. I'd logged its Top 50 chart entry a month earlier but didn't rate it – too much like Karl Denver. I thought no more about The Beatles although, like Billy Fury, they came from Liverpool. One plus point, at least.

There was absolutely no challenge to the supremacy of Billy and Elvis in 1962. Much I as loved Elvis, and it was almost out of habit since I'd been listening to his stuff for several years by now, it was Billy Fury who offered solace. Collecting each single was only part of it. Fury had something that got under my skin. I was certain he was just like me somehow. Me, the proverbial shy and sensitive child who never much cared for mixing with others. He, too, I imagined, was a solitary and vulnerable soul. But more than that, there was an underlying sombre mood in all his songs which I could identify with.

They were sad songs and he had such a melancholy way of singing. In every one of them he was essentially miserable. They were love songs, and had to be; other than daft novelty hits, all pop was about boy/girl relationships. But in Billy Fury's case he'd usually lost the girl of his dreams or was worrying that she was about to ditch him. Lovelorn or loveless, that's Billy. Like in 'Halfway to Paradise', 'so near yet so far away', thwarted as ever. In 'Last Night Was Made for Love', the title neglects the following line – 'but where were you?' – as he imagines his girl with someone else. In modern-day parlance, this was bedsit music, and Fury, ever the pessimist, always insecure, was the first in a tradition that would later include Scott Walker, Neil Young, Tim Buckley and Morrissey, among many others. The most melodramatic example of this is 'I'm

Lost Without You' from January 1965, by which time I'd shamelessly rejected him.

This was far from the case as I reached my twelfth birthday in June 1962 in a very confused state of mind. Falling in or out of love may not have been my prime concern yet, but like Billy Fury I was usually fretting about something, neither happy nor unhappy but half-way between, resigned to things the way they were. At the age of twelve you have no other choice. Everything is limited and frustrating at that age, even being a pop music fanatic.

I was out on a limb and out on my own. I was never one for joining things, so fan-club membership wasn't for me. Nor was keeping a scrapbook of photos. That was for girls. It never dawned on me, either, to try and track down the earlier singles. It never occurred to me that you could. Once records dropped out of the charts they simply ceased to exist. Any Billy Fury LPs, and there was only one that I knew about, *Halfway to Paradise*, were out of my price range. There had to be more to this life.

That July, Billy's first film, *Play it Cool*, went on release, and I had to be there on the first Friday it opened at the ABC in Eltham. I loved going to the pictures, particularly westerns, to which my dad would take me, and the Elvis pictures, to which my sisters reluctantly allowed me to tag along with them. In my usual selfish way, no one was coming with me to see the Billy Fury film even if they'd wanted to. Back then, once you'd paid the price of admission you could sit in the theatre all day if you wanted. I saw *Play it Cool* through twice and have never seen it since.

It was a flimsy affair. Billy played Billy Universe who, with his band, The Satellites, was heading to Brussels to play a gig. There was a plot of sorts involving a stuffy heiress trying to patch things up with her estranged boyfriend, but essentially it was an excuse for Billy to sing a half a dozen songs. There were also guest encounters with Shane Fenton (later Alvin Stardust),

Bobby Vee and Helen Shapiro. It hardly lived up to the poster proclaiming 'Top Twisters V Hot Swingers in Musical Battle Royal'. It was a Michael Winner film, after all.

It was lightweight fare even to an impressionable twelve-year-old. I felt just a little let down by it. The high point was Billy singing his then current single, 'Once Upon a Dream'. Even that was a rather wet, dreamy ballad, but it was still the best song in the film. The others were throwaway, especially a jolly musical routine in which he sang 'The Twist Kid'. I expected more.

The Elvis movies were tons better. I saw most of them from *Blue Hawaii* through to *Roustabout*. There were usually two or three a year, all essentially the same whether Elvis played a lifeguard, a racing-car driver, a fisherman or a fairground worker. But they were always lively, larger than life and full of bright new images for someone brought up on a south-east London council estate. And Elvis did fill the screen, always playing a moody bugger, always getting into a scrap but always coming good in the end and getting the girl. Besides, there were always killer songs.

My resolve as a fan was being tested, and things were to get worse. The family went to Great Yarmouth that August, where, by pure chance, Billy Fury was in summer season. Maybe there was a god after all. We booked tickets for the final Friday before coming home. Normally not one to reveal my emotions, I was noticeably excited.

Walking to the theatre at the end of the pier we passed droves of people walking back the other way. I thought little of it until we arrived to find a young girl outside, sobbing her heart out. I wanted to sit down beside her and join in. The show had been cancelled owing to Billy Fury's ill health. We trudged back to the B&B in silence. I was inconsolable. I should have expected it really. He was always being forced to cancel dates. The most regular stories about Billy in *Record Mirror* were apologies for cancellations. His poor health was well documented. A childhood fraught with illness, specifically a bout of rheumatic fever, had left him with a weak heart. I wasn't sympathetic. I was pissed off. I went to my room and cried. After the bitter disappointment, I was glad to get back to school.

In October Billy redeemed himself with his most sleazy, sultry track to date, 'Because of Love'. It was announced as a track from Elvis's upcoming film *Girls Girls Girls*. What a coup, I thought. And they were obviously mates. A photo appeared in *Record Mirror* of Billy and Elvis on the set of the movie, both holding gold discs. It was one of the few I cut out and kept. This confirmed everything. They hung out together. I knew you'd never catch Elvis knocking round with Cliff, but Billy Fury? Of course, it made complete sense. Looking at the photo now, an obvious publicity shot if ever there was one, Fury looks petrified and Elvis bored. It didn't help the single either: it peaked at 18.

There were no further Fury singles that year, but I more than made do with Del Shannon's 'Swiss Maid', 'Sherry' by The Four Seasons and 'It Might as Well Rain Until September' by Carole King, half of the Goffin/King team that supplied Billy Fury. World events once again played on my still-overactive mind for the rest of the winter, as John F. Kennedy, the young saviour of American politics and the Western world, stood up to the old bear Khrushchev over the presence of Soviet missiles in Cuba. I tried to understand the issues involved but couldn't. We were on the brink of war again, this time over an island that was good for nothing except producing cigars. I didn't even smoke cigarettes.

1963 was to be a really testing time. There was no Billy Fury record to spend my Christmas money on but there was a new Del Shannon, 'Little Town Flirt', a rare instrumental, 'Diamonds' by Jet Harris & Tony Meehan (more Duane Eddy than The Shadows), and 'He's a Rebel' by The Crystals, the first single I bought on the strength of hearing it just once – it sounded like nothing I'd ever heard.

At this stage I'd still buy any and every Billy Fury single. 'Like I've Never Been Gone' was no exception. It had a great pop sound, a careful balance of guitar, piano and strings, pounding drums on the chorus and a great vocal. I was beginning to notice these things. Alarmingly though, record-buying had ceased to be my exclusive domain. My private world was being invaded. Until now I'd had no schoolfriends who shared my obsession with pop. Almost overnight, they all did, but I didn't want to know. I was completely out of step with everyone else at school. Not in front but lost in another era.

Every kid in class was suddenly buying Beatles records. 'Please Please Me' had spent most of February and March in the Top 5. Then came Gerry & The Pacemakers, Billy J. Kramer and the rest. By the time 'From Me to You' hit the top spot in May, the whole school was Beatle mad. I stubbornly resisted their cheeky charm. I denied them more than thrice and reacted by seeking out The Cascades' 'Rhythm of the Rain', Tommy Roe's 'The Folk Singer', Skeeter Davis's 'End of the World' – all gloomy songs – and, as if to really prove the point that I knew more about pop than they ever could, Buddy Holly's 'Brown-Eyed Handsome Man'. This was someone I'd been listening to for six years, not flash-in-the-pan Merseybeat stuff.

Thankfully, Billy Fury and Elvis showed no signs of flagging. Presley's first release in the wake of Merseybeat, 'Devil in Disguise', went straight to the top. Fury's overwrought 'When Will You Say I Love You', with its mock-Tchaikovsky piano introduction, could still manage a month in the Top 5 flanked by The Beatles, Gerry, Billy J. and Freddie & The Dreamers. Now here was someone you really could take seriously – Freddie Garrity was no more a pop star than Arthur Askey.

The summer holidays brought relief from the constant chiding at school, though secretly I suspected I was fighting a losing battle. A new *Playfair Cricket Annual* and the arrival of one of the truly great West Indian teams helped take my mind off it all. I went to the Fifth Test at the Oval with my dad and got to see Trueman and Statham bowl in the afternoon session, and Hall, Griffiths and Lance Gibbs taunt England in the morning. The West Indies won the match and the series. Another early lesson in life.

To cap it all, Billy Fury released a single that no amount of loyalty, let alone wilful, stubborn resistance to The Beatles, could persuade me to buy. 'In Summer' was totally untypical of anything he'd yet done and truly awful. I hid my head in shame, though others were more faithful and it was his last Top 5 hit. I couldn't believe it. Whatever possessed him to record this utter pap? Starting with a 'dum dummy dum dummy dum dummy dummy do' girlie chorus, he then sings, 'When I get tired and feeling blue/I think of all the things I can do in summer.' Thank God school was out.

There were more worthy records – The Crystals' 'Da Doo Ron Ron', my second of theirs, and the trashy, bizarre 'Pipeline' by The Chantays. I also gave in to a new strain of Merseybeat, The Searchers' 'Sweets for My Sweet', a sound deliciously new with its pacy rhythm guitar. So what if it was Merseybeat, it wasn't The Beatles.

Back to school for my third year. The Beatles released 'She Loves You' and I still couldn't or, in truth wouldn't, accept them. I was really falling behind. My singles collection was everything to me. Who needed LPs? Everyone else had the *Please Please Me* LP by now. Some had even seen The Beatles' Merseybeat package at the Woolwich Gaumont in the early summer. I'd yet to see any live rock'n'roll. So much for the headstart I had.

Billy Fury also released another terrible single. Not as irredeemably bad as 'In Summer', but 'Somebody Else's Girl' was still a weedy, trite pop song. Two in a row I rejected. If I wanted big ballads, Roy Orbison was now the man. I bought

'Blue Bayou' instead. I also read about Phil Spector for the first time. 'Then He Kissed Me' was another great Crystals single, but better still was The Ronettes' 'Be My Baby'. I'd put it on the turntable and leave it to play again and again. Spector was an unfathomable figure. A producer, a role I couldn't grasp, yet he was more important than the artists themselves, and the sound he achieved was outrageous and massive. It literally shook the speaker in the dansette.

Then the moment of truth. A Billy Fury tour was announced in *Record Mirror*. He would be playing a nearby Bexley Heath cinema on Friday 11 October, a short bus ride away. I went there the following Saturday eager to get an advance ticket. At last. Unless he falls ill again.

I went to the early show filled with trepidation. He was backed by The Tornados, more than a token beat group, so it would be rocking. And Joe Brown was on the bill, too. My sister Sheila had 'A Picture of You' and 'That's What Love Will Do', both of which I coveted. The rest of the package comprised Marty Wilde and Karl Denver. I went alone, of course, telling no one at school. This was my secret pilgrimage.

I arrived early and sat while the cinema filled up. Used now to the company of schoolfriends of my own age, the hand-holding couples and huddles of girls that drifted in were so old. Not even my sisters' age – more my parents'. This lone thirteen-year-old also seemed to be attracting quizzical glances. It was my first experience of paranoia.

Karl Denver opened the show. I'd never liked his stuff or his 'famous' nasal wail. He ended, after a dreadful, interminable comedy routine, with 'Wimoweh', the audience, much to my embarrassment, singing along. I was getting fidgety. Joe Brown & The Bruvvers were next up and the girls went berserk. I slid further into my seat as he went into his Cockney patter, telling them to 'shut their cake 'oles'. This was not rock'n'roll. The set leaned heavily towards the comedy stuff, 'I'm Henry the Eighth I Am', 'Jellied Eels', a George Formby number and his *tour de force*, 'Hava Nagila'. This was music hall, gimmicky stuff like playing the guitar behind his neck. He might as well have set fire to it on stage.

Marty Wilde looked and showed his age. His voice was weak and strained and flat. After making derogatory quips about The Beatles he had the gall to play 'I Saw Her Standing There'. What if Billy Fury was as bad as the rest? It was all so slick, yet so tacky. Things picked up as The Tornados ran through 'Telstar', 'Globetrotter' and the like, but by now we were waiting for Billy Fury.

At last a buzz of excitement. He was the star, after all. He walked on and it reached fever pitch. The girls went wild – screamingly wild. I just sat there, riveted, craning to see the stage amid a sea of waving arms and bobbing heads. His every gesture, every arm movement brought further hysteria. What must it be like at Beatles concerts, I wondered?

As to what he played, it's a blur of memory, but it was rock'n'roll/R&B stuff mostly. 'That's All Right, Mama' and 'Sweet Little Sixteen' were in there somewhere along with some new songs, well new to me. Unlike everyone else that night he didn't just run through the hits, though he had every right to. He said little, and there was certainly no daft comedy stuff. He was cool. What a relief. Yet I went home feeling empty, unfulfilled. I was masquerading in the wrong generation.

Two days later it all became clear. At 8.30 on Sunday 13 October, I sat down along with 15 million other viewers to watch *Sunday Night at the London Palladium*. Just like every other Sunday, in fact. But this was different. On the Friday I'd seen rock'n'roll reduced to the level of show-business entertainment. I was about to witness the process in reverse. This was the night The Beatles topped the bill at the Palladium, the pinnacle of so many careers before. It was history in the making, and the news reports and newspapers reflected this the next day. The phrase Beatlemania was coined by Fleet Street to describe the pandemonium outside the theatre, and the rest you know.

I saw it all in a blinding flash the moment John Lennon mockingly told the predominantly young Beatle fans in the usually staid audience to shut up. The adults applauded, a vain gesture, attempting to fight a losing battle against the hysterical army of kids. It was them and us. I could be part of 'them' no more. That internal struggle was over for me at long last, as Lennon stepped to the microphone and launched into 'Twist and Shout'. Why fight the inevitable? The next day it was all anyone at school talked about, and I joined in. I didn't mention that I'd seen Billy Fury two days before.

It wasn't until the end of the year that I bought my first Beatles record, 'I Want to Hold Your Hand'. I didn't really need to, as there was no escape from hearing them on the radio. Anyway, all my new pop-hungry friends had all the Beatles records. I could go round to their homes and hear them, borrow their copies and tape them on the Philips reel-to-reel I got for Christmas.

Treacherously, I passed over Billy Fury's December release, 'Do You Really Love Me Too', with no remorse whatsoever. I did pick up a copy of the latest *Fury Monthly* though, a fan magazine that had started up earlier that year. I never bought it regularly, even though it boasted that it was always '100% Billy'. Its content was mostly photos (increasingly of Billy with furry animals) and inconsequential stuff aimed at girls. I could live without Billy's advice page since I didn't have boyfriend trouble. This issue led off with an editorial lambasting his fans for deserting him in favour of The Beatles. Fury himself said he thought they were a 'gas', while the magazine, rather hypocritically, carried advertisements for Beatles Calendars and other memorabilia.

No more the loner, 1964 was a great year. I no longer fretted over world events. Even Kennedy's assassination a month earlier didn't spoil my new found sense of fun. Soon I was able to increase my spending power: I did milk rounds, a Saturday job at the Co-op, collected money for a football lottery on the estate. By taking sandwiches to school you could be excused school dinners and pocket the money, a shilling a day. It all went on records. By now I was buying every Beatles single automatically, same with The Searchers and The Rolling Stones. My rock'n'roll background steered me towards the new influx of R&B groups, The Animals, The Pretty Things, and, towards the end of the year, the group I'd eventually consider my favourite – The Kinks.

There was so much I had to possess that year, so many classic one-off singles – The Nashville Teens' 'Tobacco Road', The Zombies' 'She's Not There', The Mojos' 'Everything's Alright', The Beach Boys' 'I Get Around', all genuinely exciting, and still more Spector singles. It was hard to keep up. By the close of the year I also had four LPs – *A Hard Day's Night*, the first Rolling Stones and Kinks LPs and *The Freewheelin' Bob Dylan*.

Dylan was the clincher in terms of defining the generation gap at home. I'd sit in my room repeating tracks as I'd try and transcribe the words to 'Masters of War'. Everything else I used to play was tolerated unless it was too loud, but Dylan, even my sisters couldn't handle Dylan. They hated his monotonous, dreary voice, his interminable songs and especially that wheezy harmonica. To the whole family Dylan was considered a 'racket', not a spokesman for the young and free-thinking.

Fourteen years old and enjoying life to the full. Thanks to the Bond films (Ursula Andress ascending from the sea in *Dr No* and Daniela Bianchi sliding under the sheets in *From Russia with Love*) and the paperback novels of Ian Fleming, we were discovering sex for the first time. Britain even had a Labour government again. Harold Wilson was elected Prime Minister that October to an extraordinary sense of optimism among all my mates at school.

I also bought my final Billy Fury single. Sometime that summer he released a cover of 'It's Only Make Believe'. We'd had the original Conway Twitty version five years earlier.

Fourteen and already old enough to be nostalgic. It was a great version, but the B-side was the real eye-opener. Jimmy Reed's 'Baby What You Want Me to Do' was a standard R&B track that the Stones or The Pretty Things probably played live. And Billy's version had that same edge, with The Gamblers, his new backing band, playing real hard. Why had he not put this sort of stuff out instead of trash like 'In Summer'?

It was a naïve wish, and I knew that it wasn't what his diehard fans wanted anyway. Unlike me, they stuck by him. Billy Fury did not sink without trace once the beat boom happened, anything but. The Merseybeat phenomenon (The Beatles and The Searchers excepted) was over in a year, whereas Billy's last Top 10 hit was in the summer of 1965 ('In Thoughts of You') and he could still muster the occasional Top 30 single a year later. 'Give Me Your Word' was the last and his final one for Decca with whom he'd recorded since the start. I scarcely gave him a thought through the remainder of the sixties, oblivious to the poor health that sent him into early semi-retirement.

Years later I was to discover his debut LP from 1960, *The Sound of Fury*, commonly regarded as not simply the first but the *only* genuine British rockabilly LP. It was reissued in 1981. By then he was critically regarded as the unchallenged greatest rock'n'roller Britain produced. *The Sound of Fury* was also the first British LP of wholly original material, the songs credited to Fury or his writing pseudonym Wilberforce. The Beatles are, mistakenly, always credited as the first to write their own songs, but it wasn't until *A Hard Day's Night* that they put out a whole LP of self-penned material.

I'd left university and was married for the first time before I grasped this astonishing fact in the early seventies. I felt genuinely proud and shamelessly smug. I'd been right all along.

Something in Arabic

MIKE EDWARDS

There is no Arab musical tradition in Britain, as there is with reggae, and the sounds, language, instruments and tone lead unpolished ears to make the unfortunate mistake of dismissing it as wailing rubbish. Second only to Egypt, Lebanon is the centre of Arab music, and from that country Fairuz (born Nouhad Haddad, probably in 1934) is currently the great Arab superstar. The country's indigenous music comes from the regional village folk cultures, from where most city dwellers relatively recently moved. Its main showcase was the Baalbek Festival, where Fairuz got her big break in the fifties. The civil war changed everything though, and Beirut's music community moved, virtually en masse, to Cairo, where the long-established Egyptian star Warda has always recorded.

Western-style singer Ofra Haza represented Israel at the 1983 Eurovision Song Contest with 'Hi'. 1985's *Yemenite Songs* was her only excursion into traditional music. She recorded her last album at The Power Station in New York, where Bon Jovi and Meat Loaf make their albums, and she's worked with Sisters of Mercy as well as being sampled by countless dance acts. 'Im Nin'Alu' reached Number 15 in the British charts in 1988.

Jah Wobble's friends refer to it as 'kebab-house music'. Jesus Jones' other guitarist calls it 'that Indian stuff', but when it comes to geography he was educationally challenged years before it became de rigueur. I've been warned off it on mental-health grounds by people who say they care about me. It causes a couple of close associates to believe that they can belly dance, with or without the appropriate belly. It seems that having a passion for traditional Arabic music does not bring out the best in one's friends.

Now I too have fallen into the trap of generalizing. Given that Arabic-speaking countries stretch approximately twice the width of western Europe with a corresponding number of cultural changes, 'Traditional Arab music' does not adequately describe the sounds that I listen to. Indeed, such a term invites more derision than asking for an Ace of Base single in a dub reggae record shop. After a time- and money-consuming search that I will explain later, I discovered that the music that can move me to tears within a couple of notes, that can transfix me to the spot as I gaze wistfully into the infinite, that strikes a deeper chord in me than any western pop music (despite fierce competition from Germans armed with Roland TB 303 synthesizers) is that of Lebanon's torch-song singers, the divas and basso profundos of the eastern Mediterranean, the classical soloists and orchestras of the Middle East, the composers and performers who provide the opposite of all that I revere in American–European pop.

I'm supposing that it'll be at about this point that I'm meant to start to get specific about the object of my passion and the reader will probably begin to understand and empathize or stand aghast. For me 'the mystery of The East' is more than just a dodgy catchphrase to advertise confectionery, foreign travel or mountain-bike frames; it describes the frustrating situation I face whenever I have to explain this passion that goes beyond words. What names I can recite will probably have the same impact that the names of medieval madrigal composers have on me. While the musical leviathan of Lebanon that is Fairuz may trigger a dim recollection in someone who inadvertently wandered into the world-music section of a Virgin Megastore while looking for a Phil Collins re-mix triple pack CD reissue, Samira Tewfiq is not a household name this side of the Bosphorus. She might not be in Beirut either, for all I know. While I'm on about it, I may as well show my hand; the other two names I know, of two more women, are Faiza Ahmed and Warda Algazaireya.

It isn't apathy or a lack of obsession that stops me from getting the information I crave; it's the fact that this music is made by and for another culture, a music that makes very few concessions to non-Arabic speakers and readers. For months I thought that Warda Algezaireya was called Khalik Hena, because those four words were the only non-Arabic ones on the album cover. Perhaps some Shi'ite in Sidon is under the belief that Lovesexy has released an album called *Prince*. (Later, Warda Algezaireya became known simply as Warda, preempting western stars of similar stature like Elton, Eric and Rod.) With few exceptions, the albums I have bought by these virtuosi yield as much information as the average western CD single: a picture, an artist's name, a title and the boring record-company jargon that you always ignore. Only in this instance, the titles are written in what looks to me like a variation of my mother's handwriting, a style where, for example, the word 'shoeshine' looks exactly the same as 'margarine'. Arabic script uses a few more dots than my mother but it's just as illegible to me.

Listening for choruses isn't much use in trying to glean facts. For a start, song structures vary, and for every Samira Tewfiq two-and-a-half-minute piece with a small number of repeated sections, there'll be Warda, outdoing The Orb with a non-stop, fifty-two minuter. Then of course there's the language. For the average Briton, there is in every language an element that bewilders; the 'g' sound in Dutch and Afrikaans, the 'j' in Spanish, the 'xh' in Xhosa, the 'sj' in Swedish and the rhyming of 'fertile' with 'turtle' in American. Arabic has '. Yes, that's ', a near lethal combination of 'g', 'h' and 'k' and something green and unpleasant at the back of the throat, the most terrifying piece of punctuation to ever come from behind, lights flashing, and say, 'pull this sentence over to the side of the road, now!' I have hours of this sound on record, CD, and tape, a sound that sits in the middle of the word and makes it too big to enter the western ear, too awkward to exit the occidental mouth.

A German friend lent me the opinion that pop songs in his own language are unpopular in non-German speaking countries, not simply because they are in a foreign tongue but because the nature of the language itself is amusical, unsuited to the application of notes, a square-peg medium for a round-hole form. While devotees of Wagner and *Heroes*-era Bowie might be moved to violence over that, the description I've given of Arabic might lead the reader to a similar conclusion of the music I am talking about. But the sheer power of expression in the pronunciation gives the lyrics, whatever they may be about, such impact. The nature of the music, its violins, cellos, flutes, ouds and tars (lute-like instruments), all doomy minor scales, bottomless pits of melancholy, an air of generations of inherited sadness, has the perfect accompaniment in words that seem to drip venom, anger, betrayal, desperation. Language will always dress for the occasion: where American blues is right to drawl and slur, it makes sense for these songs of a similarly degraded people to be staccato, blunt, hard. As for me understanding it, I'd say Yasser Arafat has a better chance of understanding John Lee Hooker.

As I glance at the sleeve of the Samira Tewfiq album that is playing now (titled something in Arabic), I see that Jamil Ass has written both the words and music to 'Allah Ou Akbar'. Knowing that 'God is Great' is by a man named Ass is a piece of information that would have sounded right for a comic like Denis Leary, but it doesn't help me gain much insight into a different world of music. I'll look at the sleeve. Samira, in common with the other artists I have photos of, both male and female, is wearing more black eyeliner than even Dusty Spring-field would have thought feasible. She has a gold-rimmed black veil held in both hands, pulling it against a prominent nose, half concealing her face, possibly in an effort to conceal the second chin she has grown since the picture on the front of her 1988 album, two years before. She stares face on, looking into the camera with a pair of beautiful, brown, almond-shaped eyes, thick black hair framing her face and continuing below the photo that is chopped just below the neck. Her fingernails are painted bright red. There is a huge green-stoned ring on her left hand. There is little discernible background, just a pale blue and yellow wall. The name Samira Tewfiq is in bright yellow and Roman script appears above her head. This album was published at the start of this decade but has design elements that scream 1970. And not in a kitsch way either.

The photos on the covers of the albums I own and have investigated are misleading. Artists in Lebanon have very long careers, it seems, and can change from attractive young women into grandmothers in the short space between albums. As a recording artist myself, I have felt this way but have never shown it so drastically. On my Faiza Ahmed CD you can hear the voice of a fallen angel and see the looks of an incompetent transvestite. Fairuz appears to have many of her album shots reprinted from passport photos. One picture of Warda shows dark, sunken eyes above sharp cheekbones, a rose held against the face by slender fingers, while another picture of her shows an Arabic Claire Rayner with a bosom impressive enough to force her to stand some distance away from the microphone stand. All of the artists seem to have about three different spellings of their name, a gambit that could vastly improve the quality of life for musicians claiming Social Security benefits in the UK.

That is the limit of the non-musical evidence I have. Albums are, however, a small source of the sounds that I love. Buying these CDs is not always a gratifying experience, as quality control is even more variable than Prince's: *Fairuz Live at the Albert Hall* could, with some notes flattened here, some sharpened there and sung in English, make a 3 a.m. Radio 2 playlist. Even my favourite pieces, which can cause my heart rate to increase noticeably, come from albums that make me thank the inventor of the 'fast forward' button on CD players. When the songs are good they are the ultimate music into emotion conduits, when they are not, they are unlistenable. I think it's the culture difference, the lack of anything other than pure music to provide the interest, that means there is nothing in between for me.

My biggest source brings me closer to the music and even further from the traditional roles of image and marketing used by the music industry. But first let me talk about cable TV. I love it – hours spent channel-surfing, watching thirty-second blasts of entirely unrelated subjects, all night long if I want. Then there are the radio stations that come with cable; all sorts of musical styles and categories lovingly beamed straight into your house, a musical equivalent of being let loose in the supermarket with as much time as you want to fill up your trolley. Yep, all these stations and channels in excellent, digital quality.

Channel 36 is MBC, the Arabic channel. If you watch the scrambled signal, by moving your head up and down very fast you can make out American cartoons with harsh, guttural voiceovers, and news reports by presenters who speak a different language from the ones we are used to but come from the same smarmy mould. The test card is pretty similar too, although there is no be-veiled girl-with-puppet picture. It starts up shortly after the readings from the Koran have finished and runs until early morning. Of course, the picture's scrambled but the music isn't. And what music it can be! All night! And in digital stereo! You'd never know who the artists were, unless you were familiar enough with them to recognize their voices or playing styles, but what would it matter? You'd react only to whether the music alone moved you or not. Someday soon, all music will be received this way, and anyone who deals in ideas that can be transferred to a digital medium is going to find it hard to make a living from those ideas.

This obsession didn't start with a bang, a revelatory moment. A follower of Krishna suggested to me that I feel for this music so strongly because in a previous life I came from the Middle East. Could this mean that I, along with a significant percentage of the western world, was once the presumably massively schizophrenic Cleopatra? In a similar vein, my maternal grandfather worked for some time on a genealogical trace of his very unusual surname, Balhatchet, ending his search with a name in a Cornish parish record of hundreds of years ago. His surmise was that the name could have been a derivation of a Phoenician name that translates as 'Keeper of the temple of Baal'. The Phoenicians were regular visitors to Cornwall, not for summer holidays, but to trade for Cornish tin, taking it back to their capital, Baalbek, in what is now Lebanon. If I were more romantic I'd leave it there. Science, however, is the most potent of modern religions, and I am a believer. I think it was a series of recycled, constantly refined influences that led me to the liqueur that is this Arabic music.

If it can be said that your parents screw you up, then mine did so in a wonderful way, a way that gave me a headstart in having a life and career obsessed with music: my parents screwed me up with The Beatles and world travel. At the age of eleven I knew what an Iranian muezzin's call to prayer sounded like live (a pain in the arse at 5 a.m.) as the Edwards family had embarked on a hippy-hangover 'let's throw it all up and travel the world for a bit' voyage. Although, to be fair on my parents, it did start as just a six-month trip to the Sahara.

As for The Beatles, despite being a *Hard Day's Night* baby, it was the records from *Revolver* onwards, etched into my subconscious by constant repetition (it was cheaper than babysitters), that got me used to the scales and sounds of Indian musicians. In my early twenties, probably inspired by channel-surfing through Asian TV shows on telly, I bought the odd cassette of sitar and saringi instrumentals as well as of some Indian singers. When I read reviews of Le Mystère des Voix Bulgares in the eighties music press suggesting that this was something radical and excitingly fresh, I bought a tape and loved it. The Bulgarians, as evidenced by some very un-European note intervals in their heartrending songs, had absorbed hundreds of years of influence from neighbouring Turkey, where, in turn, music had been influenced strongly by Indian scales. It felt as though I was getting closer to something but hadn't quite got there yet.

During the mixing of the second Jesus Jones album, an engineer played me a cassette by Hossam Ramzy, an Egyptian percussionist. It was an audio CV and featured some of his work on Peter Gabriel's *Passion* album, the soundtrack for *The Last Temptation of Christ* film. If you have this album, you'll understand my ravings about it. If not, you might remember the cinema trailer for the film, which relied heavily on the same piece of music the engineer played to me, the piece that starts the album. It's an astonishingly atmospheric, scary combination of thunderous ethnic drums and percussion, moody synth drones and an achingly beautiful Armenian deduk (flute) melody. That melody, as well as some of the other pieces on *Passion* and the setting of the film, gave me the biggest clues as to what I was looking for and where I might find it.

Ofra Haza was an obvious person to start with. I was aware of her after her hit 'Im Nin'Alu' had been sampled by Coldcut for their 'Not Paid in Full' re-mix for Eric B. & Rakim (which, incidentally, I also blame for exposing the break beat that became the most overused sample in pop – fifteen songs in the Top 20 of December 1990 used that same sampled drum pattern, and it's still being overused now). I bought Ofra's *Shaday* album which, on the whole, in a musically disappointing way, confirms her as being the Israeli equivalent of Madonna. There is one overriding difference between the two sirens: Ofra Haza is a good singer, in fact, a phenomenally talented singer.

Buy *Shaday*! Buy it for track number five, 'Love Song' (not an auspicious title, I agree). Pay over the odds for this two-and-a-half minute track if you have to, but buy it. It's an a cappella solo of presumably Hebrew words from The Song of Songs in the

Bible, set to a tune written by her manager (if only my manager could do the same for me) and recorded steeped in reverb. The sound of it can stop in his or her tracks anyone who has a heart. If I haven't heard it in a while it'll bring tears to my eyes, partly because of the deep melancholy of the tune but mostly because of the sheer greatness of a melody sung so that every inflection is worth a page of musical notes. Janis Joplin said of Otis Redding that he could tell a life story in the singing of the notes A to B, two semi-tones. Ofra Haza can show you another world in that eastern idiosyncrasy, a quarter-tone, and she does it every few seconds on 'Love Song'.

As with all obsessions, there is never enough. I bought more Ofra Haza albums until eventually the rhetorical question of whether I'd do the same for Madonna got too much for me.

The world music section of Willesden Library is a lonely place, apart from the Irish section, but I spent hours there, wading through the mis-filed calypso records, the reggae hits of the seventies, the sleeves featuring Greek men in unfeasible footwear and more eternally emigrating Irish folk. From this random assortment I dug out records of varying interest from Syria, Iran, Iraq, Tunisia, Egypt and, finally, from Lebanon. My first love was the aforementioned Samira Tewfiq, from an album with a black and white picture of her at, well, who knows when in her career. Each track would start with a short instrumental or percussive section. This would yield to an all-out choral assault, a cast of tens with the voices of hundreds camply belting out the chorus until the star enters, all nasal soprano and (to me) tangential melodies. Now the next bit is fun, but it could still be a parodic piece written for the film of *Lawrence of Arabia*. At roughly a third of the way in, all of the percussion stops, the violins drop to a low drone, and a flute or another violin or maybe a tar will start improvising around the drone, bringing some real magic out of those other-worldly scales. Then the singing starts and your breath stops. I remember sessions in the back of the tour bus in America, after shows, travelling across the homeland of rock'n'roll, passing through all those once mythical places like Chicago, Phoenix, San Francisco, with the five of us sitting in the back lounge, no lights but for glowing cigarette ends, all of us spent from the energy expended on stage, mellowed by the after-show beers and spellbound by that voice, those half-alien notes, the strangeness of the language and the bitter-sweet feelings that they combine to create.

The obsession grew with the discovery of Warda Algezaireya. Where Samira Tewfiq is plaintive, never quite subtle but restrained when the occasion demands, Warda is a drama queen, singing every line like it's an announcement of the end of the world. Her skill is that she also imbues the same lines with all of the waste and futility of human effort that might occur to you on the brink of Armageddon. There is a song by Warda called 'Kelmet Itab' which has a section six minutes in where you can hear strong echoes of Cocteau Twin Liz Frazer's excellent vocal for This Mortal Coil's 'Song to the Siren'. If you know and like that song, listen to Warda – it's the difference between Go Karting and Formula One or grape juice and wine.

At around the same time I first heard Fairuz. From what I can gather, Fairuz is the giant of Lebanon's music scene, a hip version of Vera Lynn, Liza Minnelli and Tina Turner with a career spanning several decades. Cinema buffs may have heard her songs. There is a scene in *Hors la Vie*, set in Beirut in the mid eighties, where the Lebanese hostage-holders demand at gunpoint that their French victim sing a Fairuz song. Personally, I would have needed a complete cessation of the artillery fire outside and about a ten-year warm-up. In *Les Amants du Pont Neuf* (French films are another subject I might yet get to write a chapter about), as the Bastille Day celebrations go on around them, the two lovers (the central characters of the film) are running across Pont Neuf with the varied soundtracks of the celebrations montaging around them. In the midst of some horribly average rock music and an exhilarating piece of Public Enemy comes a voice of outstanding beauty that towers above the other musical offerings and had me leaping up and down on my seat the instant I heard it. Although there was no mistaking it, I checked the credits anyway, just to confirm that it was Fairuz.

It's easy to recognize Fairuz's voice. She is so much gentler than all the other Lebanese female singers I've heard. There is no harshness, no nasal quality to Fairuz's voice, just a pure, pitch-perfect tone. When she sings those descants that start so high and hits every note on that bewitching scale perfectly before finally resting on the same note as the music, it makes you see through the dull, soulless vocal gymnastics of Screaming Whitney Houston and countless other 'soul' singers. Had Otis Redding heard some of the male singers in my collection he might very well have taken the controls and crashed that plane himself.

There are plenty of other singers who reach the same standards as Fairuz, Samira, Warda and Faiza, but what can I tell you about them? I can tell you that track number ten on one of my tapes is one of the most disturbingly emotional passages of singing that I, and possibly you, have ever heard and that it is by Deep Voiced Bloke. If I were Morrissey I might give it some snappy, punning title, but neither of us would know anything more about it. I have recordings of instrumentalists that would shame the abilities of many professional musicians in Britain, but I don't even know their names, let alone their unintelligible song titles.

There have been only a few instances where I have discovered the meaning of the dramatically delivered lyrics of some of the songs, and I've been underwhelmed at the results. Listening to a favourite Fairuz piece, it sounds as though she is relaying the deaths of every one of her children. In fact, the text concerns a shepherd who's getting a bit peeved with standing alone on a hillside for twelve hours a day. Another piece, sung

by one of the many anonymous males I have recorded, is full of
such sorrow and conviction that it triggers vague but definite
guilt in me, runs along the lines of 'I shall take my loved one a
red kerchief and ask her to marry me'. A little closer to the
mark is another Fairuz song that tells how the mountains
overlooking her home town are full of sorrow to see the people
emigrating from the land of the cedar tree. I suspect romantic
licence here, as the mountains surrounding the Bekaa Valley
are probably a little sicker about the precious people bombing
the cedars to oblivion every couple of decades, in the ever
recurring 'my God is bigger than yours' debate. However,
having heard women in this country sing along enthusiastically
with sexist seventies rock songs, heard racists sing 'Free Nelson
Mandela' and even some shiny, happy types reciting R.E.M.
songs like they actually know what they mean, I've long since
come to the conclusion that lyrics are just pegs to hang the
tunes on – and these tunes, with the likes of Fairuz singing
them, are awe-inspiring.

Hearing these Lebanese singers encourages and discourages me
in equal amounts. To sing like them, I'd have to sell a complete
village of souls as well as my own to the Devil. But I have to
try and have done. Still do. The results are pretty pathetic, as
my voice doesn't have the power of expression, the technical
ability to leave gravity and bounce off the stars like Fairuz's.
   Not being able to reproduce the sounds I hear is frustrating,
often more so because I'm sure some of the moods I have are
compatible with this music. You may have observed that these
songs are not jolly; the words 'sorrow', 'melancholy' and 'sadness'
crop up in this chapter perhaps more often than they should
when dealing with a subject that causes me such euphoria. I
have a propensity for gloom, for mild depression, and the sound
of these songs allows me to wallow in that. During the writing
of the third Jesus Jones album, *Perverse*, and in the wake of its
very successful predecessor, I went through one of my bleakest

periods ever, for reasons I'm not entirely certain of, possibly ones that have to do with living in a wet, dark, northern European capital and others that gave me strange feelings of empathy with Kurt Cobain when I heard of the reasons for his suicide, although I'd never had strong feelings for him before.

In that period, more than anything else, I'd listen to three Sonic Youth songs from their *Daydream Nation* album (also pretty doomy stuff) and every bit of Fairuz's singing that I possessed. Her influence, Warda's and others, ended up on *Perverse* any way I could get it on there. For the Lebanese you can understand how sadness could be the pervasive feel of their music, living in a region which has probably the most turbulent history in the world, a history that repeats with a harshness worse than the razor-edged boomerang in *Mad Max 2*. As for me, to quote Matt Johnson of The The, 'I'm just another western guy, with desires that I can't satisfy.'

The chance that this melancholic music might encourage depression in me is the reason a couple of friends have instructed me not to listen to it, particularly when I'm writing. It's advice I'll decline because when I feel good it makes me feel better, and when I feel bad it seems so right to feel worse, as though if I get low enough it'll purge me. At least, unlike heroin, it doesn't damage me physically. To further that dubious analogy, I've tried the methadone treatment by listening to more modern-sounding music from the same area but, at the terrible risk of sounding like Lenny Kravitz, it just doesn't have the passion, the soul, the mystery. There is also the nasty habit of modern Arab musicians to get the latest effects pedal from the west and turn the controls up to stun.

Not that it is all bad. Ofra Haza has made some valiant, often great efforts with Don Was producing, and Cheb Khaled from Algeria had a sizeable European hit in 1993 with a song that mixed his own Rai style with hip hop and house very effectively.

This passion for Arabic music is shared by other more

notables from the west. Led Zeppelin were fond of the odd eastern dalliance and I read a fairly recent interview with Robert Plant where he answered the question of what wish he would like to come true by replying that he'd like to re-form Om Khalsoum's orchestra. (Om Khalsoum was an Egyptian diva, revered throughout the Arab world but, at the risk of some sort of fatwa, a bit screechy for me.) 'Ethnic sampling' has become a buzz phrase in 1994, as people working with dance music try to expand the boundaries of modern pop and try to follow the commercial success of Enigma and the like. Who knows, it could even help rock music to shuffle geriatrically into the present.

However, I don't think I'd like to hear countless samples of Samira Tewfiq singing 'Batalt el Hob' or an anaemic, plagiaristic take on 'Khalik Hena' (perhaps because of my own failures in that area). If she is still alive, I don't want Fairuz to come to London to perform a diluted, westernized version of her greatness. I'm unsure of how stable Lebanon is now, how advisable visits by Europeans to that country are, but I have this romantic idea of sometime, when I'm not quite so busy, hopefully in this decade, taking my experienced Digital Audio Tape player to some smoky den in Beirut or Baalbek or Tyre, seeing the scenes that the records have promoted in my imagination and witnessing, in the flesh, some of the greatest sounds this planet has ever produced.

Being an obsessive, the sort of person who sits in company and says, 'Wait, wait, wait, you've got to hear this next bit,' I've always been the sort to try and get others to share my obsessions by subtle means or coercion. So in case any of this gets you even a little interested, some of these artists' recordings can be found in the world music section of larger record shops. They're quite easy to find: just ask for the belly dancers.

Sin City

SID GRIFFIN

Born Cecil Ingram Connor in 1946, Gram Parsons dropped out of Harvard to form The International Submarine Band. By the time their album, *Safe at Home*, was released in 1967, Parsons had joined The Byrds as keyboardist. His very brief tenure ended when he refused to join The Byrds on their South African tour.

With fellow ex-Byrd Chris Hillman, he formed The Flying Burrito Brothers, whom he was fired from in 1970, addled by drugs. His solo career produced two masterpieces, *GP* and the posthumously released *Grievous Angel*, which virtually defined the country-rock genre he'd invented with the Burritos.

Parsons died on 19 September 1973 from a heroin overdose after a lifetime of sustained substance abuse. He'd always said he wanted his ashes scattered at the Joshua Tree National Monument. After the funeral his road manager, Phil Kaufman, and his valet, Michael Martin, stole Parsons' body from LAX airport in a hearse and burnt it at Cap Rock in the Joshua Tree National Monument.

Almost ten years ago. I'm strolling down the Sunset Strip in Los Angeles. Night is falling and I'm on my way to the legendary Whiskey A-Go-Go to see a band, God knows which one. My own group, The Long Ryders, is currently the second most successful indie band in Europe, kept out of the top spot by The Smiths. The sun's setting is beautiful, there is a light breeze, it's almost summer and the traffic has died down in that half-life time between the business day and a wild night out.

Head down, I'm walking quickly lest anyone recognize me. I

am wearing my prize possession, a white Levi's jacket with a Sin City motorcycle club patch on the back, one of the two dozen made by a group of Houston motorcycle/Gram Parsons fanatics called, logically enough, the Sin City Boys, back in 1972. Gram was given one when he played Houston's Liberty Hall. Emmylou Harris has one, Linda Ronstadt still has hers. They sent me one as a token of their gratitude when my biography of Parsons was published. The Long Ryders are kicking ass in Los Angeles, and as members of both the neo-psychedelic Paisley Underground and New Sincerity cowpunk movements, we are in good standing. I live, work and play in the town of, in the shadow of, with the endorsement of my hero: Gram Parsons.

As I near the Whiskey I see two young Californian males, mid-to-late teens, dirty T-shirts, dirty feet, dirty hair, sitting on a low wall between a major record store and a gas station. Obviously rock fans, possibly going to the same show. I'm hoping they don't notice me, don't slow me down to ask any questions.

As I'm passing by them I notice they both brighten up considerably. The first guy hits the second on the shoulder and nods towards Sid Griffin, musician, author, Long Ryder.

'Wow,' he says with a certain awe, 'that guy's a guitar player. And the jacket . . . Sin City, cool.'

'Sin City? What's that?' asks the second would-be Butt-head.

'That's a song, dumb ass.'

'Who by?' I hear the sound of a derisive snort as they grow fainter.

'AC/DC! It's on *Powerage*. Don't you know anything?'

The sun shines bright on my old Kentucky home. Or so it seems with hindsight, so it seems in dreams, scattered reminiscences and the distorting filters of time. In London NW3 I am an ocean away from a warm slice of homemade cornbread with honeybutter. But hey, I knew the job was dangerous when I took it.

It's like this, see. I was born in the year the highest number of Americans were birthed, 1955. The peak and the real end of the baby boom at the same time. Kentucky was then twenty-sixth of the fifty states in size and population, and it still is. My old man and his father built the house I was raised in a few years after the shooting stopped in the Pacific and my dad gave up his commission. My parents have lived nowhere else in married life but that home with the flagpole by the front door. They are still there now, bless them. Frequently they fly the American flag, even if there isn't a holiday. That house is where I was raised, certainly not to be a musician, certainly not to adore Gram Parsons. But that's what happened.

My first memories are of the late fifties and this kid on the next street asking me if my pop was Gus Grissom the astronaut. I remember my folks taking me to see Eisenhower speak on behalf of Nixon in the 1960 Presidential election campaign against John Kennedy. We took the elder brother from next door. He became car-sick and puked repeatedly and violently most of the way there. I don't remember seeing Ike, just reaching up and holding on to my pop's hand for dear life. I was so small then, I remember seeing only people's knees and their hands clutching umbrellas and handbags.

Sundays meant not only church but Sunday School, where kids like me would discuss Bible stories memorized from a comic-book styled text the night before. My mother would query me for the correct answers like regular school homework. I can still remember Old Testament story after story and even tell you what they mean and how/why/what we should learn from such lessons and how this could guide our lives. Then we'd have Sunday lunch as a family, and I would spend the rest of the afternoon doing something constructive like playing baseball, arguing about baseball, reading baseball statistics or throwing buckeye nuts, acorns, water balloons, the occasional round stone or anything small enough to be lifted by a young soft hand and thrown at passing cars.

Around 5 p.m. on Fridays, Saturdays and particularly Sundays there was a seemingly endless round of country and western series on TV. *The Porter Wagoner Show*, where Dolly Parton got her start singing and pushing boxes of Breeze ('the detergent with a free towel or washcloth in every box'), *Hayloft Hoedown* with Randy Atcher and Cactus Tom Brooks, *The Wilburn Brothers Show* with Teddy and Doyle Wilburn, and other lesser-known variations on the theme with names like *Barnyard Jubilee*, *Tobacco Country Jamboree*, *Town Hall Meetin'* and *Dixie Hayride*. Lord have mercy the powers that be even gave a show to Mel Tillis, and the poor man has a chronic stutter.

For the first half of my life this embarrassed me greatly. As a youngster I didn't like music much but I did like records. I'd been pretty ill a couple of times and to keep me quiet my mom bought me some records about the American Civil War. It seemed that almost every week in the early 1960s brought about some centennial of a major Civil War battle, and an LP would be issued in commemoration with Ralph Emery or Burl Ives or Edward Everett Horton doing the narration, the songs of the Northern Blue on one side, the songs of the Rebel Grey on the other. The Devil was obviously a Confederate because they had all the good tunes. Odd the Confederacy being the losers as all their songs are so happy and up-tempo, while the songs of the victorious North are slow, lugubrious and sanctimonious. Perhaps my Sunday School lessons were right, the pious do win out in the end.

A serious illness struck me in my teens. I was flat on my back in hospital when my Uncle Henry brought me a gift of The Byrds' new album, *Sweetheart of the Rodeo*. 'I described you to the fellow in the record store,' said Uncle Henry. 'He said he thought you would like this.'

At first the fellow in the record store was wrong, dead wrong. I hated it. Hated it. It reminded me of those low-budget country TV shows on Friday, Saturday, Sunday around 5 p.m.

I had heard The Byrds before, and though I had enjoyed

them they did not particularly stand out from the morass of sixties music jingle-jangling from our radio. There was clearly a key element missing in their formula, and new member Gram Parsons supplied this ingredient. I was no great fan of C&W either, but this new combination of country and jangle gradually seeped in. I loved it.

I was forbidden to enter the University of Kentucky because my parents and sister (being older and born aged 35, she is really not a sister but a third parent) decided that if I went there I would simply hang around drinking beer. They were right. Where else, ahem, did their only male heir with mediocre grades wish to go to college?

I thought of the Gram Parsons song 'Hickory Wind' which led off side two of *Sweetheart of the Rodeo* with 'In South Carolina there are many tall pines. . .' and figured, hey, I like pine trees, I love the South, and then someone told me the legal age for alcohol was only eighteen in South Carolina (it was twenty-one in Kentucky). I was sold. I told my dad about the University of South Carolina (they also had a good basketball team) and thanks to the poor-to-average academic standards they maintained then, I was in.

First thing I noticed when I went to a school 500 miles from home was that I didn't know one, not one, of my 22,000 fellow students on the campus. Hmmm. This was gonna be a problem. Where could they be? When in doubt in Sid Griffin's world, go to a record store. Possibly one that played hip discs like either album by The Flying Burrito Brothers, the group Chris Hillman and Parsons formed after exiting The Byrds post-*Sweetheart*.

Even in conservative pro-Vietnam Dixie every state university had some hippy running a bookstore/health food shop/co-op/ record store just off campus, usually a hippy who decided academia wasn't for him and dropped out, only to find starting a record shop was a 9-to-6 grind and made you a pigdog capitalist in the eyes of fellow hippies, students and various hangers-on who wanted you to show some People's Power and simply give your wares away.

The name of my favourite shop escapes me. The South Carolina campus had three, count 'em, three, hippy record shops all reeking of incense and each with Peter Max-styled murals painted on the outside wall. Friendless freshman logic dictated that if I bought enough records and magazines from these misplanted Californians, I would sooner or later venture a comment which would start a conversation which would spark a debate, which would fuel a quasi-intellectual fire by whose flames my first deep almost-an-adult friendship would be bonded.

It didn't happen, even though they played The Flying Burrito Brothers all the time in addition to lesser-known country rockers like Hearts and Flowers, Country Gazette, Pure Prairie League, Heartsfield, Old and in the Way, New Riders of The Purple Sage, The First National Band and Poco. But I still have an almost mint collection of every issue of *Creem*, *Crawdaddy*, *Phonograph Record* and *Rolling Stone* from this era.

Earlier in my academic career at the university something happened to cement my obsession with Gram. He died. On my birthday. Actually his death certificate says the day after my birthday, but that's when the authorities got to him, so I figure he died late 18 September and not early 19 September.

Nothing like a death to let you know where you stand on an issue. I decided I was for him. In fact when the one guy I had made tentative pals with and I saw Gram's picture on the front of the afternoon newspaper as we strolled across campus we knew he was dead and that it was spectacular as there was no other way he would make the front page. This is a sad commentary on many, many things.

What can I tell you? Everything I suppose. Gram had done, to my knowledge then, five albums. All of them were terrific, all right, most of them were terrific, with *Burrito Deluxe* being kind of a let down after the classic southern grandeur of *Gilded Palace of Sin*.

It was difficult being a Gram Parsons fan in those days. I, out of desperation more than anything, went with the aforementioned tentative pal to see The Nitty Gritty Dirt Band, then a considerable commercial force in American country-rock. As I sat chilled to the bone in the university's basketball arena staring at the darkened stage, singer Jeff Hanna announced the next number as being written by Gram Parsons. The Dirt Band then broke into 'Blue Eyes'.

My pal and I looked at each other in great dismay and profound amazement, since two and two now made five. Parsons was dead and gone, fartin' dust, pushing up daisies. He, unlike Jimi Hendrix, left behind a finite body of work: *Sweetheart of the Rodeo, Gilded Palace of Sin, Burrito Deluxe, GP* and *Grievous Angel.* What the hell was Hanna talking about?

A chance glance through the cut-outs and promo copies at hippy off-campus record store number two brought me face to face with a promo copy of Gram's first solo album, *GP*, straight from the Warner Bros press office in Burbank. Tucked in the gatefold sleeve was a black and white promo sheet listing the tracks, telling radio which ones to key in on and giving a brief Parsons discography. Listed first and most obviously was *Safe at Home* by something called The International Submarine Band.

I looked everywhere. I took to the back pages of *Creem, Crawdaddy* and *Rolling Stone*, then all in their near-prime. I wrote in my dormitory room late at night to more nefarious draft dodgers and tape pirates than a heretofore honest student should ever admit to doing. Catalogues, if I may be so bold as to call them that, came in from NYC, San Francisco, Hollywood, Long Beach, White Plains, Eugene, Virginia and Myrtle Beach, South Carolina.

One day a catalogue listing bootlegs arrived in my student mailbox from Kornyphone, the label whose trademark logo was a head of a pig wearing shades and headphones with musical notes dancing around his head. We can safely presume the pig was rockin' out.

Late one night, craftily avoiding the books in my room lest I accidentally study and find myself in a well-paid job, I pulled out the catalogue and there it was, in bold gold letters with fireworks going off all around it, *Safe at Home* by The International Submarine Band. I sent for a copy and it arrived seemingly years later. Being a bootleg of the original release, it had a plain white cover with only a pink sheet laid, not glued or pasted, on the front with track listings, timings and a small sketch of a pig's head wearing shades and headphones with musical notes all around it. First track, 'Blue Eyes'! Jeff Hanna, I'm right behind you!

That the album is less than thirty minutes long and less than Gram's best work didn't matter, it existed, it was mine, there were four new Gram tunes and six covers to be digested and, best of all, I had a copy and no one else did. No other student would know how to get one unless they read the same back issue of *Crawdaddy* I had, and off-campus hippy record stores (murals and all) couldn't stock it as it was a bootleg and naughty naughty. Life was sweet as I laid the platter upon those who thought *Cricklewood Green* by Ten Years After and the debut by Captain Beyond were good albums, hip to own. This was an out and out illegal recording and, like marijuana, in those bell-bottomed days, a certain insider's status was granted to all those students who had such items in their possession.

Safe at Home completed the Gram Parsons discography for anyone in those days. He recorded six albums in his short life of 26 years, and University of South Carolina sophomore Sid Griffin knew them all by heart, who played on them and what bands they were from, where the cover versions originated from and who wrote them, what the lyrics were to each song. It's part of fandom, yet when Your Hero and Icon is deceased it is also a dead end. (Unless of course your hero is Hendrix, in which case it is obvious someone followed him around at all times taping every jam, outtake, experiment, utterance and interview.)

American college students are a restless, searching breed.

Many in society at large no doubt share the view of the late Richard Nixon, who once memorably described those studying at American universities as 'bums'. Sophomore Sid Griffin fell between the two points, my net worth being more than a bum, but I must admit times when my shadow seldom fell on the floor of McKissick Library.

Which is not to say I wasn't involved in research. Within months of his sad passing, six albums was no longer enough to satisfy my Gram Parsons addiction. No way. There had to be more GP out there somewhere. There still is, as I'm currently involved in finding the first album sessions the ISB did at Gold Star in Hollywood in the summer of 1966. But how to find it? If some balding professor can get me to leap through hoops of fire academically for no immediately apparent purpose other than a soon-forgotten grade, why not use this accumulating knowledge to do something really useless, which won't help me at all later on in life? Like finding more country-rock by a dead guy. Or so I thought then.

My appetite was whetted when A&M issued a Burrito Brothers compilation called *Close Up the Honky Tonks* with un-released tracks. Then the Dutch got in on the act by doing yet another Burritos compilation with still more unreleased tunes where Gram sang. The dust had yet to settle when A&M retaliated with *Sleepless Nights* (the original title of *Grievous Angel*), a Flying Burrito Brothers outtakes album with three previously unheard tunes added from the *Grievous Angel* sessions. I devoured all three LPs, sought to dye a blonde streak in my hair like GP, but was talked out of it when two guys off the swim team who lived near my dorm said they'd kick my ass up to Monck's Corner (near Charleston over 100 miles away) if I did anything that cissy. And yet like the pre-teen Sid with his well-worn *Sweetheart of the Rodeo*, I grew restless and felt there had to be more Gram out there. But where? It was now early 1977, graduation was looming, change was in the air.

*

In California they had all sorts of people without real haircuts or jobs. Or futures for that matter. Many of them played country-rock, some with Gram himself. Many of the somewhat younger generation of pickers performed this new punky CBGBs music, looking like The Standells or worse.

Ergo much of the summer of 1977 was spent in a sweat-soaked bed in my old room in my parents' house, staring at the ceiling wondering about my future. My folks had gleefully removed all beat-group posters and photos upon my entering college four years earlier, including one of Hendrix wearing a scowl and a dashiki onstage somewhere; I was never a big fan, it was mainly there to bug them. Kids, eh? To my horror, the room where I grew up was now a guest room with no Sid Griffin personality and all the flavour of a Ramada Inn. In California I could again have my own room yet not have dad tell me hurry up and put that tie on, we're late for church.

The only thing to do was to be like Gram and move there. I'd have to leave the South and I'd have to do it by my lonesome, the old high-school band not interested in competing in Hollywood's rock wars and my lone real buddy from college convinced graduate studies and a PhD were the way to go. Ha. The fools.

September 1977 and after repeated warnings to Mom and Dad I actually packed my Chevy Chevette, stuck a U-Haul trailer on the rear full of records and guitars, kissed Mom goodbye and drove off to California by myself. Although I dressed smartly that morning in a small effort to placate my worried mother, I was wearing the orange Flying Burrito Brothers T-shirt I'd sent away for underneath the red and white striped button-down she'd bought me. I was twenty-one. It must have broken her heart. I knew she was against it, driving two thousand miles across America by myself to Los Angeles, leaving her, my old man and Kentucky possibly forever. They had spoken about it to each other at the dinner table as if I wasn't there, and Pops always replied yes, but his sister grew up and left home, she doesn't live in Kentucky either and anyway Sid's a man now and I cannot tell our son what to do with his life or exactly how to lead it. Sid has either learned the values you and I have tried to teach him or he hasn't. Besides honey, going to California on his own will either make him or break him, it's a test of his character.

Well said, Dad, and thanks.

Since seeing The Beatles on *Ed Sullivan* I'd always wanted to be in a band – nothing else in life was going to be for me. And that's the way it has always been. When I had no real band happening I'd write about pop music or fool around in radio till I could put something together and strike again. That the guys I grew up with did not share this dream and ambition is still something I cannot quite come to grips with. I feel certain that deep down inside they too would like to be The Flying Burrito Brothers or the Stones/Faces/Muddy/Hank, and that the big difference between myself and them is not talent or desire or honesty but the fact I had the nerve to attempt showbiz and they didn't. Inside I'll always believe everyone has a secret wish to perform, to hear an avalanche of applause, their name shouted repeatedly until it bounces off the clouds and comes back to earth with an echo.

I had taken a map of the United States and circled all the cities west and southwest of Kentucky that I had always wanted to visit. That some of them were not on the way to California, or in any geographic way related to the city circled before them, was no sweat. I was going to see Memphis (again, admittedly), Little Rock (site of desegregation battles in the 1950s), Texarkana (no reason), Quitman (home of Sissy Spacek, then my favourite actress), Dallas (to check out my own grassy-knoll theory), Fort Worth (missed the exit on the freeway, still haven't been there), Austin (Doug Sahm, Jerry Jeff Walker, Thirteenth Floor Elevators), El Paso (because of Marty Robbins' great ballad), Clovis, New Mexico (where Norman Petty recorded Buddy Holly), Santa Fe (no reason in particular),

Phoenix (ditto), Death Valley (never seen a desert), San Bernadino (mentioned prominently in 'Route 66') and finally Los Angeles, where ex-Byrds walked the streets like normal folk and they let musically challenged people like Sid Griffin form bands and play clubs specifically set up for rock music. And surfing too, which I had always wanted to try. Of course, I was awful.

California represented freedom, sunshine, Gram, The Byrds, the entertainment industry in all its glory and with all its horrors, an adulthood which allowed and perhaps even encouraged adolescent behaviour and my only chance.

So I split, then formed a sixties punk band as my way of playing rock music which was snotty but not so nihilistic (or downright bad) as the short, sharp, shocking punk of the day. The Unclaimed. The Unacclaimed, my Kentucky pals called it. One of the first sixties retro bands, people now tell me. More than once, hunting for rare singles I've seen the lone EP with me on it hung on a wall next to the very first Talking Heads single or some rare Costello B-side, priced way beyond any sane person's budget. We were legends in Italy. What an honour.

The Byrds' influence on rock then was not as strong as it is today. Only Tom Petty carried the flag, and Gram Parsons was more famous for dying spectacularly in the desert than anything else. When I picked up albums from that dark era pre-Sex Pistols and saw men dressed in satin scarfs and tight silk pants I knew I could never play rock music again without the energy and commitment I'd been shown by punk, yet I ached to play a little C&W and was too embarrassed to admit to any of my spikey- or bowl-haired friends I actually liked the stuff.

Thanksgiving, 1981. I quit The Unclaimed after deciding to form my own band. The original ad placed by myself and a bass player named Barry Shank (who quit before we recorded but we cut his beautiful 'Ivory Tower' anyway) read 'Drummer and lead guitarist wanted, Creedence meets The Clash'. Translation: we're gonna have both twang and punch in our music.

Shortly after placing this ad I saw ex-Byrd Gene Clark in the Great Western bank at Sunset and Crescent Heights. I was too scared to speak to him but I did lean over and see the check he was cashing was for $50. I considered this a good omen.

When Barry Shank and I quit The Unclaimed we didn't know anything other than that we would dedicate our lives to being musicians. Lifers, for better or worse. Barry was last seen working on his PhD at Yale University, alma mater to George Bush and Bill Clinton. I was last seen loading my own amp into the Mean Fiddler on a Saturday afternoon. To each his own, I can only wish him the very best.

'Creedence meets The Clash.' Or so our advert for musicians proudly read. After the usual no-hopers and unemployed Vegas players looking for anything, anything at all, Greg Sowders showed up to audition for the drummer's chair. He wasn't a great drummer then but he learned real fast and had an amazing chameleon-like ability to adapt just enough from a given style like Cajun or heavy metal and then add his own brew to come up with something pretty darn original yet potent as well.

Greg Sowders probably didn't know tons about Gram/Burritos/Byrds when I met him, but he was willing to learn and he quickly became a spark-plug in terms of his cheery personality. And he taught me more than a few lessons about music and life by the time the band ended. I'm still learning from him today, as a matter of fact.

We stumbled on Stephen McCarthy for lead guitar. He showed up at his first Long Ryders audition thinking we'd be hotshot LA players. He was fresh from Virginia and was still learning about Southern California. Stephen played guitar in the style of The Byrds' Clarence White like no one else (Chris Hillman told us Stephen played those licks closer than anyone he had ever heard before) and was the band's best singer. He also played pedal steel, lap steel, mandolin and banjo. Sometimes keyboards too. He was so modest he once asked me if I wouldn't put some of his instrumental credits after my name instead of his because he was afraid of looking like Mr Everything on the album sleeve. Hell, he was a band in himself and he was wildly enthusiastic about my idea of wedding Gram to The Damned, CCR to The Clash. He's too polite to say it but I think he was surprised how average Greg and I played when he met us.

We became known as Parsons acolytes and so I'd been asked to do the liner notes to the initial release of *Gram Parsons and the Fallen Angels Live 1973*. Oddly enough this brought The Long Ryders' name (which I took from the movie, and yes, the 'y' is from The Byrds) to public attention, and critics started writing about us and Rank & File as the beginning of something new in post-punk music. Jesus H. Christ.

Since I did those notes *Gram Parsons and the Fallen Angels Live 1973* has been issued four different times; LP, LP with extra EP you sent away for, CD and CD longbox with EP tracks included. *Safe at Home* has been reissued four times by three different companies. I wrote the liner notes for it the last two times. Quite a cottage industry, my Gram Parsons liner notes.

Hollywood is many things and it is certainly heaven for those of us who are interested in the history of twentieth-century entertainment and interested in collecting records. So if you are obsessed with a recording artist who lived and worked in the Hollywood area you can create your own heaven and play detective all you want.

I discovered that The International Submarine Band put out two singles prior to *Safe at Home*. One was tied in with the Alan Arkin movie *The Russians are Coming, The Russians are Coming*, and the other was simply one of rock's many rolls of the dice in 1966, a one-off single issued because Gram had connections in Greenwich Village and knew someone who knew someone who owned a record company. The next quest was the tricky part, how to find these four songs without which I would not be able to live a fulfilled and contented life.

The world had once again reached a point where there were no new Parsons recordings being unearthed. I knew Gram had recorded in 1971 at A&M with Terry Melcher producing, and it was common knowledge that GP's vocals for some *Sweetheart of the Rodeo* tracks were erased and replaced with Roger McGuinn's after a contract dispute with The International Submarine Band's label, LHI. Despite me hounding CBS about the *Sweetheart* tracks I got nowhere. A&M was better; I actually talked my way into the tape vault underneath the A&M lot but someone, apparently Parsons himself, had checked the tapes out of the library years ago and they were never returned. Hell, I even called Terry Melcher and he said he had no idea where the tapes were but I shouldn't worry about it, as the sessions were terrible. Didn't Melcher realize this was Gram we were talking about? How could the sessions have been anything less than fascinating?

At the old Capital Records swap-meet, held in the parking lot of Capital Records on the first Sunday morning of each month, I bumped into a greasy-haired, unshaven man who told me that if I came by his office on North Cole in Hollywood he might have something for me. He looked and sounded like a man who dealt in narcotics with friends in high places in Peru.

I went there and was immediately taken aback. It was filthy. Though it was technically an office, it had no toilet or washing facilities and he lived there. Records were on cheap metal shelves everywhere, many bootlegs and most of the others admittedly rare but wildly overpriced. The first Germs album was blaring from a crummy plastic portable record player. Record player, not stereo. The kind you could kick down the stairs and it would still play some music.

I stepped in like nothing was out of the ordinary. He ushered me into a even stinkier side room, more a big closet really, and handed me a 7-inch single. It was a bootleg with a xeroxed sleeve of four songs recorded by an early Byrds (therefore pre-Gram) line-up. Got it, I announced with as bored a tone as possible. Can't let these Hollywood slick types think they've got all the goods on us Kentucky boys. 'How 'bout this then?' my host yawned back at me.

Though the sleeve was a bootleg it was two-colour with a nice reproduction of the band on it, a band I did not recognize, posed as they were around a ladder. But in red letters on a white background on the right it read INTERNATIONAL SUB-MARINE BAND. It was the two early singles on a bootleg 45. The Holy Grail. Well not *the* Holy Grail perhaps, but one of 'em and certainly the latest. I almost fainted.

'That's twenty-five bucks,' greasy hair said. 'But to you for coming out here, twenty.' He coulda said fifty for all I cared. Where else was I ever gonna hear this stuff? I gave him a wadded up $20 bill I had taken out of my wallet and put in my opposite pocket in order to be able to show him my almost empty billfold and then say hey, I only got ten bucks, why don't you take that? On my way out I got an autograph from the LA indie legend who was then mopping the goddam floor like a high-school janitor and raced out of the door to find I'd locked the keys in my car.

The Long Ryders were starting to move. Originally we had a lot of psychedelia in our sound because I've always loved it, it was fashionable then and if you screwed up playing it onstage you could always act as if it was supposed to sound like that. But after the first couple of albums we saw bands like The Rain Parade and The Three O'Clock doing much better with it than we ever would, so we left it to them. The country aspect to our sound was new to almost every LA punker who heard it, and there was no way even a great band like, say, The Dream Syndicate could follow us into that realm, which for a while was only us and Rank & File.

A Burritos bootleg tape of a performance at the Avalon Ballroom in February 1969 fell into my hands, and not wanting to do one of Gram's own tunes and being forever subjected to requests for it (as opposed to requests for our stuff), I thought it would be a good idea to cover a tune the Burritos covered in their Avalon set. It was. We decided on Mel Tillis's 'Sweet Mental Revenge', which Hillman and Parsons probably knew from the Waylon Jennings hit version. The Long Ryders learned the Burritos' version note for note.

I had a wonderful girl named Bobbi Kaminski sew me a Confederate-flag jacket from three rebel flags bought in LA. I wore it at our first UK gig in Portsmouth. I also dropped and broke my beloved Rickenbacker twelve-string there. Snapped the neck. The next day at soundcheck in Dingwalls no less a person than Elvis Costello sent over two of them for me to use until my guitar was repaired. What a guy, eh?

At Dingwalls we knocked 'em dead. Got the reviews to prove it. The *NME* reviewer was so design-blind he criticized me for wearing a Townshend Union Jack jacket. Every night on tour there were audible gasps and shocked looks as we raced on-stage, me in that coat. Rock'n'roll live is only half music, Flamin' Groovie Cyril Jordan told me, the other half is visual, give 'em something to look at and I thought I was. Until Liverpool.

On 16 October we played the university there. In order to save money a hotel was booked in the Dingle, a very poor, rough part of town. It looked like a bomb had hit it fairly recently. I got lost walking around shortly after we'd checked in and found myself in front of a very, very familiar looking pub. I'd never been in Liverpool before. Suddenly it dawned on me. This was the pub on the cover of Ringo's *Sentimental Journey* album and his house was number four around the corner. I was a long way from home.

I went back to the hotel to share my discovery and I found the band outside with the tour manager looking at the van with much scratching of heads. Someone had broken in the van and taken all the cassettes, hand-luggage and all the clothes hung on the bar we'd installed across the back. I had taken my clothes in so I wasn't worried ... until I asked the roadie if he'd taken my stage clothes in. Er, no. He had not. The hotel manager had seen a Rastafarian hanging around the van looking suspicious and then had heard a bang and a crash and looked out to see no Rastafarian.

Someone had smashed the glass on the far side of the van, opened the door and taken the first things they had been able to get their hands on. My white Levi's Sin City jacket was stolen and my Confederate-flag jacket was stolen, the tour barely half over. What a Rastafarian thief would make of such a sartorial collection I don't know, but I cannot imagine him, dreadlocks flying, wearing that loud red, white and blue rebel-flag jacket anywhere but a Halloween party. What happened to these jackets I never saw again? Did he try to dump them at a used clothing store or Oxfam? What on earth was his lot in life, so poor he had taken to stealing clothes (not food or money or tape decks) out of filthy vans?

I was crushed. Two good jackets, two good ideas down the drain. All I wanted to do was continue the Burrito sense of sartorial humour started by their psychedelic garb, designed by Nudie, on the cover of *Gilded Palace of Sin*, and now I only had the photos to prove I'd actually gone out and had the stuff made. What an empty feeling.

In the meantime a real LA scenester was diagnosed with bone cancer back in West Hollywood. Michele Myer came down to Los Angeles with Rodney Bingenheimer to follow The Byrds when she was still a Catholic schoolgirl.

Michele's god in life was Chris Hillman. God. There is no other word and it is in fact the word she would use to me to describe Chris. I met her in 1979 when I was playing with The Unclaimed and she brought Cyril Jordan and ex-Animal Eric Burdon (whom I later ended up rooming with) to hear us. She walked to the lip of the stage as I was tuning my twelve-string and said, here, you look like you would enjoy reading these. She threw a fat manila folder at my feet. I took it home. It was stuffed with original teen-zine Byrds clippings from the sixties. She'd clipped every single piece of trash written about The Byrds since the year dot, and her apartment was full of the stuff. She was letting some of it go to me as a gesture from one true believer to another.

Although Michele Myer was brutal to many people as a booking agent at The Roxy, The Starwood and Madame Wong's West, she was always nice to me. She helped folks like The Blasters, X and The Plimsouls get going by giving them such good gigs, something she would later do for The Long Ryders. I've never seen a woman swear like Michele, and sometimes right after yelling at some poor bass player on the phone she'd turn to me in her office and smile and say something quite kind. She knew I loved the Burritos too (she sang backup on their 'Hippie Boy' after Gram invited her to join in at the session) and was always going on and on about how Gram would've loved my band.

Like all too many people in America she could not afford health insurance, so when the bone cancer was discovered she faced huge medical bills and even rejection by some hospitals and doctors knowing she would have difficulty paying. What a world. It was decided by some kind soul in Hollywood that, since Michele had helped so many people out, why not have a benefit performance to help pay her medical bills? We were asked, I said yes of course, and of all people Chris Hillman volunteered his services.

Most people on the bill were young, like Andy Taylor from Duran Duran, Steve Jones from The Sex Pistols and Dweezil Zappa. The only band I know Michele really liked musically on the entire bill was The Long Ryders, though she liked all the rest personally. She was overjoyed that Chris Hillman, who had retreated to the Ventura area having had his fill long ago of all things Hollywood, wanted to do the show.

Then a miracle happened. Chris Hillman asked if he could play with The Long Ryders. I thought I'd died and gone to heaven. The stipulation was we'd have to go on first because there was no way he was going to hang around and listen to heavy metal. We rehearsed four new Long Ryders tunes from our next album *Two-Fisted Tales* and then Chris came in to the rehearsal and we learned some Byrds/Burritos classics.

That none of the young girls in the audience knew who we or Chris Hillman were was weird enough, that they had no idea it was a benefit was stranger, that they cheered like crazy every time Andy Taylor moved his hair was worse. We tore through our new tunes to little applause (I should've seen the end coming right then and there, but we lasted another year), Chris came out to only polite applause and then for four songs we were The Byrds, we were the Burritos. Or so it felt. Stephen McCarthy and I took turns singing Gram's parts, Hillman gave me a quizzical look when I sang a verse of 'You Ain't Goin' Nowhere' in a Roger McGuinn voice, McCarthy hit his Clarence White licks like nobody's business, and I hit a harmony so off key on 'Have You Seen Her Face?' I still shudder when I think about it.

But I've got a killer photograph of that evening. Hillman is at the mike looking like Chris Hillman and I'm right behind him on guitar looking just like some guy trying to pretend he is in The Flying Burrito Brothers in 1969. Ah, success.

The Long Ryders were at the beginning of the end, though I thought we were about ready to crack this thing and really cash in, like R.E.M. had a few years earlier. Our next-to-last American tour took us to Tipitina's in New Orleans, a converted warehouse down by the river with a bust of Professor Longhair on display where you entered. My kind of joint.

Our gig went well, as they always did in New Orleans. The next day was a day off with nothing scheduled and we'd been there so many times there wasn't much in terms of tourism we hadn't seen. Out of nowhere I remembered that Gram Parsons, or what Phil Kaufman's matches and kerosene left of him, was buried in New Orleans, and this noteworthy grave was off something called Airline Drive or Airport Lane.

Our roadie Mike Lemon found the cemetery by using, of all things, the yellow pages. (We always liked to hire bright roadies, made us look good.) And so he, myself, Stephen McCarthy and someone else whom I can't recall for love nor money journeyed out to Gram's gravesite on a lazy Louisiana afternoon with nothing much else to do but visit tombstones.

I've made pilgrimages to Sylvia Plath's grave, Eddie Cochran's, Churchill's, those of several Presidents, Brian Jones's, and of course Graceland. This seemed at first to be more of the same.

We piled in the van and drove off arguing over who would navigate through town. An hour later we were on a straight road leading out towards the airport. Many New Orleans cemeteries have the graves above ground, as burying the dead is impossible in those parts of the city reclaimed from the mighty Mississippi and, since the town is only a few feet above sea level, the water table is so close to the surface that any casket six feet under has a tendency to rise to the level of the soil, sometimes breaking through the topsoil, after a storm or heavy Dixie rain.

Stephen was the first to spot the above-ground graves in the distance on the left. It was an eerie sight for anyone used to graves being underground. Most, but not all, of the graves were marked by statues or broad tombs. Some did seem to be buried just beneath the earth's surface (only just). At the caretaker's cottage we inquired as to the final resting place of the late Cecil Ingram Connor Parsons. The fellow inside had never heard of him. 'How about Gram Parsons?' I said. Oh that's over yonder, we were told, and the caretaker produced a xeroxed map of the cemetery, placing an X in red marker where the Grievous Angel's soul rested for all eternity, sleeping the sleep of the just.

We drove over and our party got out. Stephen had the map,

and I failed to notice that Mike Lemon was carrying a small ghetto blaster. No one could find the grave. Try as we might we didn't see anything, going over the same ground, time and time again. Finally Stephen rang out with, 'I got it'. I raced over.

The final resting place of Gram Parsons was a shocker. No Jim Morrison-like shrine of melted candles, empty wine bottles and spray paint, no Eddie Cochran schmaltzy tackiness, no Churchillian dignity, no Elvis overstatement, none of the above. Gram's 'grave', if you will, was a greying stone smaller than a brick resting flush on the ground with 'Gram Parsons' in weathered block print on its face. This stone was about an inch below the surface of the grassy topsoil, positioned so that seeing it was impossible from a distance of more than a few steps. No wonder it took so long to find it.

I'd heard Gram had a simple grave, that his stepdad was a cheapskate who wanted all the money for himself, but this was ridiculous. (The Gram Parsons Foundation in Memphis ran a collection for a new GP gravestone which, I believe, he has since received.) I weakly sat down on the long grass beside the stone and brushed away the dirt and grassblades which lay on his name. Jets roared overhead on their flightpath to the airport nearby. You could hear the cars from the highway quite clearly. The heat was intense and a man on the other side of the cemetery was having trouble working a powersaw as he attempted to trim tree branches away from the tops of statues and graves. It was awful, truly awful.

Then I heard music softly playing. Mike Lemon, who knew little if anything about Gram, did know that Stephen McCarthy and I really loved this dead man's music, so he had brought along a cassette of the live album I'd annotated six years before. We were in a graveyard so he refrained from turning it up too high but the effect was overpowering. I felt tears starting and turned away from the others. No one said a word and for twenty minutes we sat there on the grass looking at the pathetic little stone and this ugly cemetery by an ugly highway, not daring to look at each other lest we all start to weep like a Veterans Of Foreign Wars meeting.

After four or five songs I reached over and switched off the machine. I simply could not take any more. Mike looked at me quizzically, as if to ask if he had done something wrong. I meekly and very briefly smiled back at him and we rose and walked to the van in silence. The four of us drove away without looking back, no one saying a goddamn thing.

The Long Ryders broke up that year and it broke my heart, though I dared not tell anyone then. After a few more empty years in Los Angeles not knowing what to do, I decided I might, I just might, want to try living abroad, some place like London. A visit to Billy Bragg brought me into contact with Kate St John, a wonderful girl I'd seen before when her band, The Dream Academy, had their only hit right about the time The Long Ryders were trying to push 'Looking for Lewis and Clark' higher and higher into the charts. I thought, as I am certain most men did, she was beautiful, and I hoped to meet up with her again. Alas, she was with someone else, and like Cyrano or John Alden before me I could not say a thing.

Now rumour had it her romance had fizzled. Mine in LA certainly had so the timing was there. Without getting all *Sleepless in Seattle*, a series of wonderfully happy events occurred which brought us together, primarily her hearing me on the radio as I guest-hosted Mary Costello's Saturday evening GLR show in London. It was enough to get us together for that first time. That always awkward first time.

It was a Wednesday. I went over to her house for lunch and we went walking on Hampstead Heath. As we returned to her house I was invited in for tea and I found myself alone in her living room as she strode off to get our tea and whatever teeth-rotting nibbles we were going to have. I began to case the joint like a detective. I inched along the many bookshelves, admiring both the prestigious and the obscure titles, making a mental note of which ones to ask about, which ones to avoid like the plague.

On the floor by the door, underneath four black shelves, lay her record collection, a motley mess pushed this way and that way, with no Sid Griffin around to alphabetize, arrange or file in any proper loving fashion. Reggae next to Steely Dan's *Aja*, battered Beatles albums next to classical titles. This was no way to live.

Of the eight or nine lazy piles spilling out towards me, one caught my attention in particular. It was almost in the middle underneath the turntable and it was the only one in any real order. I deduced these were the titles most frequently and indeed recently played. Bending over to flip through the initial part of the row I was startled by the familiar light blue of *Grievous Angel*, Gram's final effort, right as she entered the room with a tray of tea and cakes. 'Do you know this album well?' I asked in all innocence.

'Oh yes,' came the confident reply. 'I've been listening to that since the week it came out, definitely a favourite, it's played all the time in this house.'

I looked her in the eye as I cradled the LP with its bent corners and worn front face, the area where the disc inside had worn a circle thereby giving Gram a bit of a halo. I was a long way from Kentucky and even further from my friends in California but I felt as if I was home forever.

Did the romance carry on? Hell, Mrs Griffin didn't raise fools, I married her. Best thing I ever did. I knew there was a reason I was listening to his music all those years.

I prepared to leave all my compadres behind in Los Angeles to move to London, to see what was over the next horizon, to check out that next rainbow for its pot of gold. I'd formed a new band, The Coal Porters, and they were not happy about me leaving them. Nor was I in many ways, but that is life.

I knew I'd better do some recording before I split, since I had no idea what calibre musician or studios would await me in London. Time was booked and we cut some Tex-Mex styled things, as I figured London might be full of Soft Cell refugees not knowing how to swing such things.

It was an emotional final session. The fellows knew what was up, knew this was it and were disappointed they'd not been with me long enough to capitalize on the Long Ryders connection and make any kind of a mark of their own in the music world. The band recorded a few things for our album and a few things I put on hold for a rainy day when I was dry and short of ideas. We also recorded some individual tracks for compilation albums, one featuring modern bands doing 1970s hits, one a collection of LA bands and a song for a Gram Parsons tribute album.

Being cynical I reasoned most folks would expect Sid Griffin to do something special for the Gram Parsons tribute album. I also guessed the other acts would do obvious material and that many of them would miss the inherent irony, the pull between rural values and the city's reality in Gram's music. I was right all round.

For our selection I chose 'November Nights', a song Gram performed (and I believe recorded, in 1966 at Gold Star on the lost album session) with The International Submarine Band but never released himself. Peter Fonda used it for a 1966 flop single, and that arrangement is the one we based our recording on. I couldn't get horn players on such short notice so I had our keyboardist play the horn riff on some horrific piece of plastic masquerading as a piano. No one but no one in the band liked the song or our take of it and several of them tried to talk me out of it, to get me to record something broader, easier, more famous. These final sessions should've been a coming together and a healing too. But we were grumpy and argumentative and I was ready to get to London and the girl ASAP.

One track makes this tribute a necessity for every Parsons obsessive. Sid Griffin, ex-Long Ryder and author of Gram Parsons: A Music

Biography, *has obviously done his homework. A Parsons recording of his own song 'November Nights' has never been found, and unless you own Peter Fonda's [yes, that Peter Fonda] 1966 cover or saw Parsons perform it live around Boston at that time, you haven't heard it. Griffin and his band The Coal Porters cover the song and don't disappoint, providing a text-book example of how Parsons gave his best music its syncopated groove by mixing up rhythms as well as genres.*

Corey Seymour, *Rolling Stone* magazine

One of my last meals in LA before coming to London was at a swank grill in the heart of Hollywood, where starlets hang out hoping to be noticed and you can hear deals being made for motion pictures at the tables around you. Everyone had a mobile phone. Except me.

I was invited there by a lawyer and a manager to meet Polly Parsons, Gram's daughter. In Phil Kaufman's book he says Gram denied the baby girl was his but changed his heart at the court hearing. Polly Parsons was then thinking about being a nurse and since has attempted a singing career, fronting a C&W band called She which was managed by Pamela Des-Barres, writer of the groupie memoir *I'm With the Band*. They have since disbanded.

As the meal went on it became apparent my brain was being picked about Gram's career. Claims were being made about Gram's royalties (he never sold records when he was alive and he is hardly a big seller now) and how they never went to Polly or her mother. There was alleged hanky-panky about a Byrd and Gram's dough and various record companies and Gram's dough and this evil lawyer and Gram's dough and some old flame of Gram's wanting his dough.

I ate my expensive yet none too filling meal in growing disgust. Gram Gram Gram Gram Gram Gram. That's all anyone was saying, but they really meant me me me me me me, or better yet, money money money money money money. There was an exciting basketball play-off game reaching fever pitch on TV and businessmen in the restaurant's cocktail bar were shouting encouragement at the players on TV. Out of the corner of my eye I saw Nick Lowe having a drink quietly. I thought of the girl I knew I wanted to marry waiting for me in London. I wanted to be anywhere but at this stupid business meeting disguised as dinner.

Shortly before the meal ended, in the middle of someone's long legal point, I interrupted saying I wasn't feeling well and would they excuse me. Before anyone could reply I pushed away from the table and was way out the door. It was a warm early evening like the one when I walked past the two long-haired kids who thought I was endorsing AC/DC in my Sin City jacket, the one stolen in Liverpool.

The hell with it. I was going to leave my beloved California with its terrific weather, winning baseball teams, powerful surf and all my many compadres. I was going to London to chase that girl. Gram was gone, he didn't need me. I'd be a Burrito no longer.

That's Entertainment

D. J. TAYLOR

They began doing dodgy, Cockney-accented, R&B covers, told everyone they were going to vote Conservative and started the Mod revival, spearheaded by acolytes The Lambrettas and Secret Affair. By the time Paul Weller jacked it in, The Jam were the biggest cult group in Britain. Weller became the voice of a white, male suburban generation, and so their singles were guaranteed Top 10 status on core-following alone, but sadly nobody else was interested and the singles would plummet into oblivion quicker than you could say 'can't crossover'. They made two classic albums, *Setting Sons* and *All Mod Cons*, and several good ones and, 'amusingly', once sent a turd in the post to The Damned. Paul Weller is now enjoying an artistic, critical and commercial renaissance. The other Jam members, Bruce Foxton and Rick Buckler, are not.

From 1978 to 1982 The Jam were My Group. They were My Group since I saw them on the *Marc Bolan Show* playing 'All Around the World', a furious piece of noise with bawled lyrics about 'youth explosions', to the evident bewilderment of their leopardskin-clad host. I bought their singles on the day they came out. I liked them for their sharp suits and their black and white shoes, their Rickenbacker guitars, the crazed way they hurled themselves around the stage, and of course the songs, which were half romantic dolefulness (an essential pop ingredient since The Beatles) and half stinging sociology. Above all, in an age that favoured bearded Californians crooning about adultery, I liked them merely for being English, for singing about council houses and watching the news and not eating your tea.

It was always a comfort to know that they were never going to conquer America.

The Jam. There were three of them: working-class lads from Woking, friends since their teens, who'd clambered their way up through the wheeltappers and shunters' clubs and the cabaret circuit – Paul Weller, gloomy, passionate, opinionated, who wrote and sang most of the songs; Bruce Foxton, who played bass with a kind of mesmerizing energy, head bobbing up above the microphone like a greyhound in the slips; Rick Buckler, who expertly held down the beat. Curiously, I liked them for this compactness, for not being over-burdened by troops of keyboard players or fanciful percussionists. When, towards the end, they tacked on a brass section and roped in Weller's mate Mick Talbot to play organ, it was a sure sign that the game was up. Paul's adenoidal voice, a guitar sound designed to strip paint off walls, Bruce's lolloping, counterpoint bass, Rick's route-march 4/4. Sparse and unornamented, fizzing and direct, it was one of the classic seventies pop noises, as distinctive in its way as Slade's raucous blare, or the roller-coaster aloofness of Roxy Music. Wham Bam, as the first *New Musical Express* cover spread in the summer of 1977 advised, Here Comes The Jam.

If I can find a context in which to locate Paul, Bruce and Rick, two-tone shoes and jangly guitars, it lies in childhood, and in particular with The Beatles. My parents were the kind of cautious middle-class people who faintly disapproved of pop music while remaining routinely aware of it, the kind – a very common category, I later discovered – who affected to loath the Fab Four but who still inexplicably bought their records. A copy of 'She Loves You' consequently rubbed shoulders on the rack next to the *Messiah* and The *Dream of Gerontius*. Undoubtedly most of this impetus came from my father. On the one hand a 'serious' singer – so competent a tenor, in fact, that it was an embarrassment to stand alongside him in the otherwise reedy throng of a church congregation – he remained a devotee of every sort of Anglo-American popular music up until but not including the advent of Elvis. There were piles of sheet music stuffed under the lid of the family piano, and one of my earliest memories is of learning to sing 'In a Mountain Greenery' and 'Chattanooga Choo-Choo' over the top of his thrumming fortissimo accompaniment. Though my father used quite seriously to maintain that The Beatles, along with jeans and fish fingers, were responsible for the decline of Western civilization, I think he sometimes found this pose rather a struggle. Certainly he liked 'Penny Lane' and the line 'in his pocket is a portrait of the Queen' ('that means a stamp,' he used to explain, sternly exasperated at the idea of Paul McCartney managing a lyrical flourish), along with any amount of tuneful mid-sixties pop: 'Excerpt from a Teenage Opera', Mike Sarne's 'Come Outside', 'Downtown'. Such eclecticism had its effect: by the time I was eleven my record collection consisted of 'She Loves You', an EP of Simon and Garfunkel covers and the 1970 England World Cup Squad singing 'Back Home'.

At the same time, though, there were stirrings of what the *NME* in its great late-seventies days would call a 'pop sensibility'. The first single I bought was Slade's 'Coz I Luv You', which came out in autumn 1971. In those days there was no ban on consecutive appearances on *Top of the Pops*: Slade were on seven times running – the week the single was released, the week it charted at Number 26, the week it rose dramatically to Number 8 ('up 18 places...' Tony Blackburn would divulge with an intent seriousness, as if he were revealing the Shadow Cabinet election results), and the four weeks it reposed at Number 1. I watched every appearance, fascinated by the boys' cheery football-hooligan demeanour (they had only recently emerged from their skinhead phase), Noddy Holder's Dickensian leer, Jim Lea's eldritch violin flourishes, the rampant shout-line ('I won't laugh at you when you boo hoo hoo coz I lurve you'). It was the beginning of a short but fervent love affair. Just as Norwich City were my football team and J. R. R. Tolkien was my writer, so Slade were my group. I bought such pop papers as printed their song lyrics or disclosed that Noddy's real name was, rather embarrassingly, Neville. In the summer of 1972 they actually played St Andrew's Hall in Norwich, a roomy old amphitheatre where we had our school prize-giving. I asked my father to take me. He thought about it, consulted knowledgeable younger colleagues at work, and then declined, but I consoled myself by scraping together the £2 necessary to purchase *Slade Alive*, their storming live set. This fixation went on for some time: I bought a large black exercise book in which to log their progress up and down the chart. But then, unaccountably, Slade blew it. Even at thirteen I was enough of a purist to think that 'Merry Xmas Everybody' wasn't quite the most rockingest, least compromising pop statement placed on vinyl. After this they started releasing treacly ballads with no power chords (the *idea* of Noddy Holder, who had a voice like a cut-throat razor, singing a ballad!). Finally they headed west across the Atlantic and became one of those British bands who failed to make it in America and ruined their careers back home in consequence.

Meanwhile, there was another set of contenders lining up beyond the horizon. Sparks consisted of a couple of oddball Los Angeles brothers named Mael: Russell (pretty-boy falsetto) and Ron (inert keyboard player), who together with three mundane sidemen – the drummer, I remember, rejoiced in the name of Dinky Diamond – exploded into the national pop firmament in mid 1974. Trapped in front of the cameras for the first time on *TOTP* doing 'This Town Ain't Big Enough for Both of Us' they seemed to me the epitome of transatlantic weirdness: Russell warbling lines of quite startling indecency, Ron motionless apart from an occasional baring of teeth, bozo henchmen thrashing on impassively in the background. Inspection of their back catalogue revealed that they'd been even more outlandish in the past: this was the watered down commercial version. The

NME, whose opinions I took very seriously in those formative days, suggested that they were a couple of prissy fruits. Plainly it was time to be moving on. But locating the new pop sensation in the England of 1975 was easier than it sounded. Pop history, famously, has revealed the mid 1970s to be a kind of desert of under-achievement and boredom, made up of pomp rock, synthesizers, castrati vocals, men with beards and Roger Dean cover artwork. Without claiming undue prescience, it was possible to make this judgement at the time. Not only were the major league acts – Genesis, ELP, Yes, Pink Floyd – completely dreadful; so were the supposedly 'interesting' minor outfits. Does anyone, I wonder, remember Greenslade or Druid or Camel or Baker-Gurvitz Army? I do, and as they quavered on about hobbits, spyglass guests and snowgeese they made *The Old Grey Whistle Test* unwatchable for about three years.

Unhappily, this sense of isolation was compounded by peer pressure. At thirteen those of us at school who were interested in pop music confined ourselves to excited conversations about *Mud Rock Vol. 2.* But at fourteen there were suddenly crowds of boys reverently exchanging Robins Records bags (Robins was the big Norwich independent shop) on the edge of the school playground, and what you thought and said about music was taken very seriously, or in my case derisorily, indeed. At Norwich School, a middling grammar school that had joined the private sector when the Labour Government removed its direct grant, musical affiliations divided up broadly along class lines. A few North Norwich hooligans went in for Northern Soul of the Wigan's Ovation/Johnny 'Guitar' Watson school. There was a solitary Teddy Boy, a Norfolk farmer's son named Andy Easton, who brought his own records (mostly obscure fifties rockabilly) to school discos and intimidated the DJ into playing them. But the great majority of the sons of the prosperous Norwich bourgeoisie, the boys I knew, favoured what was known as progressive rock. Not only did this label take in horrors such as Pink Floyd, but it extended to possibly the worst group in the history of the world, an ensemble much favoured by Norwich Schoolboys, named Barclay James Harvest. They had beards. They came from Oldham. They played mellotrons. They specialized in reedy abstractions with titles like 'Crazy City'. I hated them.

Intermittently, bright spots flickered into view. A boy called Pete Cadman, one of a notorious Norwich School clan, numbers of whom had been expelled for what was laconically referred to as A Drugs Episode, lent me a copy of the first Velvet Underground LP. Captain Beefheart turned up about this time, too, by way of a recommendation in the *NME Book of Rock*, another publication I took very seriously in those days, although you could go badly wrong with it, as happened when I tracked down an obscure and unlistenable recording by much-vaunted Norwegian jazz-rock outfit Burnin' Red Ivanhoe. There was also a glimmer of home-grown talent in the shape of Dr Feelgood, who really were the business in terms of sound, even if one had to endure cartoon lyrics about the singer walking twenty yards behind his girlfriend the better to monitor her gyrating buttocks. The Feelgoods played St Andrew's Hall too, in June 1976, but it was the night before my O level French oral so I couldn't go. However, the wet, enveloping blanket of progressive rock fell heavily over one's social life in these years (I remember being sternly rebuked for liking Sparks by a boy named Dick Shelton on the grounds that none of their album tracks was more than five minutes long). It fell still more heavily over primitive attempts to participate in the world of pop itself. For about six months, in 1975, as the nervous owner of a Hofner Les Paul (it cost £25, which was all my savings and twenty weeks' Sunday paper-round money), I was a member of A Group. There were four of us: Pete Barnes on vocals, Dick of the distressingly prog-rock tendencies on bass, a boy called Richard Frostick, whose father, the Lord Mayor of Norwich, could occasionally be seen donning his mayoral chain outside in the hall while we rehearsed, on drums, and myself. At early rehearsals, amplification being in short supply, everything was channelled through a 20-watt record player. Later, somebody borrowed the physics lab's AC 30 on long loan. As fledgling rock superstars, our chief worry was fixing on a resonant enough name. We started out as Mithril (I was still reading Tolkien), changed quickly to Hulk, thence to Mole, subsequently to Wave. Musically, we played D. J. Taylor originals, for example the Status Quo tribute 'Night Train to Memphis':

> It's the night train to Memphis, burning on its wheels of fire
> It's the night train to Memphis, and the music gets higher and higher

In fact, with two guitars and a microphone plugged into a Sony stereo, the music got lower and lower, but it was the spirit that mattered. There was another one called 'The Angels are Coming', about motorcycle violence, which began 'Heading out of Newport Pagnell on a souped-up Saturday morning ...' I left, or 'quit' as we used to say in imitation of the music press, in the summer for what I proudly informed the playground cognoscenti were musical differences – the other three hankered after those Pink Floyd numbers – but was at least as much to do with their refusal to countenance the admission of my friend Bob (who as it happened could scarcely play a note) on rhythm guitar. I haven't seen any of them for fifteen years, but when last heard of Dick was a dentist and Pete and Richard were accountants, which just goes to show. Curiously, there were people at school who went on to make some sort of career in the music business: Ian Thirkettle, rechristened 'Stan', played guitar with the immortal Farmer's Boys; Tom Fenner drummed for Microdisney; while Simon Denbigh, half of a sixth-form comedy duo named Pratt and Denbigh, graced both The March Violets and The Batfish Boys.

But this was 1975. All that – like exams, university and the tumbling world – was before us. The Jam, too, lay silent beyond the pop horizon. And yet I knew they were there, knew that at some point there would be another group, *the* group, whom I could claim as my own, that Paul, Bruce and Rick with their suits and their Rickenbacker guitars would come careering over flat fields that currently echoed to the sound of Be Bop Deluxe (who I thought were crap, but everyone else liked) and *Wish You Were Here*. All this was the purest speculation, of course. The stirrings to the North and West went unreported. The fact that as I quietly shelled out £1.50 for a secondhand copy of Captain Beefheart's *Bluejeans and Moonbeams*, Lydon, Jones and Co. were planning their assault on Tin Pan Alley, and that 200 miles northwest Howard Devoto and Pete Shelley were forming Buzzcocks, would only become apparent years later. Until well into 1976, the only data I possessed on The Sex Pistols was a story that had appeared in a February *NME* under the canny headline DON'T LOOK OVER YOUR SHOULDER BUT THE SEX PISTOLS ARE COMING! But this was of scant interest to someone who had just made his print debut with a measured contribution to an *NME* symposium on that vital topic Should Gabriel have left Genesis?

Punk exploded, or rather fizzed gamely, on to the Norwich School scene on the morning in late November 1976 when somebody first played 'Anarchy in the UK' on the Sixth Form Club gramophone. To the majority of earnest seventeen-year-olds soberly trading copies of *Tales from Topographic Oceans* in the foreground, the effect was like that of a Free Church elder suddenly detecting a whiff of incense floating across the ceiling of his austere Highland chapel. As it happened, I didn't much care for it myself. I was an intransigently conservative schoolboy – another band I formed shortly before this time was called Woolwich West in celebration of a Tory by-election victory – and I found the idea of yobbish teenagers who couldn't sing whining on about anarchy deeply distasteful. But all over the place the statutes were being kicked away. John Peel had already unbent sufficiently to start playing The Damned's 'New

Rose' among the quarter-hour slabs of self-indulgence by Gryphon and Tangerine Dream; various superannuated fogies were lining up in the music papers to complain that they (the punks) couldn't play and that it (the music) wouldn't last; and you just knew that it was all going to change, that the day of the bearded synthesizer player was over, that Rick Wakeman, ELP and the rest of them were on the way out.

Meanwhile there was the problem of finding something one actually liked. I thought the Pistols were a bunch of yobs, and nodded approvingly over press reports of the police break-up of their Jubilee night excursion on the Thames. The Clash seemed the worst sort of art school pinheads, forever going on about something called 'constructive violence' (apparently if you hit someone and he stopped doing something you didn't like, then this was a good thing) to respectful interviewers. The Damned were a self-destructing joke even then; The Stranglers looked suspiciously like old men caught in a propitious time playing recycled Doors riffs. That left The Jam.

The *NME* cover spread WHAM BAM HERE COMES THE JAM! had them peeking out jauntily from behind a street corner. Even Paul, whose gloom quickly became a feature of group interviews, looked cheerful. Bruce and Rick were clearly revelling in it: you got the feeling that after years on the club circuit the knowledge that they were finally pop stars was a shade overwhelming. Best of all was the revelation that the boys *actually intended to vote Conservative at the next election.* This famously unforgivable remark, made by Weller with the aim of annoying the more political ensembles like The Clash, I took at face value.

But faced with a kind of noise that one hadn't heard before and certainly not at this speed, and a degree of political and social awareness that had been conspicuously absent from the music of the mid-1970s, nearly everyone was making mistakes of this sort: it was my then hero Charles Shaar Murray of the *NME* who, reviewing some early Clash waxing, tetchily remarked that if this was a garage band then they ought to be speedily returned there and the motor left running. Even then, though, despite the suits, the ties, the shoes, the Rickenbacker guitars, that majestic second single 'All Around the World', despite the Conservatism, I hesitated about The Jam. Old loyalties died hard. Mid 1977 found me listening – shameful to relate, but accuracy demands it – to Status Quo's *Live* and Fleetwood Mac's *Rumours*. There were other, more pressing anxieties, such as A levels, school plays and the pursuit of an unyielding siren from the Norwich High School for Girls named Diana Sutton-Jones, in the face of which pop music tended to take a back seat. Later on, listening to other people talk about their schooldays, in mixed North London day schools or Grimepit Comprehensive, South Yorkshire, I used to marvel at the ticket-collector-on-the-Oblivion-Express existences some of them seemed to have enjoyed ('So then me and this chick got really stoned...'). I spent the years from sixteen to nineteen worrying about Oxbridge exams, my chances in the Eastern Schools Public Speaking Championships, and whether the head-master disliked me insufficiently to make me a prefect.

The Jam, too, were having an unsatisfactory time of it. The second album, I dimly discerned somewhere between putting down an essay on the use of the phrase 'Kingdom of God' in the Synoptic Gospels and picking up *Waiting for Godot,* was slightly inferior to the first. February 1978's 'News of the World', the fourth single, didn't even sound like The Jam, the reason being, I later discovered, that it was Bruce who wrote and sang it. Only later did one learn how near it had all come to falling apart: how Paul, transfixed in love, idled away the hours writing unrecordable songs with titles like 'I Love to Paint', how Bruce gave a maudlin interview to *Sounds* in which he canvassed the notion of giving it all up and opening a guest-house, how Rick did whatever it is that drummers do when the other two thirds of the band is having an identity crisis. 'David

Watts', the fifth single, an old Kinks number, which I heard a few times over the summer, in between taking A levels and waiting for the results, didn't sound too bad. But the blinding flash of revelation, the moment when I divined for all time that my heroes had come at last, arrived in October 1978 when, looking up from some knowing excursus on the personal government of Charles I (I was doing Oxbridge entrance in Modern History), I chanced upon The Jam performing 'Down in the Tube Station at Midnight' on *TOTP*. Even now, sixteen years on, that song still seems an extraordinary achievement for a twenty-year-old, which is the age I calculate Weller to have been when he wrote it: bleak imagery – the song is about a man being attacked by a gang of fascist thugs in a deserted subway – mordant, tightly controlled lyrics, the awful pathos in Weller's voice as he reaches the finale. The result, or so it seemed to me, was genuine poetry. At any rate it was a long way superior to the cautious little ironic fragments one read in the *Times Literary Supplement*. A couple of days after the Oxbridge exams, which passed in a blur of nerves and influenza, wanting to treat myself to something alluring, I splashed out on their third album, *All Mod Cons*, then getting rave reviews.

Eventually I got into St John's College, Oxford, after a calamitously traumatic interview in which an edifice of historical untruths carefully constructed by my chief tormentor, a Mr, later Professor, now Sir Keith, Thomas, and gamely accepted by my credulous younger self was finally sent crashing around my ears (comparing notes much later, we discovered that the severity of the interview was in inverse proportion to your performance in the exam: at any rate the boy before me who wandered out benignly to announce that 'they asked me what I wanted to talk about' was never seen again). Later, again, I used to marvel at the accounts people gave of what they did in the nine months off between school and university ('So then I had to have antibiotics for the saddle sores . . . Of course you could only see the llamas from the highest passes. . .'). I spent the first nine months of 1979 working in a bookshop in Norwich, where I covered library orders in cellophane – 'quite possibly the dreariest manual task known to humankind – checked the movements of the light-fingered clientele and tried not to antagonize the formidable Mrs Gliddon, wife of the shop's diffident owner. But in the evenings, when not brooding over the gas-fire or writing a (need I say) unpublished autobiographical novel called *Tomorrow Belongs to Me*, there was always The Jam. With my first week's wages – £25, about twice as much money as I'd ever seen in my life – I bought the first album, *In the City*. With my second week's wages – I was a prudent young man with a horror of extravagance – I bought the second album, *This is the Modern World*. And with the aid of concert reviews, liner notes and the ever-helpful *NME* – which after a short period of thinking them the black sheep of the New Wave had now decided that The Jam were A Good Thing – I set about getting to know my idols. Paul, it quickly became apparent, was The Face: frontman, opinion-former and muse: Bruce being confined to the occasional B-side or album-filler. It was Paul who dropped the acid comments in the newspapers. In interviews, while Paul discoursed about politics and the books he was reading, Bruce and Rick came across as nice blokes who liked a drink and a laugh. None of my subsequent research refined this assessment of moody frontman and keen, companionable sidekicks. The other key characteristic – key, that is, to anyone who had grown up in the serious mid-seventies albums culture, when 'well-produced' was about the highest compliment that could be applied to a record – was that The Jam were a singles band. The albums gave the impression of being written in some haste in the studio, and had a tendency to harbour Foxton originals with hopelessly naff lyrics or obvious makeweights like 'Music for the Last Couple' on *Sound Affects*. But the singles rarely failed. 1979 was a vintage year: 'Strange Town' in the spring; 'When You're Young', with its classic line about the world being your oyster but the future a clam, in the summer; 'The Eton Rifles' in the autumn.

Meanwhile, time was moving on. They had punk gigs by this stage at St Andrew's Hall, hugely violent affairs with fighting in the foyer and punch-ups in the crowd. The Undertones played there on their first tour in March – five scrofulous Irish lads with pudding-basin haircuts and old pullovers who beamed with delight when you applauded, ran out of songs during the encore and were reduced to finishing with a version of Gary Glitter's 'Rock and Roll (Part 2)'. But then the autumn came, I said goodbye, not unregretfully, to the bookshop, despatched the manuscript of *Tomorrow Belongs to Me* to the first of the several publishers who weren't going to publish it, packed my possessions into the boot of my father's old Morris Marina, and was driven away to the dappled lawns and sun-drenched quadrangles of Oxford, or rather the rainy sidestreets and freezing accommodation blocks of Oxford, the putting away of childish things and the beginnings of adult life.

Somehow, though, The Jam followed me; somehow Weller's voice was there amongst the wide-eyed dishevelment of the first term, its two dozen essays and exam-strewn conclusion; somehow one still fingered the *NME* out of a sheaf of more august publications in the hope that there might be news of an album or a tour or – even better – a page of Paul replying with inarticulate sincerity to a respectful interlocutor.

Probably a little of this had to do with the heightened sense of class awareness that being in a place like Oxford, and, more important, being with one's fellow-Oxonians, aroused. (I can remember sitting in the TV room when The Jam were playing 'The Eton Rifles' and hearing a peacock voice which belonged to a girl named Kathy Shipsey shriek, 'Hamish, you were at Eton – what are these chappies on about?' What Hamish said in reply I don't recall.) Certainly it had nothing to do with one of the traditional reasons for favouring pop music, that of infiltrating your way into the affections of the opposite sex. None of the girls I knew at college liked The Jam. It was too loud, the singer sounded too miserable, and anyway you couldn't hear the words. Female musical taste at Oxford was depressingly uniform. In three years there I didn't find a record collection that failed to yield up Al Stewart's *Year of the Cat*, the obligatory Cat Stevens album (usually *Tea for the Tillerman*) and The Eagles' *Hotel California* (years later, invited to supper for the first time with the girl I was subsequently to marry and flicking patronizingly through the record sleeves, almost the first thing I uncovered was, sure enough, Mr Al Stewart: worse, Rachel had even attended one of his concerts). No, The Jam were a boys' band. In footage of their live shows seething masses of lads in parkas coursed back and forth like football fans on the terraces. And liking them was on a par with liking football or some other ritualistic sectarian pursuit. Oddly Weller both conciliated this collectivism and sharply exposed it. Half the songs drew on the group ethos – 'Saturday's Kids', 'That's Entertainment'– but the other half were highly personal and apparently authentic. Anyone else who sang, in relation to a love affair, that he wanted to be like Peter Pan would have been hooted out of the studio: Weller seemed to have enough conviction to get away with it.

And so, amid the bitter mornings and the misty afternoons – it rains all the time in Oxford, and the fog rising up along the Thames Valley is a consumptive's nightmare – The Jam survived. By this time, of course, they were not merely one among a number of promising New Wave bands, but the Big Thing. 'Going Underground', the first single of 1980, went straight in at Number 1, thanks partly to the adroit record-company marketing ploy of including a free live EP, but also partly to unprecedented fan commitment: it was selling 30,000 copies a day in the week of release. The annual *NME* Readers' Poll became The Jam first, the rest nowhere. Best group. Best singer/guitar/bass/drums. Best single. Best album. Best live act. The presence of an occasional piano fill on *All Mod Cons* soon had Paul marked down as best keyboards. Curiously, despite elitist attitudes towards every other art form, I liked this solidarity, liked the popularity and the sight of Paul's bony, cheerless face staring from posters. I even started to try and look like him: the dark jacket, the fags, the white shirt and black tie, the silk scarves. Such was the depth of my ardour that it survived even exposure to the withering sensibilities of Paul Oldfield. Oldfield, known as Davros after his uncanny resemblance to the head dalek in *Dr Who*, an English postgraduate of saturnine appearance and ever more precarious tenure, had what were at this stage the most extreme musical tastes of anyone I had met. An early fan of punk – he was supposed to have worked in an alternative record shop in the heady days of early '77 – he had quickly moved on to its obscure post- and post-post variations. He liked (well – listened to) bands like Rema-Rema and Dome, the Wire spin-off, bands whose records came in stencilled sleeves from unheard of indie labels, and whose performances consisted either of savage shrieking above rumbling bass lines or spiky electronic doodlings. Needless to say, he didn't like The Jam.

Despite this stern tutelage, I persevered (and Oldfield wasn't infallible: he bought the first Altered Images single before he discovered that they were a pop group, and an early-eighties hankering after something called 'radical dance' was jettisoned when ABC went commercial). As it turned out, The Jam took most of 1981 off. There was just a brace of, to my exigent mind, not entirely top-flight singles, in particular 'Funeral Pyre' which, so far as I could deduce, didn't have a tune. When they returned early in 1982 with *The Gift* it was clear that something was wrong: some foursquare Jam classics, certainly, but also some pastiche calypso, Motown approximations and weedy Stax keyboards. Bruce and Rick sounded slightly bemused, muffled down in the mix by trumpet players and overdubs. Finals were looming, the rejection slips from advertising agencies and publishing houses lay across the desk, but I listened on as the snow fell over front quad, the smell of paint lingered in the air, and the decorators worked to repair my room, which had been wrecked by a burst pipe. Summer came with its protracted stake-out in Examination Schools – ten three-hour papers in seven days. The rejection letters were cascading in now – from journalism training schemes, oil-company marketing departments, university post-graduate courses: 1982 was a bad year for graduate employment. I left Oxford in June 1982 to spend six months fretting at home and writing the occasional piece about what it felt like to be a graduate on the dole, which was quite a lucrative sideline in those days.

Elsewhere, as it turned out, equally radical disturbances were in store for settled ways of existence. The Jam produced a late-summer single, 'The Bitterest Pill', not one of their best, and then suddenly, there it was – the headlines on the front page of the *NME*, the stony, impassive faces, the rumours and denials (it was all Paul's doing, everyone knew), fission and recrimination. Curiously, I hardly thought about The Jam's demise. I was too busy applying for the assistant editorship of *Scouting Weekly* or jobs with firms of religious publishers. There was a farewell tour, a wonderful extended appearance on an early edition of *The Tube*, a valedictory single, 'Beat Surrender'. In the same week, as it happened, I got a job – not *the* job, but at any rate paid employment, in a public-relations agency off Oxford Street. That Tuesday, the day the BBC singles chart was announced, I was in Banbury on the return leg of a week-long commission to investigate *The Spectator*'s then practically non-existent circulation, but I made sure I was in W. H. Smith's record department when they posted up the new chart positions. The Jam went straight in at Number 1, as I had known they would, but the warm glow of fulfilment (even then, at twenty-two, they were My Group) was balanced by the knowledge that some sterner realities lay at hand.

I kept up with them. Come the spring I queued for four hours in the mud of Brockwell Park for a CND concert which saw the unveiling of The Style Council (I was right-wing Labour by then, so I could just about stand the politics).

Strangely, I'd never seen The Jam live: Norwich and Oxford were well away from the big concert circuit. They played two numbers, and it was scarcely worth the wait. Where were the jangly guitars? Where were the poppy melodies? The laboured off-white soul now proffered by Weller, Mick Talbot and assorted backing singers seemed a poor substitute. Bruce had a brief solo career, bounced around the *TOTP* studio to a likeable-sounding single called 'Freak', and then disappeared. Rick fronted a band called Time UK, recorded a single which Mike Read played a bit, and then was gone. Weller was doing Labour Party benefits by this time, crooning sweetly about *cafés bleus* and his ever-changing moods, and The Smiths sounded a great deal more interesting. But I never forgot them.

The half-dozen albums and the row of singles in their glossy sleeves stayed in the record rack, and I watched out proudly for Paul on the Band Aid video. As late as 1988, when somebody asked me whom I most admired, I toyed with and then rejected names such as Peter Ackroyd and Martin Amis before coming up with Paul Weller. After Polydor had thrown The Style Council off the label I went to one of his first solo gigs (he looked a bit lost and uncertain, plainly exasperated by the parka-clad hordes at the front clamouring for 'Strange Town') and watched approvingly over his later renaissance. And in early 1994, by an extraordinary stroke of pertinacity, I even got to interview Bruce and Rick. The excuse, a flimsy paperback life and times, was literally that. I simply wanted to meet them, to be able to say to my brother (another diehard), ultimately perhaps even to my son, that 'I have sat and talked to Bruce Foxton and Rick Buckler'.

I sat in the pub outside their management offices in Cleveland Street nursing a pint of Guinness in the gravest anticipation. What would they be like? Would they really speak to me? It was painfully apparent that, seventeen years on from their first *TOTP* appearance in mohair suits and footrule ties, time's ravages had been at work. Rick had lost most of his hair. Bruce had that frail, etiolated and slightly gangsterish look of the middle-aged man adrift in the young man's world. The good humour, recalled from a score of music-press interviews, remained. The eleven-year journey away from The Jam turned out to have taken a predictable route: lean times in cheap rehearsal rooms with bands that never made it, badly handled business ventures (Rick), unsuccessful songwriting (Bruce). Bruce currently plays bass with Stiff Little Fingers, another band of seventies leftovers.

Rick, meanwhile, has settled for a furniture-restoration business down Woking way. 'The expectations everyone had for us after The Jam split were far too high,' he plausibly suggested. For a moment I wondered about inventing some furniture that needed restoring, a biggish job that would probably require the attendance of the boss himself . . . then I let it go.

I liked them enormously, liked them for their scrupulousness – resisting the temptation to be nasty about Paul, or Paul's dad, who as manager could easily have been cast as the villain of the peace – liked them for their apparently genuine pleasure in the fact that I had bought their records and stuck their likenesses on my bedroom wall. Rather than harbouring gross resentments over The Jam's demise, which sundered three of the most potentially lucrative careers in British pop, they were merely bewildered. You grow up with someone. You start a group. It matches, exceeds and then far surpasses your modest expectations. And then your mate Paul, whom you knew in the old days of playing cloakrooms for £5 a night, not only walks out on you, but won't speak to you again. Weller, notoriously, has not communicated with his former sidekicks for over a decade, and there is, as Bruce wistfully put it, a limit to the number of Christmas cards you can send someone.

The Jam. They were the last of my adolescent enthusiasms, the last great English pop group, with the possible exception of The Smiths. There have been other great English pop groups –

Magazine, XTC, Madness. None of them quite possessed, or wanted, The Jam's command over their environment, the same awareness of their past. Even as I write, rock critics are shaking their heads over Blur's candidature for international celebrity on the grounds that their influences are from this side of the Atlantic, without realizing that this is what makes them special: doleful love songs, sardonic stuff about watching television, going on holiday and being young.

The Jam. Paul, Bruce and Rick. I couldn't bear it if they reformed. It would be like meeting your twenty-year-old self at a party. When I play their records now it is mostly for their evocation of past time – fog over the South Parks Road, grainy Norwich dawns and all the rest of it – and Weller seems inferior, in terms of technical accomplishment, to late-seventies rivals like Howard Devoto. But at the time they were the best, 'my park, my pleasaunce', as Gerard Manley Hopkins used to say of Oxford, and a chapter in my life came to an end when they broke up.

Johnny Too Bad

MARK COOPER

He's a jazz man, he's a folkie and he's been a drinker. Singer songwriter John Martyn has been most things, apart from commercially acceptable. Now in his twenty-sixth year of recording, the Glaswegian has amassed a huge back catalogue of quality and distinction. He's the ultimate cult artist who can tour anywhere, any time and still draw a reasonable audience.

He made a succession of albums with his first wife Beverley, in the seventies, but his naturally slurred delivery masked some serious drinking and drug problems.

In a brave but abortive bid to break through, he had a couple of albums produced by Phil Collins – including arguably his best work, *Grace & Danger* – and Eric Clapton recorded the lovely 'May You Never'. Nothing happened commercially and, in 1988, Martyn was told by his doctor to stop drinking or die. He dried out and now lives in something approaching domestic bliss, recording his always beautiful music as and when he feels like it.

Once you pass a certain age, you get a shock every time you look in the mirror. I don't know if this is a particularly male trait but my mental picture of myself seems permanently stalled somewhere around an idealized seventeen. I never quite recognize the forty-something man with the receding hairline who stares back at me these days because I'm always expecting to see a golden youth with long, curly hair, unlined skin and an ever-present smile. No matter that when I actually was seventeen I was still recovering from terrible teenage acne and could only dream of being allowed enough hair to cover the collar of my school shirt: in my mind's eye I will always look rather like John Martyn on the cover of the first album he recorded with his wife Beverley in 1970, *Stormbringer!* Truth is, the best I could hope for back then was to look a bit like John Martyn on the sleeve of his 1969 solo album *The Tumbler*.

In early 1969, Martyn looked positively boyish, as if he'd only just run away from home. The cover shot of *The Tumbler* has him standing in front of a wide-angled lens, framed against green trees and a blue sky. On the back, he's standing beside a small river. He's wearing wide-bottomed trousers, a waistcoat and a white, open-necked shirt. Paul Wheeler's sleeve-note poem has John 'clambering, bumbling, splashing, twiddling and tumbling' about like a gleeful child. The sleeve and the music wear their late-sixties, summery innocence proudly but, nevertheless, John's hair still only barely covers his ears. It's like looking at one of those mid-sixties sleeves of American bands on the cusp of psychedelia: they've already taken their first trip but their hair hasn't quite had time to grow yet and their clothes are still more preppie than jumble-sale chic.

Later that year, John and Beverley went to Woodstock and recorded *Stormbringer!* Now John looks like a full-blown member of Island's hippy family, with long locks to match those of Stevie Winwood or Richard Thompson on the sleeve of the label's cheapo-cheapo 1969 compilation, *You Can All Join In*. His curls disappear into the fleece of his Turkish coat, and Beverley, black-haired, beautiful and also clad in one of the coats you simply had to hitch to Istanbul to own, rests her head dreamily on his shoulder. They are sitting on the grass at dusk in summer and they look idyllically happy at a time when happiness was almost confrontational, when a smile and a peace sign were thought enough to levitate the Houses of Parliament and make the straight world realize the obvious error of its ways.

Oddly enough, it wasn't the dreamy Beverley who impressed me most at the time. I already knew most of Brian Patten's love poems by heart and could mouth the words to all manner of love songs, but girls – real girls – were still mostly far off and untouchable as far as I was concerned. John and Bev looked the complete couple and such intimacy was completely unimaginable to me when I was seventeen. No, what really impressed me on the sleeve of *Stormbringer!* was the fact that John wasn't wearing any socks. 'Cool' was not a fashionable term back then, even though we all read Kerouac's *On The Road* with feverish hunger, but John's bare feet and dirty gym shoes were definitely 'far out'.

Of course, I already knew John Martyn rarely wore socks because I'd been going regularly to Soho's Les Cousins club to see him play since the previous summer. In fact, I tried rigorously to avoid socks myself when I wasn't stuck at boarding school at Cranbrook in Kent, trapped in a ghastly brown tweed jacket, grey trousers and a tie, endlessly combing my hair in the hope that it would grow magically over ears that, according to my peers, stuck out like those of *Mad*'s Alfred E. Newman and over collars that never quite hid the spots on my neck.

John Kendall-Carpenter, an ex-England rugby international, was Cranbrook's headmaster in that era and John Kendall-Carpenter ran the school as if it were still the fifties, or, indeed, the thirties. 'There is some ability here which needs directing towards justifiable targets,' he wrote in one of my reports. 'I am not pleased to discover that he has been discourteous in class, and I warn him here and now that if there are recurrences of it in the future, I will give him a good spanking for juvenile behaviour.' This was the end of the summer term of 1969 – the same summer I'd skived off school one Saturday morning, hitched a lift to the local train station with my friend Dave Roberts (who during the next two summers hitched with me to Turkey and then to India), and went to see the Stones in Hyde Park. We marvelled at King Crimson, the butterflies and the Hell's Angels and got back to school in time for tea.

Two worlds were definitely colliding but, fortunately, we hadn't been missed. Kendall-Carpenter would definitely have thrashed us for that escapade but then he thrashed us for anything he termed 'insolence'. That could mean being caught smoking in the upstairs room of Mrs Humphrys' village cafe or simply wearing the wrong facial expression during assembly. He embodied arbitrary, despotic power and we loathed him. To depose him, however, was unimaginable, and I was far too protected to even dream of running away.

According to my house master's report for the Autumn Term of 1968, my main interests were folk music and rugger. The 'folk music' of that report was all the rage at Cranbrook, thanks to the acoustic guitars of two boys in the year above me – Sean McMillan and Ted Holden. We'd all grown up on The Beatles and the Stones and our particular boarding house, Cornwallis, was infiltrated very early on by Jefferson Airplane, Love and Moby Grape thanks to my friend Angus's holiday in San Francisco. You couldn't actually play that stuff yourself, however, or hope to ever be that far out. The new folk music was a little more accessible. Sean McMillan was my elder brother Nigel's best friend and Ted was soon going out with one of my closest friends, Susie. Sean used to wear a fireman's coat (very hip after 'Granny Takes a Trip') and a neck scarf and he could sing. Ted was more the guitar virtuoso. He knew enough about tunings to play Al Stewart's 'Ivich' (written after the Sartre character from *Roads to Freedom*), John Martyn's 'Seven Black Roses' (in which you had to intermittently slide the capo down the guitar's neck to alter keys) and even Paul Simon's version of Davy Graham's 'Anji', then the litmus test for any aspiring acoustic guitarist. The acoustic guitar was somehow the symbol of everything we all dreamed of being, the talisman of that other world that lay beyond school, the world where boys just a tiny bit older than you could grow their hair, throw a sleeping bag over their shoulders and, well, just 'ramble'.

'Rambling' was pretty big with us back then. Sean and Ted did a great version of Tom Paxton's 'Ramblin' Boy' as well as his 'I Can't Help But Wonder Where I'm Bound'. We all longed to be 'bound' somewhere, to be out on that open road instead of trapped at school for prep and early bed. Paxton and Dylan embodied the dream, but they were American and not exactly available. Somehow we heard about Cousins, and my best friend Gordon, a dayboy with infinitely greater freedom, even went there. I already knew about John Martyn, Al Stewart, Ralph McTell, Roy Harper, Mike Chapman et al. thanks to the listening booths of Bromley's W. H. Smith's, where I'd hang out as often as possible in the holidays, asking to hear all the new releases. I was itching to see the singers, but I was still only in the fifth form and my parents were happier with the idea of the local tennis club.

Finally, in March 1968, I got to go to my first 'popular music' concert. Shamefully, it was Esther and Abi Ofarim at the Royal Albert Hall; there were seventeen encores and my mother and little sister came too. Despite the happy couple's undoubted triumph and Esther's interpretation of The Bee Gees' 'Morning of My Life', the whole business still seems a little sorry to me even now.

Fortunately, Esther and Abi acted as something of a bridge-head and, a few weeks later, Gordon and I went to Cousins for a Saturday evening session featuring Mike Cooper, who now lives in Rome and combines a love of Hawaiian music with avant-jazz leanings. Back then, he was a country-blues specialist with a National steel guitar, a Western moustache and a big, quavering voice. I still remember 'Electric Chair' which had driving slide and an unfortunate hero who kept begging the judge to send him direct to the ''lectric chair'.

Cooper was impressive enough, but Cousins itself was awe-inspiring. First and foremost, it was in Soho, the very heart of London, and secondly, it was profoundly Bohemian without being the least bit frightening. The club itself was little more than a long, rectangular cellar with a small stage near the entrance. It cost around seven shillings to get in and, as they didn't serve alcohol, it didn't matter that everybody else seemed older than us. Instead there was terrible coffee and sad cheese rolls and, on Saturday nights, an all-night session from midnight till 6 a.m.

Jansch, Renbourn and The Young Tradition had all played there regularly in the mid-sixties and now it was home for a new generation of singer-songwriters. Yet Cousins wasn't really folkie then: Lol Coxhill would come by after busking at the South Bank and blow his sax, The Third Ear Band were regulars and I once saw Davy Graham put down his guitar and devote twenty-five minutes to explaining why the Vietnam War was profoundly unjust to an apparently rapt full house. I promptly made it my spiritual home, and for the next two or three years I went there almost weekly.

John Martyn and Al Stewart were regulars among regulars at Cousins in the late sixties and I first saw Martyn a week or two after I'd seen Mike Cooper. John was great mates with Andy Mathews, Cousins' owner/doorman. He'd hang around the entrance chatting loudly to Andy and swapping personae at the drop of a hat, switching from Scots to Cockney to Posh. He was big, nervous and speedy all at once but, above all, he seemed to embody all the eclectic freedoms of the club itself. Cousins didn't exactly separate the performers from the audience, and John would bounce onstage, throw open his guitar case and start chatting to the crowd while he changed strings. In 1968, his repertoire was a mixture of blues standards like 'Winding Boy' and 'Cocaine Blues' and his own originals, which were deeply romantic, and in the case of 'Fairytale Lullaby' and 'Sing a Song of Summer', on the Donovan side of twee. The voice hadn't developed its trademark blend of growls and slurs as yet, but what was already extraordinary about Martyn was the sheer physicality of his guitar playing. Even when he was singing ditties to all things nice, Martyn hammered the guitar strings with his fist, constantly yanking the bass strings with his claw of a thumb and slapping out rhythms that were already far funkier than those of his peers. Al Stewart and Roy Harper were lyricists, and we hung on every rhyming couplet and every new composition like they were sermons from the mount, but Martyn was already the music itself. He'd rock back and forth on his stool – wild, free, and just a little bit crazy, yet somehow more human than the others, more like yourself.

I had been a disaster at music at school since the age of seven, when I was officially pronounced tone deaf. Until the age of thirteen, I had a sixty-year old music teacher named Miss Smith who sat at a piano and ranked our class in ability along two rows of folding wooden chairs. I sang every note horribly out of tune and was permanently stationed in one of the last three chairs in the second row. Nevertheless, after I'd seen John Martyn a couple of times, I decided that I simply had to learn the guitar. No matter that to this day I cannot tune a guitar, I acquired a little acoustic and set about trying to master the odd chord and the difficult art of fingerpicking. As a small boy, I had spent hours throwing a soft cricket ball against our kitchen wall to practise my forward defensive. Now I applied the same dogged patience to the guitar. I had no rhythm and no ear, but after a couple of years I could play the opening flurry of Al Stewart's 'Love Chronicles', most of The Incredible String Band's 'You Get Brighter' and various doodles that I regarded as the bedrock of my developing repertoire. John Martyn's songs were almost all in tunings that defeated far more accomplished guitarists than me but I could 'hammer on' and slap the strings in pale imitation of his style. I was a lot better at simply rocking back and forth on a stool while clutching the guitar. It might as well have been a tennis racquet, but if you can't imitate the skill, sometimes you have to make do with the manner. After all, the guitar was only the pathway to being less like a schoolboy, a pointer to a world where you would never have to wear socks.

By the spring of 1969, I'd seen John Martyn five or six times at Cousins and I was beginning to wonder if he was ever going to change his set. I could get a smile out of Andy Mathews and loved the stoned feeling of staggering out into the dawn to see polythene bags of peeled chips sitting in front of unopened Soho cafés. Gordon and I would wander down to the Embankment and stare across at the Festival Hall while sharing a tea stall with the odd tramp. I'd even skived out of Cranbrook a couple of times after lights out and hitched up to London for the occasional unmissable all-night line-up, the teaming of, say, Mike Chapman, Third Ear Band, Marc Brierley, Sam Mitchell and Jackson C. Frank. Cousins was everything that Cranbrook and Bromley wasn't, and I couldn't wait to get out there and ramble, footloose and fancy-free.

Unfortunately, my A levels were set for the summer of 1970 – more than a year away. After an enthusiastic physics master followed me up to the sanctuary of the upstairs room of Mrs Humphrys' café and caught me smoking, I decided I had to keep a low profile in order to survive. My parents had finally taken my brother away from Cranbrook in circumstances which still fill me with fraternal pride: one Sunday evening at church he simply failed to kneel or so much as sit down for prayers on the grounds that enforced worship is necessarily a contradiction in terms.

I loved the schoolwork, English and history particularly, so I started working at night – high in the roof of Cornwallis in the privacy of the lower-sixth study with the dansette spinning Cream, Dylan and Martyn's 'The Tumbler'. I dozed in class during the day, my reports becoming increasingly gloomy, but I was surviving.

Meanwhile various like-minded spirits had decided that it was time to start our own Cousins at Cranbrook. A local singer-songwriter was booked for the first Saturday night session, some tables and chairs were set up in Big School, Cranbrook's old assembly hall, Ted and Sean opened the evening and a good time was had by all. It was a ghastly parody of everything I now held dear but it was better than nowt. I got a phone number from Andy Mathews at Cousins and we promptly booked John Martyn for the second evening for the princely sum of £25.

John didn't drive and he was picked up from Staplehurst, the local railway station, by a friendly master. He was dressed pretty much like he is on the sleeve of *The Tumbler* and only carrying a guitar case when he arrived. Like all aspiring middle-class hippies, I clung to the rather Puritan belief that when 'you got nothing, you got nothing to lose' and was greatly impressed by this lack of baggage.

I'd seen John bouncing onstage at Cousins enough to be used to the abandon with which he moved but, up close, the way he swaggered upstairs to Big School seemed positively dangerous. He was bold and free but also tangibly nervous and highly strung and obviously capable of almost anything. He promptly threw open his guitar case, which contained a couple of paperbacks, various articles of clothing and innumerable packets of guitar strings, and proceeded to re-string his instrument, testing each one by pulling it a good two or three inches from the fretboard and letting go. The odd one broke and he shrugged philosophically. We chatted about Cousins and Al Stewart, and about his nocturnal train rides to Hastings where he then lived and where he'd return after gigs on the early-morning milk train.

Meanwhile the boys in Big School were chattering with excitement. John Martyn can only have been three or four years older than many of us at the time but he made records, he had long hair by the school's standards and, most importantly, he clearly never had to do what he was told. Our fun was only being spoilt by one thing, the presence of a young music teacher called, I believe, Les Johnson. Mr Johnson walked around the school with his nose in the air and a cravat round his neck, exuding a distaste for Cranbrook's bourgeois values. This should have made him our natural ally but unfortunately he was also a snob, whose every rarefied gesture indicated that he only approved of classical music, sherry and certain symbolist poets of the nineteenth century. Tonight, Les Johnson was sitting among the boys and talking loudly in an alternately waspish and disparaging tone. Here was our freewheelin' world made manifest and we had to put up with this idiot wrinkling his nose.

John did two sets that night and Johnson whispered loudly to his acolytes throughout the first. During the interval, I muttered something to him about Johnson's attitude, which during the course of the evening had come to symbolize everything I hated about school. After all, for all Johnson's affectations of individualism, it was only because he was a teacher that he could behave like such an asshole. Calling attention to this display of petulance was like a red rag to a bull to John, who could probably smell antiquated authority in every pore of the building. A couple of songs into the second set, right after 'The Gardeners', a jokey Gothic tune about things behind the wood-shed, Martyn suddenly laid down his guitar and stared menac-ingly at Johnson. 'Who are you looking at, petal?' he enquired.

The whole room withdrew into a stunned but sniggering silence as Martyn proceeded to shred Johnson and his dandyism very publicly and very personally. I can't remember much of what he said but I do remember its menace and his refusal to let Johnson off the hook. It was brutal. The teacher stuttered a couple of lame ripostes and soon left the room. Martyn carried on with his set as if nothing had happened and then disappeared into the night, heading for Waterloo and the milk train.

I was impressed and a little frightened. There was nothing twee or polite about this John Martyn; the man I'd met seemed to feel things deeply but be barely in control of his own emotions. He sang about love but his rage was palpable. Perhaps I was realizing that, to my enduring chagrin, I would always only be able to feel like a critic. Everything in my minor public-school upbringing had taught me that profundity and originality was something to study and admire either in the past or in those most distanced and Olympian of beings, poets, artists and musicians. John Martyn was very much of the present; he wasn't much older than me but he seemed party to a wild and sacred fire that I found almost shocking. He wasn't inhibited by the English disease of politeness. He wasn't mediated, there was virtually no gap between his emotions and his music and he didn't seem to apologize very much. I could still identify utterly with his music, but the man himself was almost scary.

John's set finally changed pretty soon after that. He stopped doing 'Sing a Song of Summer', married Beverley and went to Woodstock. A few months later the couple launched *Stormbringer!* at the Queen Elizabeth Hall with a full band. Nick Drake opened the show, staring at his feet, playing extraordinary finger-style guitar and disappearing as quickly as possible as though to deny he'd ever been there at all. John later wrote 'Solid Air', one of his most enduring, smoky songs, for Nick, but that night he smacked an electric guitar while the lovely Beverley sang the extended, muscular funk of 'Sweet Honesty', another arrogant gauntlet thrown at the feet of our elders' hypocrisy. The couple made another album together, *Road to Ruin*, whose sleeve notes informed us that 'We think we can safely say *quite categorically* that this music has nothing to do with dying or anything like that ... Lots of love, John and Bev.' Briefly, they were the royal couple of a certain kind of hippy optimism.

Bev soon retired to raise their kids while John's music continued to ferment. He'd discovered the Echoplex, a simple device that enabled him to send spiralling loops of sound out of his guitar, set up recurring bass patterns and rhythms and then throw back chords and clusters of notes in answer. The Echoplex was stunning in a small club like Cousins and it became the mainstay of Martyn's act throughout the seventies. You couldn't really call him a folkie any more – not least because his vocal style was gradually turning into a husky, slurred blend of growls and caresses. By 1973's *Solid Air*, he sounded like a blend of jazz singer and drunk.

I survived Cranbrook and got a place at Cambridge despite failing my French A level, a subject I'd lost interest in with the arrival of a fatally weak teacher named Blunt whose nickname you can guess. I didn't really want to go to university. I wanted to travel the world for the rest of my life, cleansing my system of anything remotely bourgeois. I wanted to ramble.

In 1971 at the tender age of eighteen, I bussed and hitch-hiked to India for four months with a small and rather awkward guitar that someone had painted blue. We smoked vast quantities of Afghan black and played Incredible String Band and John Martyn songs on houseboats in Benares and Kashmir. At least, Dave did. I continued to doodle and wonder why my doodles never quite transformed themselves into 'Seven Black Roses'. I knew I didn't understand music's most basic vocabulary, but my inability seemed not only cruel but also frankly incredible. This, after all, was what was later dubbed the Aquarian Age and everything was supposed to be possible. Everywhere we went young travellers with hair now well past their collars flashed us peace signs and smiles. The journey cost just over £100 and I lost two and a half stone. When I came back I almost felt like somebody, even though I knew I would never be able to play guitar and still hadn't fallen in love.

John Martyn played Cambridge regularly between 1971 and 1974. He was now touring with double-bassist and fellow anarchist Danny Thompson, and the pair raged around the country on a never-ending spree, bellowing, tumbling and mimicking while making probably the best music of their careers. Martyn recorded three marvellous albums, *Bless the Weather*, *Inside Out*, and *Solid Air*, that gradually shook off any traces of tweeness and seamlessly blended folk, jazz and funk in a manner that would only ever be matched by Tim Buckley and Van Morrison. Above all, his music carried an extraordinary emotional openness. Onstage and in his songs he frequently seemed like the violent man of his *Johnny Too Bad* cover with more than his share of rage bottled up inside, but somehow his overriding wish for love and loveliness still drove the music, even as times grew darker and more cynical. Love was now militant in John's music, and while he frequently behaved like a drunken stevedore on stage, his music was naked male emotionalism.

As for me, I fell in love for the first time to *Bless the Weather* and, like John Martyn, had to start working out why I couldn't be always smiling and where all the rage and confusion was coming from. I was in ferment in those years, feeling everything on my fingertips and questioning everything. In the summers, I hitch-hiked twice through the Middle East to keep my rambling ambitions on the boil. During term time, I studied, partied and sat up all night discussing the meaning of life through great clouds of smoke. We listened to the Dead, Dylan, the Velvets and Van Morrison but also to John Martyn. I'd outgrown most of the other singer-songwriters and Cousins was winding down, but John's music remained a kind of shadow diary of my emotional weather. I'd stopped wanting to be like him years ago – that kind of fandom seemed like an insult to the religion of individualism to which I rather pompously subscribed – but I still felt he was singing my life.

Cambridge finished and I worked as a postman for a few months then spent six months travelling round South America with my friend Mike. My first love affair finally broke up not long after I returned and I was completely devastated. I'd lost my soul mate: Evie and I weren't going to be together forever like John and Bev. Meanwhile everything was ending. Hippy culture was stale and smelly, England was in the grip of recession and my friends all seemed to be knuckling down to their careers. It was, as they say, the end of an era. I knew it was time to start wandering the world in earnest, but nobody else seemed to agree and I wasn't very good at being alone. As a compromise, I applied to a couple of American universities and headed off for Kent State, Ohio, in the Bicentenary year of 1976. A few weeks before I went, The Sex Pistols played the Screen on the Green in Islington. I was visiting my friend Julian in a flat just around the corner that night but, for some reason, we decided not to go.

I stayed four years in America, the last three of which I spent at the University of California in Santa Barbara. My eight months in Ohio were a cold and lonely disaster, even though I did get to go to Boston at Christmas, where I saw John Martyn opening for Mose Allison in a small club. He was bigger, bearded but still bouncy.

Punk happened while I was studying for a PhD and teaching English to unwilling undergraduates in Santa Barbara. Somewhere around 1978, I cut my hair short and started wearing black. I began writing the odd review for *Record Mirror* back in London, kicking off with The Sex Pistols' last gig in San Francisco. Paranoia, speed and putdowns fuelled the music as if in direct contrast to the dawn of the seventies. John Martyn had sung beautifully of 'One World' in 1977 but although he was now clearly going to stay the course, he was like a voice crying in the wilderness. I played his albums in what he calls the 'small hours' and, like every aspiring New Waver, wore shades during the day. I also finally gave up playing the guitar.

The story's almost over now. I came back to London in 1980 and started writing about music for a living. John Martyn split up with Bev and documented the sorry tale in 1980's yearning *Grace & Danger*, left Island Records, made a couple of glossy albums for Warners (one produced by Phil Collins), and eventually went back to Island in the mid-eighties. He started wearing a suit onstage and touring with a band. I became disillusioned with having to write for a living and worked in record companies for a few years. Sian – 'the mother of Mark's children', as she sometimes introduces herself in order to 'place' our relationship –and I went on our first 'date', to see John Martyn at the Dominion,

Tottenham Court Road, in November 1985. I'd grown up on music that my parents always thought I'd get over. I seem to be from that generation that never got over it.

I've met John Martyn twice in the nineties. In 1990, I interviewed him for *Q* Magazine. We met in the Chelsea Arts Club, where he was swanning round the pool table, talking in his myriad voices and showing off. He'd finally quit drinking a few months before and proved deeply and thoroughly uncomfortable with the interview process. So, for once, was I. Doing interviews is rather like doing 'tricks' Jin another line of work: you get complete strangers to expose themselves to you for a short amount of time and then you never see each other again. I didn't remind John of his gig at Cranbrook because I knew he'd have forgotten it. Instead I acted modern, distant and professional and asked him whether he still subscribed to the rambler mythology. John's music has never surrendered to the merely analytical and, fortunately, he refused to recant. 'I'm still living that life,' he cheerfully admitted. 'I love the idea of the travelling singer; it's half the reason I'm doing this: the man with his guitar against the world, the lonely beacon, the railroad tracks running into infinity, a guitar and a gunny sack ... I'm still right into that.'

I couldn't really talk to this man whose music had touched me so much over the years, but then my communion has been with the music, not the man. He still seemed wild, trembly and untamed and I secretly loved the fact that he wasn't prepared to surrender much of himself for idle chatter in a magazine.

A couple of years later, I'd started producing BBC2's music show *Later With Jools Holland*. John had a re-recorded retrospective album coming out and I booked him for the fifth show of the first series, alongside the particularly odd mixture of The Inspiral Carpets, The Tyrell Corporation, Joan Baez and a new young singer-songwriter called David Gray. John was an hour late and, despite the fact that he was supposed to be still on the wagon, he swept into TV Centre, calling for stimulants and looking to party. He was portly now, inclined to sweat and, despite being in full braggart mode, visibly nervous and insecure.

When we finally recorded the show, the saxophonist Andy Sheppard and Jools sat in with him, his classic song 'May You Never' came alive again and John positively burned. Most of the artists came to the Green Room after we'd recorded the show to watch it go out on air at midnight. John sat in the corner, looking exhausted and watched himself on screen. He grew teary during his own performance, either because he was shocked at having to look at himself in the mirror of television or because he could feel the music still burning. I went over and congratulated him and had to reassure him how good he was.

The beauty of John Martyn's music is that he doesn't seem to protect himself very much or censor his emotions. He's probably a monster to live with but his heart and soul is in every note he plays. I don't know the man and, frankly, I don't wish to, but I guess I know his soul pretty well through the music. He's gone his own sweet way, he's become a master of a kind and, when I look back over the years, I realize I'm absurdly, tearfully, grateful to him. Here, after all, is a man who's never been afraid to wear his heart on his sleeve. As the song says, 'You're just like a long-lost brother to me/You know that I love you true ...' May you never indeed.

Notes on Contributors

John Bauldie is a freelance writer and sub-editor. He has had three books about Bob Dylan published and received a Grammy Award nomination for his liner notes to the Dylan box set *The Bootleg Series Volumes 1-3*. He lives in Richmond, Surrey, and likes David Blue, Phil Ochs and Bolton Wanderers.

David Cavanagh is a journalist who became besotted with The Triffids as a student in 1984. Eventually, in 1989, he interviewed them for *Sounds*. He found the experience strange but rewarding. Since then he has written prolifically for *Select*, *Q Magazine*, *Mojo* and *Volume*, without ever really experiencing the same feeling.

Mark Cooper is forty-one, going on seventeen. He lives with Sian and their two boys, Luke and Cian, in Acton, West London. He is the music producer for *The Late Show* and producer of *Later With Jools Holland*. He writes regularly for *Q Magazine*, *Mojo* and various newspapers.

Mike Edwards, born lucky, 1964. Rejected education for rock at eighteen. Rejected by rock until 1988. Formed Jesus Jones, got record deal. Wrote three albums, treated like royalty by EMI after second. Does re-mixes, production, narrates award-winning radio series, DJs, mountain-bikes, skateboards, daughter-raises, plays computer games, writes soundtracks. Needs sleep.

John Fordham is a freelance jazz critic, writer and broadcaster. He writes for the *Guardian* and *Q Magazine* and broadcasts regularly for the BBC Radio 4 arts programme *Kaleidoscope*. He interviewed many of the world's jazz legends for the 1990 BBC TV series *Birdland* and has written several books, including a biography of Ronnie Scott, the record guide *Jazz on CD* and the illustrated history *Jazz*.

Sheryl Garratt is the editor of *The Face* magazine in London. She is now happily married and her fantasies about baby-faced young pop stars these days involve getting them on her covers, not under them.

Sid Griffin is a musician, freelance writer and occasional disc jockey, author of a Gram Parsons biography and ringleader of the late-lamented Long Ryders. He now performs both solo and with his new band The Coal Porters. A native of Kentucky, he lives in exile in Hampstead.

Tom Hibbert has written for *Just Seventeen* magazine and ... oh I don't bloody know. I'm forty years old for God's sake ... Will this do, 'mini-biog' wise?

Mick Houghton is a one-time journalist and three-time loser. Has spent the last fifteen years with the stigma of being a music-business publicist, a shameful profession despite working with very cool people like Julian Cope, The KLF, The Jesus & Mary Chain and Sonic Youth. Currently seeking a publisher for a collection of his best press releases.

Sean Hughes is predominantly a stand-up comedian who has published his own highly successful collection of poetry and prose – *Sean's Book* – and has succumbed to writing pieces such as 'Titanic Motives' for peanuts, rather than earning vast quantities of money in television commercials.

Danny Kelly is editor of *Q* Magazine. Once, he edited the *NME* and worked for British Rail. He supports Tottenham

Hotspur, likes rap, has appeared on national television and is currently reading a book about Bomber Command. Although allegedly of Irish descent, he has never tasted Guinness.

Steve Lamacq is a journalist turned radio presenter who worked on the *New Musical Express* for five years before joining *Select* magazine and then Radio 1FM. He saw his first live band at the age of twelve (The Lurkers at Chelmsford Chancellors Hall), and claims to have once seen 197 gigs in one year. His doctor says he should eat better and 'slow down'.

Stuart Maconie is from Wigan and is a writer and broadcaster. His writing appears mainly in *Q* Magazine, *Mojo* and *Select* and he appears regularly on radio and TV where he foists his unwanted opinions upon others. Contrary to the belief of most taxi drivers, he is not, nor has he ever been, Andy Kershaw.

Lucy O'Brien is a writer/broadcaster/music journalist. She has published two biographies, *Dusty* and the best-selling *Annie Lennox*. She is currently working on the definitive history of women in rock and pop, due to be published in Britain and America by Penguin.

David Sinclair is chief rock critic of *The Times* and a contributor to *Rolling Stone* and *Q* Magazine. He edits the Global Music Pulse column in *Billboard*, broadcasts weekly on Greater London Radio and is author of *Rock on CD* (1993). A few copies are still available.

D. J. Taylor is thirty-four and was born in Norwich. His books include two novels, *Great Eastern Land* (1986) and *Real Life* (1992), and a critical study, *After the War: The Novel and England since 1945* (1993). Although he claims to have stopped listening to pop music in 1987, he 'quite likes' Blur, Sugar and The Fatima Mansions.

READ MORE IN PENGUIN

In every corner of the world, on every subject under the sun, Penguin represents quality and variety – the very best in publishing today.

For complete information about books available from Penguin – including Puffins, Penguin Classics and Arkana – and how to order them, write to us at the appropriate address below. Please note that for copyright reasons the selection of books varies from country to country.

In the United Kingdom: Please write to *Dept. JC, Penguin Books Ltd, FREEPOST, West Drayton, Middlesex UB7 OBR*

If you have any difficulty in obtaining a title, please send your order with the correct money, plus ten per cent for postage and packaging, to *PO Box No. 11, West Drayton, Middlesex UB7 OBR*

In the United States: Please write to *Penguin USA Inc., 375 Hudson Street, New York, NY 10014*

In Canada: Please write to *Penguin Books Canada Ltd, 10 Alcorn Avenue, Suite 300, Toronto, Ontario M4V 3B2*

In Australia: Please write to *Penguin Books Australia Ltd, 487 Maroondah Highway, Ringwood, Victoria 3134*

In New Zealand: Please write to *Penguin Books (NZ) Ltd,182–190 Wairau Road, Private Bag, Takapuna, Auckland 9*

In India: Please write to *Penguin Books India Pvt Ltd, 706 Eros Apartments, 56 Nehru Place, New Delhi 110 019*

In the Netherlands: Please write to *Penguin Books Netherlands B.V., Keizersgracht 231 NL–1016 DV Amsterdam*

In Germany: Please write to *Penguin Books Deutschland GmbH, Friedrichstrasse 10–12, W–6000 Frankfurt/Main 1*

In Spain: Please write to *Penguin Books S. A., C. San Bernardo 117–6° E–28015 Madrid*

In Italy: Please write to *Penguin Italia s.r.l., Via Felice Casati 20, 1–20124 Milano*

In France: Please write to *Penguin France S. A., 17 rue Lejeune, F–31000 Toulouse*

In Japan: Please write to *Penguin Books Japan, Ishikiribashi Building, 2–5–4, Suido, Bunkyo-ku, Tokyo 112*

In Greece: Please write to *Penguin Hellas Ltd, Dimocritou 3, GR–106 71 Athens*

In South Africa: Please write to *Longman Penguin Southern Africa (Pty) Ltd, Private Bag X08, Bertsham 2013*

READ MORE IN PENGUIN

A SELECTION OF MUSICAL HITS

The Dark Stuff Nick Kent
Selected Writings on Rock Music 1972–1993

Never afraid to flirt with danger and excess, Nick Kent didn't just know how to write about rock stars ... he lived in their shadow. From the debauched turbulence of the Rolling Stones on tour, to the violence that surrounded the Sex Pistols, from the tragedies of Brian Wilson and Syd Barrett to the epic survival sagas of Neil Young and Iggy Pop, Nick Kent got close to everything that was mad, bad and dangerous to know about rock 'n' roll.

Keith Richards Victor Bockris

'Victor Bockris, who wrote brilliant biographies of Andy Warhol and Cassius Clay, is the biographer Richards deserves; a fluid, supple, generous writer who never descends into puffery or ascends into sarcasm ... Richards and Bockris are definitely as good as it gets' – *Spectator*

Pet Shop Boys versus America Chris Heath

In 1991 the Pet Shop Boys – the pop group notorious for its humour, intelligence and prudence in the face of stardom – went to tour America, the land that idolizes the famous. The book that resulted (with pictures by Pennie Smith) is a gripping document of modern celebrity.

The American Night Jim Morrison

'A hellfire preacher, part-terrified, part-enraged and mainly fascinated by the drawbacks that being merely human entails ... refreshing' – *Sunday Times*. 'A great American poet' – Oliver Stone

Unforgettable Fire: The Story of U2 Eamon Dunphy

When *The Joshua Tree* topped the charts in twenty-two countries, U2 became the hottest band in the world. 'Zoo TV' took their fame to sublime heights. Half Catholic, half Protestant, the band embodies the conflict and anguish of a divided Ireland – across the world their music is the voice of hope for millions. '*Unforgettable Fire* is a beacon ... in a cynical world' – *Time Out*